# THE
# FREE
# LIST

# THE
# FREE
# LIST
# Property
# Without
# Taxes

*Alfred Balk*

*Russell Sage Foundation*
1971

PUBLICATIONS OF RUSSELL SAGE FOUNDATION

*Russell Sage Foundation was established in 1907 by Mrs. Russell Sage for the improvement of social and living conditions in the United States. In carrying out its purpose the Foundation conducts research under the direction of members of the staff or in close collaboration with other institutions, and supports programs designed to improve the utilization of social science knowledge. As an integral part of its operations, the Foundation from time to time publishes books or pamphlets resulting from these activities. Publication under the imprint of the Foundation does not necessarily imply agreement by the Foundation, its Trustees, or its staff with the interpretations or conclusions of the authors.*

HJ
4182
.A27
B 35

© 1971 RUSSELL SAGE FOUNDATION

Printed in the United States of America
Standard Book Number 87154–083–5
Library of Congress Catalog Card Number: 78–129147

# Acknowledgments

A nyone who writes a book is indebted to many people. My thanks first should go to the staff of the Russell Sage Foundation, especially Doctor Orville G. Brim, Jr., president, and Doctor Wilbert E. Moore, sociologist, for their interest and encouragement. Shortly after I reported on church wealth and tax exemptions in the October 1967 *Harper's*, Doctors Brim and Moore invited me to broaden my research, with Foundation support, to encompass the entire spectrum of tax-exempt real property. During my residency at the Foundation—appropriately, rental quarters in a commercial building and thus not part of the exempt-property problem—they and other staff members offered much helpful guidance. But I had complete freedom in research and writing, and the ultimate responsibility for what appears in this book is mine.

From the start it was apparent that data were scarce and that assembling data scattered throughout thousands of taxing districts was beyond our resources. We agreed on an objective:

v

MONTEITH LIBRARY
ALMA, MICHIGAN

to provide a sampling, an introduction to the subject and perhaps a general map of territory meriting further exploration. That is all this book purports to be.

Listing everyone who was generous enough to provide information by mail, by phone, or in personal interviews would require another book. The staff of the International Association of Assessing Officers—especially Paul V. Corusy, executive director, and Leo A. Droste, research director—was exceedingly helpful in innumerable ways, and I was enormously impressed by their professionalism. (The IAAO's files and publications, together with the Joint Reference Library under the same roof at 1313 East Sixtieth Street in Chicago, probably constitute the largest repository of current information on the subject.) John Shannon and Allen D. Manvel of the Advisory Commission on Intergovernmental Relations also deserve special mention, as do the local and state officials named in Chapter 11. Ronald B. Welch of the California State Board of Equalization, for example, graciously spent much time with me on a busy day when he was to appear at a legislative hearing, and Colorado State Senator Ruth Stockton traveled to the Capitol in Denver on a hot summer day between legislative sessions to assist members of the state's excellent Legislative Council in recapitulating extensive hearings on exemption problems.

Gratitude also is due Pamela Susskind and Deborah W. Beers for assistance in research; Vivian Kaufman, my secretary, and her Russell Sage colleagues Helen Fitzsimmons and Marjorie Painton, who assisted in transcribing of dictation and in typing of manuscript drafts; and my wife Phyllis and my daughters Laraine and Diane for their understanding during my lengthy periods of travel and, on my return, enforced seclusion with notes and typewriter.

# Contents

# THE
# FREE
# LIST

# 1

# The Unexamined Sieve

*The world is not the way they tell you it is.*
—"Adam Smith," *The Money Game*

THE UNIVERSALITY of the above contribution to philosophy may not have immediately occurred to its author. Its intended context was the world of stocks and bonds—the speculators, lenders, brokers, and others who comprise the variegated universe of Wall Street. Yet its message might hold true of almost any other subject, including one unavoidably close to millions of American homeowners—their property tax.

It is the conventional wisdom that *ad valorem* (i.e., "according to the value") taxation of real property—land and the structures attached to it—means that taxes are levied proportionately on the valuation of each owner's holdings, thus fairly distributing the burden of the tax. To this end a ponderous but durable machinery has been set up: A tax assessor estimates and lists a valuation for each property; an appeals or review body alters or affirms it; a "mill levy" per thousand dollars of assessed valuation is uniformly applied; and taxes are apportioned or collected accordingly. In some eighty thousand American taxing jurisdictions utilizing the property tax this, in the words of market observer "Adam Smith," is "the way they tell you it is."

In the real world, however, a number of variables intrude. One of the more important yet least examined of these is a legal status known as *immunity* (for governmental property) or *exemption* (for nongovernmental property) from taxation,* that is, the privilege of being *excused from paying any property taxes on all or part of a parcel of real estate*, thus requiring the remainder of the taxpaying community to make up the difference. Meanwhile, of course, community services still are provided to the exempt property.

By law or custom, a number of categories of property long have occupied places on this "free list": governmental buildings, parks, streets, highways, public schools, colleges and universities, houses of worship, cemeteries, hospitals, and the like. But in recent years this exemption roster has been extended far beyond these rather conventional classifications. Hence, in New York City, when one gazes on the seventy-seven-story Chrysler Building, third highest skyscraper built by man, he is looking at the world's tallest tax exemption. For reasons to be explained later, while neighboring skyscrapers pay millions of dollars annually in real estate taxes toward support of governmental services, the 1,048-foot Chrysler Building—whose thousands of weekday inhabitants receive equivalent services—pays none. In 1973, with the completion of the twin 110-story towers of the World Trade

---

* Henceforth in this book *exemption* and *immunity* will be synonymous.

4

Center in Lower Manhattan—which then will be the two high-est buildings in the world—the title of "tallest tax exemption" will pass to them.

In fact, by careful planning, one now can live much of his life on tax-exempt property. (Here, as elsewhere in this book, I refer to exemption from real estate taxes only, not personal property or Federal or state taxes unless so specified.) He would start, of course, with birth in a tax-exempt hospital, followed by baptism in an untaxed church and education in tax-immune public schools. Later, he would traverse the continent on tax-exempt highways or by airliners serving tax-exempt airports, sleeping only in tax-exempt hotel/motel rooms. These could range from the Logan International Hotel at the Boston Airport to Holiday Inns in Boaz, Greenville, and other Alabama com-munities, or a Best Western establishment operated by the Self-Realization Fellowship near Willits, California. This assumes that one chose not to avail himself of the many university, church, YM-YWCA, or other nonprofit organizations' recrea-tion and conference centers along the route. At appropriate times, he could eat and drink regally in tax-exempt dining rooms, clubs, and recreation camps and retreats operated by exempt organizations. Meanwhile, in Utah (and other states) he could augment menus with surplus produce sold by tax-exempt "welfare farms" of the Mormon Church, or, in the Chi-cago area, with cola from an exempt-branch bottling plant (Pepsi-Cola) and groceries from a tax-exempt supermarket (Kroger).

If our exemption connoisseur were a veteran living in a designated state, he could enjoy all community services while paying only a fraction of regular property taxes—or none. If he were a factory owner, or wished to become one, he could choose

5

among states that not only would finance his enterprise with low-interest, tax-free bonds but also would allow freedom from all or most property tax for a specified period, after which, if he wished, he could move on to another such tax haven. And when he was ready to retire, if he did not already live in a state where all or part of his realty taxes might be forgiven, he could console himself by retiring in style to a tax-exempt luxury or semi-luxury high-rise apartment in California, Florida, or similarly hospitable jurisdiction and allow other aged or younger homeowners to help subsidize his comfort with their property tax payments. To complete a cradle-to-grave odyssey in tax-exempt properties, he then could be interred in a tax-exempt cemetery beneath a gravestone that had been displayed in and engraved at a tax-exempt showroom.

This is how sievelike the United States property tax exemption system has become. Indeed, *Fortune* magazine, in an article titled "Tax-Exempt Property: Another Crushing Burden for the Cities," described real property exemptions as "coming to be recognized as a national scandal,"[1] and the *Milwaukee Journal*, in comment typical of that of several highly respected large-city newspapers, declared in an editorial headlined EX-EMPTIONS THE BIG EVIL IN THE PROPERTY TAX SYSTEM, "Private nonprofit activities have succeeded politically in gaining a hoard of exemptions, many of them questionable or excessive."[2] Comparable concern has been expressed in similar reports in *Newsweek*, *U.S. News & World Report*, *The Wall Street Journal*, *The New York Times*, and CBS-TV, among other national media.[3]

Associations ranging from the United States Conference of Mayors and the National Association of County Officials to the

National Education Association and National Association of
Real Estate Boards have likewise voiced alarm.[4] A National Education Association study, for instance, characterized real estate
exemptions as "a kind of 'no man's land' in governmental relationships," adding, "In the opinion of the committee the time
has come in most states for a review of the facts with regard to
tax-exempt real estate. . . ."[5] Eugene P. Conser, executive vice-
president of the National Association of Real Estate Boards, ad-
monished that "abuse of the exemption privilege granted by
law or constitutional provision is now running rampant."[6] And
the Advisory Commission on Intergovernmental Relations, in a
section of *The Role of the States in Strengthening the Property
Tax* insouciantly titled "The Limits of Property Tax Philan-
thropy," declared:

> The seemingly endless procession of narrowing the
> property tax base has progressed so far, and in such di-
> verse directions, as to necessitate some forthright deter-
> mination not only on where it should stop, but how
> much of it should be repealed. The questions raised . . .
> are directed at the perennial giveaway system that is con-
> fusing local tax administration, frittering away the tax
> base, and unequally burdening local governments by
> yielding to special pressure groups, by shifting the tax
> burden without due regard for equity and justice, by the
> reckless misuse of exemptions . . . and by the piling up of
> concealed subsidies with little regard to their mounting
> cost and its effect on the local governments and the nar-
> rowing group of fulltime taxpayers.[7]

Many public officials are equally critical. New York State
Senator Roy M. Goodman, former New York City finance administrator, told the Municipal Forum of Washington: "Tax

7

exemption in our cities is out of control. The majority of the public does not realize [its] far-reaching implications. . . ."[8] Allegheny County, Pennsylvania, Solicitor Maurice Louik, after reviewing exempt properties in Pittsburgh, termed the total "staggering,"[9] and Minnesota State Representative Ernest Lindstrom, chairman of a legislative tax-exempt property study subcommittee, told his colleagues: "It appears that we have reached a point in time when the whole field of tax-exempt property has got to be reexamined."[10]

Several recent state studies have reached similar conclusions. A California Advisory Commission on Tax Reform report to the governor, for one, noted: "The Commission is firmly convinced that a searching review and reduction in the number and types of property tax exemptions presently applicable to particular types of property ought to be accomplished. . . ."[11] A study by the Bureau of Business and Economic Research at the University of Maryland concluded, "The property tax base of the state and its subdivisions is shot through with exemptions . . .";[12] and an Iowa survey stated, "It seems clear . . . that the general trend in Iowa . . . has been to liberalize exemptions from taxation allowed upon property, which . . . of course, increase the burden upon nonexempt property."[13]

"The problem is serious," says Paul V. Corusy, executive director of the International Association of Assessing Officers. "The tax base is being eroded."[14]

"The whole exempt-property situation," adds Alfred Willoughby, executive director of the National Civic Association, "is a mess of inequities."[15]

Why these criticisms? Why, indeed, did the United States Supreme Court in June 1969 unexpectedly consent, for the first time in its history, to review one class of property tax exemptions, those bestowed on churches?[16] Let us examine these questions, and let us begin by discussing the amount of real estate—and the apparent tax loss—associated with the real property "free list."

# 2

# The One-Third Untaxed

Standing beside the enormous concrete chamber of a canal lock, I once heard an attendant proclaim its water level with the cry: "Thirteen feet deep and rising!" Applied to the nation's exempt property, the call might be: "One-third exempt and rising"—or at least rising in various jurisdictions where data are at hand. Somewhat extraordinarily, in this presumably advanced era of computerization, instant communication, and ubiquitous records, no precise nationwide exempt-property data are available; only informed estimates.

*Fortune* in its May 1969 report declared: "In 1968, according to one solidly based estimate, almost one-third of all potentially taxable real estate in the U.S. was entitled to some kind of exemption (and this does not include the huge land areas—e.g., nearly 97 per cent of Alaska—that remain in the public

domain)."[1] One-third also has been advanced as a likely ex-
empt-to-total valuation ratio by the International Association
of Assessing Officers[2] and by Martin A. Larson and C. Stanley
Lowell, co-authors of a study under partial auspices of Americans United for Separation of Church and State, *The Churches:
Their Riches, Revenues, and Immunities.*[3]*

> \* IAAO Research Director Leo A. Droste began with valuations of
> taxable realty compiled by the U.S. Census Bureau in *Taxable
> Property Values*, and with data furnished by various state agencies
> responsible for *ad valorem* tax administration. The Census Bureau,
> after establishing that property assessment ratios averaged 32.6
> per cent of actual market value nationally, translated total 1966
> assessed taxable valuations of $393 billion into a market value of
> $1.210 billion ($1.2 trillion). Droste, using assessed valuations of
> exempt properties available for several state and local jurisdictions,
> then weighted urban and nonurban jurisdictions' ratios of exempt
> to taxable valuations and arrived at an approximate exemption
> ratio of one-third. Adding one-third to the taxable real estate
> market valuation of $1.2 trillion gave a total of $1.8 trillion, of
> which $600 billion was exempt.
>
> Larson and Lowell worked from exempt- and taxable-property
> inventories in fourteen cities, applying their own weighting to
> valuations on the basis of samplings of assessment reliability on
> selected individual properties. They then extrapolated, by a formula
> never thoroughly explained, arriving at a total market valuation of
> $1.738 trillion for all real property. Of this, according to their
> samplings, 32.6 per cent or $569 billion was exempt—$398.5 bil-
> lion of it publicly owned, $170.9 billion nongovernmental exempt.
>
> Will S. Myers, Jr., analyst for the Advisory Commission on In-
> tergovernmental Relations, proposed a slightly lower figure to a
> 1967 Tax Institute property tax symposium. His estimate was based
> on figures from Dr. John W. Kendrick of George Washington
> University, updating a national wealth inventory done for the Na-
> tional Bureau of Economic Research and published by the Joint
> Economic Committee of Congress as *Measuring the Nation's
> Wealth*. Dr. Kendrick, in *Morgan Guaranty Survey* for August
> 1966, had estimated that real estate represented just under 70 per
> cent, or about $1.5 trillion, of the nation's wealth in 1964; and
> that governmental and nonprofit organizations "held somewhat
> more than 22 per cent, or about $330 billion of this real property,
> practically all of it exempt." Myers then reviewed how he had

At current rates, then, Larson and Lowell calculate, taxes foregone on all exempt real property totaled 12.3 billion or $310 per family (not property owner) in the nation. Of this $8.6 billion or $217 per family was attributed to publicly-owned property; $3.7 billion or $93 per family to nongovernmental exempt realty.[4]

Confirming these totals, however, or placing the flesh of details on them is somewhat akin to working a jigsaw puzzle in the dark. Only eighteen states have compiled exempt-valuation inventories—and only a dozen or so on a regular basis.[5] Among these the accuracy of valuation, geographical comprehensiveness, and degree of detail are frustratingly uneven. An Iowa survey in 1955, for instance, described available valuations as "extremely rough,"[6] and Maine officials, in a survey questionnaire sent them in connection with this book, confessed to "gravest doubt" about valuations they reported.[7] In New Jersey and North Dakota, laws requiring valuation of exempt property have been almost totally ignored, and in Colorado, despite a reporting law, only ten of sixty-three counties completed exempt-valuation abstracts for the State Tax Commission for the 1967 tax year.[8]

California, for one, meticulously requires local officials of every county to compile nongovernmental realty exemptions and dispatch annual summaries to the State Board of Equalization, which then publishes them.[9] But no valuations are in-

---

verified these estimates by use of U.S. Census reports for locally and state assessed taxable real estate values. Left unsaid was the point that, were all real property exemptions for industry, veterans, the aged, certain farmers, and other owners of property outside the nonprofit sector added to the basic $330 billion exempt-valuation figure, the exemption total might be elevated above $400 billion— nearer to the $500 billion estimate by others.

cluded for government-owned real estate, Federal, state, or local
—by far the largest category of exempt/immune property (at
least half to two-thirds of most urban counties' valuation, and
more than that proportion of the acreage of some Western
states).[10]

Indeed, American governmental bodies, except for many
school districts—whose accountability to voters is both frequent
and direct—seem not to know the valuation of their own properties. As noted in *Measuring the Nation's Wealth*, Federal
censuses of wealth were made every decade from 1850 through
1900, and in 1904, 1912, and 1922, including valuation of exempt
property from 1870 through 1922. But only a national total was
published; some categories were sketchily drawn; and the surveys were executed "without social accounting objectives in
mind," and so they were dropped.[11] There was, in fact, no serious effort to inventory Federal real property in detail until the
1930s, when the impact of Federal ownership on state and local
taxation became a prominent Depression-era financial issue.
Then came the Federal property acquisition boom of World
War II, and in 1953 the General Services Administration, at the
behest of the Senate Appropriations Committee, began issu-
ing annual or biannual Federal property inventories, at first of
realty owned or leased in the United States, and later throughout the world as well.[12]

The GSA inventory, published in separate summary sec-
tions for owned and for leased property, makes no pretense to
precision. As the 1968 *Inventory Report on Real Property
Owned by the United States Throughout the World* states:

> Estimated costs (preferably at date of acquisition)
> are used when actual costs are not reasonably ascertain-
> able . . . without considering depreciation, obsolescence,

13

or economic changes of value. . . . No costs are included [for] public domain.[13]

State and local governments and most of their subdivisions in general follow the same procedure: real property inventories, if they exist at all, amount to listings of properties' acquisition costs or original cost of improvements—which may date back a century or more.*

Nongovernmental exempt valuations are almost as haphazardly made and maintained. Indeed, in some jurisdictions it appears that once a property passes into the exempt sector, it not only is not assessed but also its address and legal description are not even maintained in the assessor's rolls. To find mention of it one must delve into property title records maintained by other officials! Exempt valuations, when listed, are apt to be at acquisition or original construction costs. In most instances these are never tabulated or even maintained in a separate exempt-property roll where they could be compiled relatively

---

* The Office of Education attempts to compile data on public elementary and secondary school property valuations—but only some three dozen states report these. Valuations for public institutions of higher education also are compiled by OE, these (also of limited comprehensiveness) for publication biannually. The Bureau of Public Roads tabulates mileage of roads and streets by state, classified by level of government responsible for it—but no valuations are attempted, and in fact dedicated streets, alleys, and highways almost never are included in exempt-valuation listings, apparently on the theory that their valuations are reflected in adjacent property. The Department of Defense publishes a worldwide inventory of its real property—summarized in the aforementioned GSA report—but valuations are on the same incomplete basis as the GSA's; the Public Health Service collects data on water and sewage facilities in communities of 25,000 population or more, but includes no dollar valuations; the American Water Works Association publishes the book value, age, and depreciation of water supply facilities, but only in samplings every five years; and so run the data deficiencies.

14

easily. Moreover, identification is usually by legal description only—a series of numbers and letters denoting lot, subdivision, etc.—without the convenience of a street address or description of buildings and their use, adding further to the inhibition of cohesive conclusions.

In ferreting for information about exemptions, then, one will find that, say, in Chicago the Cook County assessor can tell you how many land parcels in the county are exempt, and how many of these are in the city, and that the number in the county has doubled in twelve years, and that 13 per cent of the parcels in Chicago's Loop are now exempt, but he cannot provide even approximate valuations; they do not exist. In Cleveland, exempt properties are listed on more than four thousand index cards; in Pittsburgh, exempt properties encompass the last pages of thirty-two separate ward listings aggregating seventy-nine volumes, but there is no breakdown of public and private exempt categories; in Richmond, Virginia, exempt-property listings and valuations comprise one volume, but are classified only under two headings ("City" and "Other"); and in Providence, St. Louis, Cambridge, Massachusetts, and Baltimore exempt properties and valuations are listed in separate volumes readily available to the public, but property descriptions, lacking cross-references for parcels comprising property entities, are cryptic and confusing. Only once in my travels in and out of tax commission and review and assessment offices could I obtain a complete listing of a city's exempt property, by property owner, address of property, and valuation. That was in Albany, New York, where a listing published as part of the December 4, 1968, issue of the *Albany City Record* could be bought for fifteen cents at City Hall.

Statewide summaries of exempt properties are available in

15

several capitals. Of these, compilations in the *Annual Report of the Ohio Department of Taxation* probably are the most universally respected for accuracy and comprehensiveness, but subcategories (churches, school districts, fraternal organizations, etc.) are of limited detail; elaboration and interpretation in bulletins of the nonprofit Ohio Public Expenditure Council are most valuable for lay interpretation of data. California, as noted, publishes statewide and county-by-county exempt-valuation summaries—entirely omitting the bulk of exempt property (governmental). Reports by Connecticut, New York, Massachusetts, and other states that tabulate exempt valuations are similarly lacking in important respects. But New York, uniquely, has data computerized so that exempt valuations can be "printed out" by city, in order of ratio of exempt to total valuations. (See Appendix.)

Then there is the added pitfall of divining the valuation base used. Despite laws to the contrary in some states, nowhere does "assessed valuation" consistently coincide with "market" or "full cash" valuation, though several jurisdictions now are attempting to make them coincide. Instead, assessed valuation may be as low as 10 per cent of market or full cash valuation; more often, some 30 to 70 per cent. Thus, to make totals and comparisons meaningful, one must know what assessment ratio is employed for valuation listings; yet this is not always evident, even when "explained" by an assessor. Consider this "explanatory" note from E. R. Welhaven, Ramsey County (St. Paul), Minnesota, assessor:

> As an explanation of the headings over the values as listed, the assessed value is that which would be applied against the tax rate were the property taxable. The adjusted market value in Ramsey County represents 35

per cent of the full market value, so that in order to obtain the full market value you would divide the adjusted market value by .35 to give you the full market value.[14]

In short, "adjusted market value" in this case is not true cash or normal market valuation—merely 35 per cent of it.

One also must know whether the listed value is based on an assessor's valuation or a self-declaration by the exempt property owner—and how recently the valuation was made. The older the valuation, the less apt it is to be relevant in a rising market, and, the more that assessment rolls are dependent on self-declarations, the more absurdly undervalued property is likely to be.

Thrust into this no-man's land of appraisal and record-keeping, one thus encounters such phenomena as San Francisco Assessor Joseph E. Tenney's stating with conviction that "about one half of our property is exempt"—but being unable to prove it for lack of valuations on such governmental property as the shorefront Presidio (a United States military reservation). "The Presidio alone could be worth $100,000 an acre," says Tenney, "and it covers a huge acreage."[15] Or in St. Louis, there is the Roman Catholic St. Louis University (enrolling eleven thousand students) officially assessed at $14.1 million, though its reported official book value is $72.1 million and the replacement cost has been estimated at $100 million.[16] Or in Denver—a state capital with large Federal, state, university, and other nonprofit complexes serving a multistate area of the West—City/County Deputy Assessor Michael Licht describes a computerized exempt-property record-keeping system that is one of the most efficient in the nation, then adds, "I'm not too happy with our exempt valuations. I would say they would be twice the listed valuation if we had the time and staff to look hard."[17]

17

Despite the unavailability of reliable national exempt-property data, however, there are islands of information that substantiate certain trends. In 1966, for instance, the Eastern Division Office of the Pennsylvania Economy League, noting that "concern has been voiced over the large segment of real estate which is exempt from local taxation," undertook a study of exempt property in Philadelphia, in conjunction with the Bureau of Municipal Research.[18] In the first section of the study, the League recapitulated the increasing proportion of exempt to total valuation from 1915 through 1966, along with dollar valuations. Excerpts from its listing show this exempt ratio progression: 1916, 13.1 per cent; 1930, 15.8 per cent; 1955, 20.1 per cent; 1960, 22.8 per cent; 1966, 24.3 per cent.

By 1969, according to Philadelphia's Board of Revision of Taxes, the exempt ratio had climbed to 24.7 per cent, with $1.621 billion of the city's $4.546 billion assessed real estate valuation exempt. (Actually, because Philadelphia assesses property at 70 per cent of market value, the true cash valuations were 30 per cent higher than official figures—and because, as we shall see, exempt properties, when assessed at all, are notoriously undervalued, the true exempt valuation and ratio would be significantly higher. A mere 20 per cent upward valuation of exempt properties, for instance, would raise Philadelphia's exempt valuation to $1.945 billion, and its exempt ratio to 30 per cent.

This upward spiral of exempt valuations as a ratio of the total tax roll appears to exist in comparable or greater degree in most localities where data are available. Consider this progression of exempt-property ratios in selected cities* in recent years:[19]

---

* For more comprehensive city exemption data, see Appendix.

### The One-Third Untaxed

|              | Year | % exempt | Year | % exempt |
|--------------|------|----------|------|----------|
| Baltimore    | 1958 | 21.4     | 1968 | 23.5     |
| Boston       | 1957 | 39.2     | 1967 | 47.2     |
| Buffalo, N.Y.| 1951 | 21.0     | 1969 | 33.6     |
| Denver       | 1963 | 18.4     | 1968 | 19.7     |
| New York City| 1950 | 24.5     | 1969 | 33.6     |
| Pittsburgh   | 1957 | 25.4     | 1967 | 32.4     |
| Washington, D.C.| 1959 | 40.0  | 1969 | 52.3     |

One could quibble about using progressive dollar sums of exempt valuation as an index since they might fail to allow for inflation or population growth. The ratio of exempt to total valuation, though, would deceive only in the event of a steeply progressive overvaluation of exempt properties or accelerating undervaluation of taxable properties—or both. If anything, the opposite has occurred. Sporadic assessment reform has tended to improve the accuracy of taxable property valuations, albeit modestly. Meanwhile, exempt valuations, especially where they consist of such farcical entries as cost of acquisition as part of the Louisiana Purchase, tend to lag farther behind market values each year.

It is clear, then, that in many localities exempt valuations are increasing faster than the taxable base—sometimes spectacularly so. The next question is why. To answer that, let us analyze which properties, by attaining places on the "free list," have caused this phenomenon, and how they came to be accorded this privilege

# 3

# Whence Came Exemptions?

EXEMPTIONS PROBABLY are as old as taxes. For it is venerable logic that a king does not tax himself or submit to taxation without his consent. Thus governmental immunity began. Church-property exemptions, too, date to the earliest tax systems, for the ancient priesthood in effect was part of incipient governmental forms. Royal astrologers, soothsayers, and more traditional priestly functionaries, in fact, received benefits far beyond exemption from taxes: James Henry Breasted records in his *History of Egypt* that the Osirian priesthood owned 750,000 acres of select Nile Valley lands, plus the right to levy taxes and own slaves for ecclesiastical estates.[1]

In India, the Brahmans' property was exempt, and in Persia Zoroaster granted priests exemptions, along with revenues that Larson and Lowell describe as "often exceeding those of the royal establishment itself."[2] In ancient Greece and Rome, temples not only were exempt but, when not state-owned, were state-supported.[3] In light of these customs—intimately related to rulers' political fears of the primitive and superstitious religions of their day—it was natural, as Leo Pfeffer has written, that "with the establishment of the Jewish theocracy after the return from Babylon . . . this exemption should be continued. . . ."[4]

Christian churches won exemption in the fourth century when Emperor Constantine (306–337), discomfited by the weak state of secular government, allied with the Church's well-organized hierarchy and exempted clericals from civil charges, and their property from taxation.[5] But, as Pfeffer points out, "It is . . . not to be assumed that religious institutions have everywhere been exempt from taxation."[6] In fact, Constantine's successors subjected church property to "ordinary taxes,"[7] and the history of Western church-state relations since then is one of rising and receding contention over tax concessions.

England's Henry II (1154–1189), in establishing Europe's first strong kingship, taxed the church, and Kings John and Henry III increased the levies. But by the reign of Henry VIII (1509–1547), churches and monasteries possessed such vast lands and revenues—three times those of the king—that Henry forsook taxation in favor of confiscation: ultimately, some thirty-five hundred properties.[8] The Stuarts and the Cromwellian Commonwealth taxed virtually all properties still in clerical hands,[9] and in France, after the revolution, expropriation of most church properties (which totaled one-third of the nation's land) was followed for a time by regular taxation, then exemption.[10]

Exemption of secular private properties has a far briefer history, dating approximately to the modern Western state and its parliamentary fostering of pluralistic institutions. Here exemption has been bestowed on the premise that "if, in the absence of a private enterprise, taxation would be necessary in order to discharge a needed function, the state may properly subsidize the institution which performs the service."[11] Exemption, then, is a subsidy, albeit an indirect and, in economic terms, a hidden one.

Exemption for institutions of higher education apparently came first, instituted by Henry VII when he "discharged from subsidies [taxes]" the colleges and universities of Oxford and Cambridge.[12] Henry also set one precedent for exemption of charitable institutions in dealing with a wave of vagrancy—then "a formidable . . . national menace"—by ordering beggars back to their native towns, where by an act of 1536 citizens were to contribute to their support. In 1597 and 1601 Elizabeth I, recognizing voluntary contributions as being inadequate, proclaimed the famous Elizabethan Poor Laws, providing that each town or parish, through its government, should care for its destitute.[13] In affirmation that this responsibility henceforth was to be on a par with public safety or national security, state funds and properties devoted to it were ordered exempted from taxes. Then, in 1601, when the Statute of Charitable Uses gave the citizenry "permission to found hospitals or abiding places for the poor or impotent," nongovernmental institutions also were exempted— though each was restricted to a yearly income of "not more than 200 pounds."[14]

The founding of the American colonies transplanted this British law and custom to the New World. Crown and colonial governmental property, of course, was indisputably exempt. And though many colonists had fled the "oppression" of state religions, they were established in every colony except Rhode

Island and Pennsylvania. Thus in Massachusetts, in addition to paying a tax for support of the clergy, residents were compelled to become Puritans or be disfranchised; and in Virginia, where the Church of England was decreed the true religion, all residents were required to pay toward support of the Anglican clergy as well as attend regular Sunday services. (These strictures were despite the fact that only 5 per cent of all Americans were church members in 1776—and only 15.5 per cent as late as 1850.[15])

Because the colonies' only schools were church-operated they, too—along with homes of ministers and laymen who taught in them—were placed under the churches' exemption/support umbrella. Indeed, because theocracies were so firmly established and, in the main, fees and fines rather than property taxes supported the first colonial governments, there is no record that exemption ever became a major colonial issue.[16]

With adoption of the United States Constitution and the exuberant challenge of creating a new society, this situation soon changed. The Constitution neither specifically grants nor prohibits exemptions—and a United States Supreme Court decision (*McCulloch* v. *Maryland*) was required to establish the immunity of even Federal property. In that case, Maryland had tried to tax the business of a United States Bank branch in Baltimore.[17] College and university properties, in the British tradition, were routinely exempted, often by their original colonial charters, and exemption of properties for general welfare/charitable purposes—essentially asylums or orphanages—also conformed to inherited British common law. Not so with church property.

The First Amendment, in a reversal of colonial practice, provides: "Congress shall make no law respecting an establish-

ment of religion, or prohibiting the free exercise thereof. . . ."
But there is no elaboration of tax implications intended, and,
as D. B. Roberison writes, "It is significant that one finds no
single reference to the question of the tax status of church property in discussions of religion in the adoption of the religion
clauses of the First Amendment."[18] Government simply is en-
joined from either suppressing or establishing religion.

But in Virginia, where Thomas Jefferson and James Madison had eloquently championed church-state separation, the
injunction against establishment first was taken as license to
dismantle colonial-era church trappings. Acts of 1799 and 1802
ordered "seizure of every type of taxable property held by
churches . . . church buildings, grounds, glebes, and other real
estate, the bells from church towers, church furnishings, books,
records of the parishes, and even communion silver . . . [with
proceeds] to be used for any public purpose."[19] Bequests to any
denomination or congregation were prohibited—and even today
the constitutions of Virginia and West Virginia require:
"The General Assembly shall not grant a charter of incorpora-
tion to any church or denomination." Though the United
States Supreme Court held the confiscation act unconstitutional
in 1815, the Virginia Supreme Court of Appeals, in an early
gesture of interposition, supported a state ruling of 1827
allowing a seizure of glebe land.[20]

Church property was not exempted from taxation in Virginia until 1840—four years after Madison's death. Kentucky
exempted houses of worship in 1816; Massachusetts in 1836;
New Hampshire in 1842; and New Jersey in 1851. But in 1850
bills were introduced in Pennsylvania's legislature to repeal laws
exempting church property; and fourteen years after the Civil

## Whence Came Exemptions?

War, in response to a Midwest-spawned drive to "put God into the Constitution," liberals presented a 900-foot, 35,000-signature petition to Congress, citing as its first concern: "We demand that churches and other ecclesiastical property shall be no longer exempt from taxation."[21] In 1875, President Ulysses S. Grant, in his seventh annual message to Congress, expressed at least partial support, declaring:

> I would also call your attention to the importance of correcting an evil that, if permitted to continue, will probably lead to great trouble in our land before the close of the nineteenth century. It is the accumulation of vast amounts of untaxed church property. In 1850, I believe, the church properties in the United States which paid no taxes, municipal or state, amounted to about $83 million. In 1860, the amount had doubled; in 1875, it is about $1 billion. By 1900, without check, it is safe to say this property will reach a sum exceeding $3 billion.
>
> So vast a sum, receiving all the protection and benefits of government without bearing its portion of the burdens and expenses of the same, will not be looked upon acquiescently by those who have to pay the taxes. In a growing country, where real estate enhances so rapidly with time, as in the United States, there is scarcely a limit to the wealth that may be acquired by corporations, religious or otherwise, if allowed to retain real estate without taxation. . . . I would suggest the taxation of all property equally, whether church or corporation, exempting only the last resting place of the dead and possibly, with proper restrictions, church edifices.[22]*

* The proposal became lost in debate over Spanish-American relations and other more publicized issues, and Grant failed to revive it; but at his suggestion Maine Congressman James G. Blaine drafted a Constitutional amendment prohibiting public aid to church-sponsored schools. "The Blaine Amendment," though never approved by Congress, was introduced in various forms into the constitutions of twenty-nine states between 1877 and 1917.[23]

25

Missouri is reported to have taxed church property, including cemeteries, from 1863 until at least 1875; an Iowa State senator in 1874 introduced a bill to tax churches; the Massachusetts House in 1876 voted on a $12,000 church property exemption ceiling, defeating it 116 to 64; and at an 1890 Kentucky constitutional convention a judge reported "considerable support for the proposition that all church property should be taxed."[24] Typical of the reasoning usually cited was an 1888 Maryland tax commission charge that exemption "fostered extravagance and saddled others with the cost thereof," with the result that a "Quaker, opposed as a matter of conscience to ostentatious display, would be required to pay taxes to support the improvident Methodist in his extravagant church buildings."[25]

Hence, building on British common law and an evolving judicial interpretation of the Constitution, an indigenous framework of law and custom for exempting property in the United States "just growed." The experience of New York State, summarized in a study document for its 1967 Temporary Constitutional Convention, in many ways typifies its ebb and flow:

> During the colonial period and New York's first 100 years of statehood, the legislature granted many ad hoc exemptions from taxation by enacting special laws or granting special charters. These special laws and other charters often were unrelated to each other and to the general revenue laws of the state. The result was statutory confusion. . . .
>
> This abuse of legislative discretion was noted especially in the post Civil War period when many individuals or corporations could buy an exemption from property taxes for a lump sum payment. The resulting public outcry for reform culminated in the appointment in 1889

of the Commission for the Revision of the Statutes of the State. . . . In 1896 the work of the revision commission was completed and the legislature enacted a general tax statute. . . . In 1901 this wave of reform culminated in the adoption of New York's first Constitutional provision expressly relating to tax exemption. . . .

The Constitutional exemption granted to properties owned by private religious, educational, and charitable institutions was approved in 1938. Until the adoption of these provisions, such property, like all other classes of privately owned property, was accorded exemption solely at the discretion of the legislature, although the legislature could not repeal exemptions of a contractual nature. . . .[26]

This enumeration only begins to suggest the range of properties now exempt from taxation in New York State. The other forty-nine states have equally distinctive exemption histories, for each, pursuant to its power to tax, independently determines which properties shall be excused from taxes by the state government or its subdivisions. Some constitutions enumerate types of property to be exempted; others mention only broad categories. Some grant exemption based on ownership; others on ownership *and* use for exempt purposes. Some place ceilings on valuations of exemption granted certain type properties; others grant carte blanche. Some provide for systematic centralized review of exemption applications; others grant local option, subject only to judicial review. And, in all of them, in implementing state laws and constitutional provisions, assessors and other officials with jurisdiction over eighty thousand taxing districts further modify and define exemptions.

The frequently surprising problems that this rather free-form, hereditary, sparsely monitored mechanism can generate are described in the next half-dozen chapters.

# 4

# "For Religious Purposes"

In a skit on NBC-TV's *Laugh In*, the owner of a small grocery store listened to a tax official explaining that property levies had increased spectacularly that year because surrounding land parcels had been exempted for religious purposes. As the official paused, leaning casually against the cash register, the grocer thought a moment, then in a flash of inspiration exclaimed, "Take your hands off my altar!"

Subsidies to, and exemption of, church property have been subjects of bitter contention for centuries. Today some national governments levy taxes on behalf of churches (West Germany, Austria, and Sweden, for instance), and The Netherlands provides tax support for parochial schools—which now enroll the majority of all its elementary and secondary school students.[1] Mexico, Argentina, Guatemala, Haiti, and other Latin American countries have nationalized all or some church property.[2] In the United States, due to First Amendment imperatives, exemption from various taxes—Federal, state, and local—has been the only major long-term financial benefit consistently bestowed on religion by government.[3]

These exemptions have been subject to numerous challenges—in this decade alone, suits have questioned property tax exemption in Rhode Island (*General Finance Corp. v. Archetto,* 1952), Maryland (*Murray, et al., v. Comptroller of the Treasury,* 1966), and New York (*Walz v. The Tax Commission of the City of New York,* 1969). But only the New York case was accepted for review by the United States Supreme Court. In it, obscure New York City attorney Frederick Walz, who described himself as "a religious person, not a member of a religious group," contended that a portion of his $5.24 annual property tax on a vacant lot (twenty-two feet by twenty-nine feet) on Staten Island "constitute[s] an involuntary payment by plaintiff to the aforementioned religious organizations, in violation of the plaintiff's right of religious freedom, guaranteed to him under the Constitution of the United States of America." The Court, in a 7 to 1 decision in May 1970, ruled against him, but in doing so it seemed to indicate only that the Constitution allows exemption, not that it requires it—at least not for all types of church property.[4] (See Appendix.)

There is little question that exemptions, in narrowing the tax base, necessitate compensatory "involuntary" payments by non-exempt property owners. Nor is there a question that owners of exempt property—in this instance, religious organizations—benefit. To defenders of the exemption, the point is that government *allows* churches to benefit, in part as a *quid pro quo* for presumed contributions to charity and fostering of moral values said to be at least as beneficial as exempt activities of secular organizations; and also because, to some, taxation would represent governmental intervention in the religious realm. The question to which Walz demanded an answer which predecessor suits did not is: *Apart* from the question of impingement on the rights of nonbelievers, does exemption violate the freedom of religious *believers* who choose not to belong to an organized faith?

Certainly the extent of exemptions granted church properties now is highly variable with locale. There are constitutional or statutory exemptions for church property in every state and the District of Columbia, but only thirty-three state constitutions expressly provide for exemption, and only fifteen make it mandatory.[5] In every state the place of worship and, as sometimes added, "necessary adjacent land," is exempt.[6] Twenty-nine states and the District of Columbia exempt church parsonages and clergymen's living quarters, though in nineteen states the exemption is not expressly provided but granted under other laws.[7] Thus in Oregon or Kansas a parsonage would be taxed; in Colorado valuation over $6,000 would be taxed; in Tennessee the principal minister's parsonage and up to three acres of land would be exempt; and in Connecticut, New York, and states with similar practices any size parsonage and any size lot would be exempt—and, in some instances, any number of parsonages for a single church.[8]

More than half the states provide general exemptions for other religious property if, as several statutes phrase it, "used for religious purposes." But definitions of "religious purposes" vary in fascinating degree. In Providence, a 1900 act exempts the Roman Catholic bishop from tax on "real and personal estate of every kind and description without limitation on the total amount thereof . . . to use, manage, improve and invest" for corporation purposes.[9] As a consequence, a deputy assessor in Providence told me, the list of income properties under this blanket exemption is "six miles long." In Minneapolis, the Augsburg Publishing House of the American Lutheran Church, which in a recent year reported profits of $399,990 on its publishing enterprise, is exempt,[10] while in Nashville the assessor has denied exemption to a whole complex of similar properties, including the Methodist Publishing House, National Baptist Publishing Board, and Southern Publishing Association (Seventh Day Adventist).[11] In Texas, church parking lots available for weekday parking at a fee are taxed;[12] in Florida, they are exempt.[13]

Almost everywhere I traveled, even within a given state, there was a surprising lack of uniformity in applying church exemption laws. In Pennsylvania, for example, parsonages not adjacent to houses of worship have been held taxable by court decree. Yet John H. Ferguson, director of the Pennsylvania State University Institute of Public Administration, reported: "Despite the clarity of the court's ruling, assessment officials in many communities continue to exempt non-adjacent parsonages."[14] In Illinois, nearly a half-century after a 1908 State Supreme Court ruled parsonages taxable because they were not used exclusively for religious purposes, a grand jury discovered the Cook County assessor was exempting parsonages in Chicago and suburbs. When they were ordered placed on the tax rolls, the Illinois legislature removed them permanently with a new exemption provision.[15]

Almost everywhere, local tax officials squirm, evade, or even try to end conversations when pressed for details of church exemptions. In the Alameda County Assessor's office in Oakland, California, for instance, this memorable dialogue occurred on the subject of $21.9 million in assessed church exemptions in the county:

"Could you name the five or ten largest church parishes?"

"I really couldn't name any."

"Just two or three of the largest downtown."

"I can't think of any."

"How long have you lived in Oakland?"

"About all my life."

"You've never noticed the larger church buildings?"

"We don't really have many showpiece buildings, like San Francisco's Grace Cathedral, or Saint Mary's, which burned down."

"Where is the Archbishop's church?"

"He has a very modest one. It surprises a lot of people. It's really very modest."

A few moments later, after further prodding, this man, who is one of the office specialists in exempt property, thought of several downtown churches and their assessed valuations: St. Francis DeSales Cathedral, $83,550; First Baptist Church, $159,400; and First Methodist Church (one block from the main business center), $220,800, of which $4,200 was taxable as living quarters.

A few minutes later he unbent enough to add: "When I first went to work in the office I used to take out the field books and plats—they had properties marked by owner then—and about every other parcel seemed to be marked with the initials RCA. I thought, 'My God, RCA owns a lot of property here.' Only later did I find the letters meant Roman Catholic Archdiocese. You won't find the books marked that way now, so it would be hard to run a total valuation."

The exemption problem is complicated by ambiguities in

definitions of "church," "religion," or "religious activities." As an example, not long ago near Modesto, California, a man named Kirby Hensley announced he was awarding himself an honorary Doctor of Divinity and forming the Universal Life Church, Inc., with his ramshackle home as "national headquarters." One ninety-minute worship service was scheduled there each week, qualifying him for property tax exemption; the rest of the week he spent with nine assistants in "evangelization activity"—mailing out credentials of ordination as a minister to anyone requesting them and enclosing $20; also four pages on how to join with any two other persons and incorporate as a church. Syndicated religion writer Lester Kinsolving reported:

> Based on Dr. Hensley's experience any three incor-
> porators could declare their home a church (perhaps
> "The Church of the Dispensation") and, in order to
> qualify as a religion, simply hold one ninety-minute wor-
> ship service every Sunday, perhaps in the form of a silent
> meditation. . . . There are few homes with a tax rate so
> low as not to justify ninety minutes . . . of worship . . . in
> exchange for tax exemption. If this appears preposterous,
> consider the wide variety of bizarre cults that are receiv-
> ing tax exemptions. In prohibiting any law "respecting
> an establishment of religion," the Constitution appears
> to forbid any legal criterion for defining just what "reli-
> gion" is.[16]

Wayne Johnson, Hennepin County (Minneapolis), Minnesota, assessor, is only one of many who has found this problem to be anything but hypothetical. "In one case," he says, "a man incorporated himself, his wife, his father, and his mother as a church. He put an altar in his basement. We checked, and in the eyes of the law it appeared he had a church. We had a terrible time getting him on the tax roll."[17]

33

How much property is necessary for certain "religious activities"? The American Bible Institute claimed exemption on 120 acres of timber, cropland, and buildings near Pittsburgh, asserting the entire area was used for training missionaries. A court held that buildings were exempt but not cropland or timber.[18] And in New Mexico, Tax Commission Secretary Jesse Kornegay ordered millions of dollars' worth of church-owned camps and summer retreats back on the tax rolls, explaining that state exemption statutes apply only to property "used specifically for worship."[19] On the other hand, in Minnesota the Oblate Fathers have been allowed exemption on an eighty-acre lakefront property on grounds it is a "rest area and retreat" for priests. "We checked this property out," says Hennepin County Assessor Wayne Johnson, "and there was one priest there. We said, 'We would like to see the exempt use here.' There are eighty acres of prime land on Lake Minnetonka that one priest was using to rest in. Should this be an exempt use?"[20]

In Nashville, Tennessee, the State Supreme Court ruled in 1962 that the Sunday School Board of the Southern Baptist Convention must pay taxes on $4.79 million in valuation devoted to an administration building, operations building, and six parking lots. The Tennessee constitution allows exemptions only for property "such as may be held and used for purposes purely religious. . . ."[21] But in Minneapolis, headquarters of the Billy Graham Evangelistic Association, the six-story Minnesota Protestant Center and the aforementioned Lutheran Church publishing house are exempt. In 1906 a clause of Minnesota's 1857 constitution limiting exemptions to "property used for religious purposes" was amended to read "church property."[22]

"What this means," one tax official told me, "is that we as

34

Minneapolis taxpayers support the worldwide work of a particular church, and maybe we don't want to."

California tax officials have had notable difficulty classifying a vast Marin County property of Christ's Church of the Golden Rule, an outgrowth of the utopian Mankind United group of the 1940s. The group, as an experiment in religious community living near the town of Willits, owns and operates a $500,000 Best Western motel, restaurant, gift shop, garage and service station, saw mill, and cattle farm. In 1961, the Internal Revenue Service, ruling that the group was not a church (it has no church building), filed for $98,000 in back Federal taxes. By 1968 the group had sold 9,600 of the 16,000 acres for which it originally had paid some $1 million, and the Mendicino County assessor was taxing $300,380 assessed valuation and exempting only $12,250.[23]

Mormon Church enterprises known as "welfare farms" also have proved controversial. As standard procedure, the Mormons —Church of Jesus Christ of Latter Day Saints—operate farms as part of their church welfare program. In their home state of Utah and several other states, the farms have been exempt; in Idaho and Oregon, among others, they are taxable. In Idaho the State Supreme Court ruled in 1954 that a 160-acre farm used to raise wheat for flour manufacture was not in "exclusive and primary use" for religious purposes, though income was for church programs.[24] In Oregon, the Tax Commission in 1961 held a 350-acre welfare farm in Multnomah County taxable, explaining that more than 70 per cent of its total produce was sold in the open market, proceeds were not distributed directly to the welfarees, and it was impossible to determine the proportion of the total attributable to efforts of handicapped, aged, and/or

35

indigent welfarees. "Tax exemption statutes," said the commission, "are to be strictly construed in favor of the state and against the taxpayer. . . . Under the rule of strict construction . . . it appears that the exemption should be denied. . . ."[25]

In addition to these problems, some religious organizations have demonstrated that they are not above exploiting their privileged position which, as Jens Jensen has written, provides "opportunities for abuse."[26] In one action at which Americans United for Separation of Church and State looked askance, the Catholic Archdiocese of Hartford purchased 121.5 acres of vacant land in New Britain, Connecticut, for $23,500. The land then was classified as a cemetery and exempted; a body was buried there; and in 1966, when the land had appreciated to $607,000, the body was removed and the "cemetery" was sold. According to Americans United, the exemption saved the church $200,000 in taxes in the years it owned the land.[27]

In a similarly fascinating case, the Roman Catholic Archdiocese of Chicago bought 320 acres of vacant land adjacent to the affluent suburb of Oak Brook, again for announced eventual use as a cemetery. In 1959, recalls Nicholas T. Kitsos, former special assistant village attorney of Oak Brook, the archdiocese then obtained a county permit to remove dirt from the property on condition garbage not be used as replacement fill. The archdiocese next arranged to sell dirt for toll highway construction for $130,000, and it signed a thirty-year lease with a sand and gravel company allowing removal of dirt, clay, sand and gravel at specified payments. These arrangements came to light only when Oak Brook sued the archdiocese and its lessee in 1967. The village charged that the property was being used as a garbage dump averaging $840,000 annually in receipts; that more than a hundred trucks a day dumped "refuse, garbage, food waste, offal, and dead animals" which "give forth a great stench"; that "great burrows and excavations" and a crane a hundred feet high created a visual nuisance; and that an injunction against further dumping as well as an order to fill all excavations were necessary to deal fairly with the village and nearby property owners, some of whose homes cost $60,000 or more.[28]

Despite repeated requests, Kitsos never was shown the declaration of exempt uses that is required for exemption, or receipted tax bills except for the year 1968. At last report, after months of delay, an out-of-court compromise was made, and the property was on the tax rolls—albeit for taxes of $1,200 for the 320 acres, compared to $1,200 per half-acre for nearby properties.[29]

Such ventures have been encouraged by Federal tax laws, particularly exemption on unrelated business income—proceeds from activities unrelated to the principal purpose for which an exempt organization is chartered. Thus, Trinity Episcopal Church in New York City owns twenty-two commercial buildings in lower Manhattan as part of its $50 million endowment; the First Methodist Church of Chicago owns the skyscraper Chicago Temple office building, most of which is commercially rented; the Cathedral of Tomorrow in Akron, Ohio, owns a plastics company, an electronics firm, and other enterprises, including the Real Form Girdle Company. There are hundreds of other examples.[30] Though such commercial ventures usually pay property tax, where special blanket exemptions exist, such as for the Episcopal and Catholic denominations in Providence, the businesses may be totally exempt.[31]

Thus, religious exemptions are a huge increment in some localities—and are growing (see Appendix). In Minnesota, churches and church property now are the largest nongovernmental category of exempt property,[32] and comparable church property expansion has occurred elsewhere. In California, for example, according to *Taxation of Property in California,* "since 1947 the assessed value of property coming under the church exemption has been increasing at a much more rapid rate than the assessed value of the state as a whole."[33] In Hartford, Connecticut, the Hartford *Times* reports, 14 per cent of all exempt valuations and 30 per cent of all nongovernmental exempt valuations are owned by the Hartford Roman Catholic Archdiocese. Despite Hartford's being the state capital with much state-owned property, the church owns more real estate than does the state in the eighty-one towns comprising the archdiocese.[34] In the small resort town of Cape May, New Jersey, in some five years Fundamentalist Minister Carl McIntire's Twentieth Century Reformation movement has acquired the two largest hotels, a complex of beach houses—in total, $1.5 million of assessed valuation.[35]

According to estimates by Larson and Lowell, total exempt real and personal property owned by United States churches now amounts to about $110 billion. Of this, they estimate Roman Catholic valuations total $60 billion; Protestant, $40 billion; and Jewish, from $8 billion to $10 billion.[36] Among Protestant denominations, the United Methodist Church alone reportedly has $4.5 billion in assets; the Lutheran Church in America, $1.3 billion;[37] and the Southern Baptist Convention $2.5 billion.[38] The Presbyterian Church in the U.S.A. usually is compared to United Methodist in size and wealth.[39]

But perhaps the fastest growing in wealth and, according to one estimate, "fast becoming, if it is not already, the richest church of its size in the world," is the Mormon church.[40] Its annual income increased 30 per cent in five years, to $110 million, according to *Fortune*, and its portfolio of business properties includes banks, department stores, radio-TV stations, a newspaper, beet sugar firms, hotels, insurance companies, and vast real estate holdings.[41] In 1962, former Utah Governor J. Bracken Lee said, "I have no guess as to [its] wealth. I do know that the net income exceeds a million dollars a day."[42] In 1968, it sold the largest single-ownership ranch in Florida—the 260,000-acre Deseret Farms, near Orlando, at the site of the new Disney World—for nearly $100 million.[43] And church representatives, in uncharacteristic candor, wrote in "Temple Square in Salt Lake City," which is distributed to all visitors to the church's headquarters complex:

> Once driven from state to state, and without means, its [the church's] assets today are substantial in temples, tabernacles, chapels, recreation centers, schools, hospitals, mission homes, *and other facilities.* (Italics added.)[44]

Indeed, America's organized religions—many admittedly poor parishes notwithstanding—have such colossal wealth and so rapidly are acquiring more that thoughtful churchmen are troubled. Doctor Eugene Carson Blake, former stated clerk of the United Presbyterian Church in the U.S.A., now general secretary of the World Council of Churches, has said:

> When one remembers that churches pay no inheritance tax (churches do not die), that churches may own and operate businesses and be exempt from the 52 per cent corporate income tax, and that real property used for church purposes (which in some states are most generously construed) is tax exempt, it is not unreasonable to prophesy that with reasonably prudent management the churches ought to be able to control the whole economy of the nation within the predictable future.[45]

39

And the Most Reverend Fulton J. Sheen, shortly after becoming Roman Catholic Bishop of Rochester, New York, declared:

> There never should be a new church built here that costs more than, say, $1,000,000. If a diocese insists on spending more for a church, it ought to pay something like a 20 per cent tax for missions. . . . The right of the poor to have a decent home enjoys priority over our right to erect a tax-exempt structure which exceeds the bare minimum. . . .[46]

Equally troubling to many is the lack of verifiable data on church wealth, as a result of both governmental and church organizations' policies. From 1850 to 1890 the United States Census obtained partial information on church property valuations, and from 1906 through 1936 four successive editions of a *Census of Religious Bodies* published by the Government gave not only valuations for church sanctuaries but also other property such as parsonages.[47] There has been no official data since then—nor do church organizations collect and release such figures. Hence, says John Copeland of the United States Treasury's Office of Tax Analysis: "The real blank area in our data now is religious organizations. All we know is what we hear from the press."[48] Moreover, says Joseph A. Pechman, director of economic studies for the Brookings Institution: "You can make reasonable progress [with data] in the nonreligious area. The religion part of it has been in the outer reaches. I think the country is getting big enough and the churches' income is getting big enough so that we ought to know about it."[49]

A survey for the CBS-TV special, *The Business of Reli-*

*gion,*[50] revealed considerable sentiment for such public reports. In questionnaires to clergymen, congressmen, and the public, there were these responses to these questions:

*In favor of required reporting of all church property and income:*
   Public, 66%
   Congress, 65%
   Clergy, 53%
*In favor of reporting only commercial (non-religious) property and income:*
   Public, 77%
   Congress, 94%
   Clergy, 91%

Policy statements of several Protestant denominations also have urged greater candor in financial matters. But at this writing the only major action at the national level has been a joint petition to Congress by the United States Catholic Conference and the general board of the National Council of Churches asking repeal of the Federal unrelated business income tax exemption.[51] There have been no such concrete steps on church property valuation or financial reporting. In fact, in Utah, when several legislators introduced a modest bill to inventory all exempt property, the 1969 legislature killed the measure by voice vote—principally, I was told, because of behind-the-scenes opposition by the Mormon Church, the most powerful single interest group in the state.

As for self-reporting, a recent action by the Roman Catholic Archdiocese of New York is fairly typical of local attitudes. The archdiocese, after months of pressure by young-priest and lay organizations to issue a complete financial statement, issued only an income-expense summary in June 1969. Relatively meaningless as such a fragment was in accounting terms, it nonetheless had strategic significance as a small first step. Next, said the president of the New York Association of Laymen, "We would hope that it [the archdiocese] would go on to give full disclosure of all its assets, including the property it holds."[52] Only one small local American Catholic hierarchy, the Baton Rouge, Louisiana, diocese, had issued a complete statement to that time. Its report, in September 1967, revealed $38.4 million in real estate, $5.8 million in other assets, and an average growth in net assets of $3.4 million annually since 1962.[53]

Meanwhile, a number of localities have taken independent action to restrict the growth of church property exemptions. Perhaps the most drastic maneuver was the Cleveland suburban village of Pepper Pike's passage of a 1968 charter amendment limiting exempt acreage to 15 per cent of the village. This occurred after eight religious institutions in eight years sought rezoning for major projects, the most recent being a synagogue seeking to build a religious school on an eleven-acre site. Passage of the amendment, 2,242 to 386, immediately brought announcement of plans for a suit to test its legality.[54]

More conventional was the decision of Maricopa County, Arizona, Assessor Kenneth R. Kunes in January 1969 to follow the letter of state law and place all church parsonages and rectories back on the tax rolls. The Presbytery of Phoenix and several individual Protestant ministers spoke in support of his drive, begun shortly after taking office, but the Greater Phoenix Evangelical Ministers Association and others opposed it. The Phoenix Gazette, however, in an editorial headlined COURAGE ON CHURCH EXEMPTIONS, supported Kunes. It said:

42

*"For Religious Purposes"*

> The existing law on church exemptions has been sorely abused, thanks to all too liberal interpretations that have gone, up to now, unchallenged. . . . By tackling a situation that has been ignored for years, Kunes takes on the political equivalent of the labors of Hercules. . . . Whatever the outcome on his decisions . . . he deserves credit and the taxpayers' gratitude. . . .[55]

In addition, in this decade at least four attempts have been made at the state level to withdraw some church property tax concessions. Every Oregon legislative session since 1963 has considered bills to charge private exempt groups, including churches, for municipal services—in effect, a maximum of 25 per cent "taxation." By Oregon Representative Richard Eyemann's estimate, the partial tax would cost the average churchgoer no more than 25 cents per Sunday; and the 1969 bill's sponsor, Representative Donald Stathos—a trustee of Medford's First Methodist Church—calculated it would raise $3 million annually in revenue. "Just as it should be the policy of government not to hinder churches and benevolent organizations," he added, "likewise it should not be the policy of government to subsidize them."[56] The 1969 bill passed the House but died in the Senate. Similar bills introduced in the Washington State legislature in 1969 and in Vermont in 1968 (there, all exempt land would have been taxed) failed to clear committees, and in 1968 a proposed amendment to Pennsylvania's constitution allowing charges for municipal services died in a committee of the Constitutional Convention. "Universities were for it at first," a convention staff member recalls. "Then eight hundred telegrams arrived in one day from Catholic institutions throughout the state and that ended that."

The California legislature, in a mild reform measure in 1969, did discontinue state sales tax exemptions for church-

43

owned and operated business (though not businesses owned by churches and leased out, or businesses in which churches merely have controlling interest); and, in another law, required churches for the first time to file a form annually listing types of income (rental, investment, etc.), but neither amounts nor names of income sources.[57]

Given these variate trends and the *Walz* decision, it seems likely that exemption of church property will be determined largely by state and local option, at least for the foreseeable future. Unless, of course, the Supreme Court dramatically reverses itself which, in the present political climate, scarcely seems possible.

# 5

# Who Defines "Government"?

If any exemption would seem uncontroversial, predictable, and beyond abuse, it would be that on governmental property. Since taxes are, after all, for support of government, what could the tax collector gain by taxing himself? Should not any government property *ipso facto* be entitled to exemption? What could be less complicated? Yet, nearly a quarter-century ago, economist Walter W. Heller, then a member of the Division of Tax Research of the United States Treasury, told the National Tax Association that "the problem of taxes on federal real estate holdings [is] one of the major issues in federal-state-local relations."[1] It remains so today—and exemption of state and some local governmental properties is no less troublesome in some jurisdictions.

One root of the distress, to be sure, is the sheer magnitude of governmental holdings. The Federal government owns 33.7

45

per cent of the nation's land acreage, and state and local governments another 5 per cent.[2] Government property is by far the largest single exemption category—including public schools and various quasi-governmental special-purpose authorities, 66.3 per cent of all exempt valuations in Philadelphia in 1966; 81.8 per cent in New York City in 1968–1969; well over 50 per cent in most cities.[3] Moreover, with population growth and intensifying demand for governmental services at all jurisdictional levels, the proportion of acreage in governmental control has increased steadily. As Heller wrote at the end of World War II:

> [Recent years] have been marked by a great expansion of conservation activity; federal entry into the field of power production, urban housing and rural resettlement; extensive public works programs to combat unemployment; vast regional development and reclamation projects, and, finally, governmental mobilization of resources to meet the ravenous demands of war.[4]

To this inventory now could be added the immense postwar highway-building boom, aerospace and medical research programs, park and recreation area acquisitions, and apart from Federal properties airport and waterfront terminal expansion, urban redevelopment, school and health-care facilities, and miscellaneous other public-serving properties necessitated by a proliferating, increasingly urbanized, mobile, affluent population.

Highways alone consume far more taxable property than is generally realized. Russell T. Wilson, chairman of the Tax Study Committee of the New Jersey State League of Municipalities, described to a state legislative commission one little-publicized effect on the town of East Orange of construction of Interstate 280: "It cost $12 million in [valuation] right through the center of the municipality."[5] St. Louis City Assessor Joseph C. Sansone adds, "Regarding the 10 per cent share of financing which the Federal government asks for interstate highways, my contention is that the city's contribution already has been made—in giving taxable property for the right-of-way."[6] According to a study for the National Commission on Urban Problems, streets and highways already occupy from one-sixth to one-fourth of city areas—and more in metropolitan centers such as New York City, where the total is 30.1 per cent.[7]

In addition, governmental properties are disproportionately distributed, and becoming more so. The Public Land Law Review Commission, for instance, reports that Federal holdings range from "as few as 7,552 acres in Rhode Island to 358 million in Alaska—98 per cent of that state."[8] In twelve states the public domain lands alone (acreage obtained in vast acquisitions from other countries and never sold by the government) comprise more than 25 per cent of the area of each state, and in aggregate more than six out of every ten acres.* Twenty other states have no public domain lands.

Other species of public property severely restrict the tax base of many localities. In Teton County, Wyoming, headquarters for Grand Teton National Park, only 2 per cent of the acreage remains in nongovernmental ownership. In Pope County in southern Illinois, 80,000 acres—or about one-third of the county's land—is part of the Shawnee National Forest. In San Diego,

---

* These "public land states," in order of ratio of Federal land to the total, are: Alaska, Nevada, Utah, Idaho, Oregon, Wyoming, Arizona, California, Colorado, New Mexico, Montana, and Washington.

47

California, 9,000 acres are Federally owned, including the San Diego Naval Base and nine housing projects and miscellaneous other properties associated with it. Indeed, as John Raymond pointed out in the *Harvard Business Review*:

> The military services and the defense agencies, after a calculated effort to rid themselves of costly installations, still maintain some 470 major bases, camps, and installations, and about 5,000 lesser ones around the nation. The Department of Defense budget for nine arsenals . . . totals $3.9 billion. . . . These arsenals employ 57,000 workers.[9]

"In some instances," the National Association of County Officials said in a statement in 1956, "as much as 20 per cent of the tax base of particular taxing jurisdictions has been acquired by the Federal government and removed from the local tax rolls in a single year."[10] This was true in 1953 when the Air Force, with one property acquisition, cut $90,000 from the tax revenues of Cuyahoga Heights, Ohio, then a village of some seven hundred persons. Village officials at first denied a permit for a building on the property, but after an Air Force threat to begin construction in any event, officials yielded.[11] Federal purchase of the pier terminal in Hoboken, New Jersey, cut 14 per cent from that city's tax base; and in Cheatham County, Tennessee, according to Judge Neil Robertson, the Army Corps of Engineers took "most of the good Cumberland River bottom land in this county" for the construction of the Cheatham Lock and Dam. "The next land that the government takes from this county," he added, "we will insist on them taking the entire county."[12]

Any capital finds its tax base significantly restricted by governmental properties. In Washington, D.C., where 54.9 per

48

cent of the land area and 52.3 per cent of the valuation are exempt, 75 per cent of the exempt valuations are Federal properties.[13] This despite a basic exemption law which, says the District Finance Officer Kenneth Back, "is probably as tight as any in the United States."[14] Organizations must apply for exemption, enclosing their by-laws and a statement of their activities; their property is investigated; they must file annual sworn statements as to continuing exempt usage; and valuations for exempt property, as well as being listed on the rolls, are reviewed along with those for taxable property every four years.

Washington's exempt rolls are swelled further by nontaxable, nongovernmental properties which inevitably cluster in a capital. Foreign governments' embassies are exempt by treaty or informal reciprocity, approved by the State Department— and in Washington, a listing of these properties fills nearly a hundred pages of the official State Department *Diplomatic List*. Fraternal, labor, trade association, and similar properties in general are taxable under District law, but over the years Congress, as the *de facto* government of the District, has legislated numerous special exemptions. Consequently, one finds in Washington statute exemptions for:

> Buildings belonging to and used in carrying out the purposes and activities of the National Geographic Society, American Pharmaceutical Association, the Medical Society of the District of Columbia, the National Lutheran Home, the National Academy of Sciences, the Brookings Institution, the American Forestry Association, the Carnegie Institution of Washington, the American Chemical Society, the American Association to promote the Teaching of speech to the Deaf, and buildings belonging to such similar institutions as may hereafter

49

be exempted from such taxation by special acts of Congress.

Episcopal residences owned by a church and used
exclusively as the residence of a bishop of such church;
buildings belonging to organizations which are charged
with the administration, coordination, or unification of
activities, locally or otherwise, of institutions and organizations entitled to exemption under the provisions of this
act, and used as administrative headquarters thereof.[15]

During one of my visits to the District I learned of introduction of a bill to exempt a half-acre of property bought by
the National Society of Colonial Dames. Its assessed valuation
was $150,000, producing some $4,500 in taxes annually. When
I asked a member of the District government if he had any idea
what might happen to the bill, he replied, "We know what will
happen—the property will be added to that exempt list, unless
there's a miracle." There was none.

In Albany, New York, where 50.2 per cent of the property
valuation is exempt in large part due to state properties, William P. Rutledge, chairman of the Board of Assessors, says, "I
can look out of my window and see nothing but exempt property." Harrisburg, Pennsylvania; Boston, Massachusetts; Montpelier, Vermont; and Trenton, New Jersey—all record one-third
to one-half of their valuation exempt, in heavy measure because
of state governmental properties and such "satellites" as Federal regional offices.

"The extent to which public property is concentrated is
material," Jens P. Jensen wrote in his major study, *Property
Taxation in the United States*. He added:

If it were distributed proportionately to taxable
property, no serious objection could be made. Such is

50

largely true of elementary and secondary school buildings; but it is often not true of state and federal properties.[16]

Indeed, as Marion Clawson of Resources for the Future
has pointed out:

> Many decisions about public acquisition of land for
> parks or other purposes are heavily influenced by, or
> even turn upon, their effect upon local tax revenue.
> Larger questions of the worth of the area for public use,
> or on the other hand the need to retain it in private own-
> ership, tend to be submerged. . . .[17]

Among examples he cites:

> In 1961 Congress passed and the President approved
> a law under which over $100 million was to be made
> available over a seven-year period, to be repaid in the end
> by revenues from duck stamp sales, for a greatly acceler-
> ated program of expanding wildlife refuges. . . . Consent
> of the governor of the state in which the land lay was re-
> quired. . . . Much of the desired land lay in North and
> South Dakota. Counties concerned, pressed for revenue
> to meet necessary costs of their governmental programs,
> objected to loss of property from their tax rolls. So the
> governors withheld their consent. A program authorized
> by our national government, with widespread public sup-
> port around the nation, came to a halt because of this
> effect on local tax revenues. . . .
>
> In hearings on the Oregon Dunes National Seashore
> proposal, citizens complained of lands going off the tax
> rolls. Much of the land was already under the National
> Forest Service. . . .[18]

The National Park Service, in economic studies commis-
sioned in connection with at least a half-dozen present or pro-

posed new preserves, has demonstrated that in most cases the allegedly disastrous effects of park acquisition are imagined. Moreover, as concluded by a Michigan State University study of a proposed Sleeping Bear Dunes preserve, because of in-park construction, increased Federal employment, and new commercial facilities outside the park, "any losses which might result . . . would be more than offset by potential economic gain."[19] Nevertheless, a National Park Service spokesman privately told me, "With all the recent proposals for new parks, whenever we have private property in the plan, we anticipate that the tax-loss argument will be used against us."

Another complication occurs when property of a city, county, or municipal corporation is located outside its borders. New York City, for instance, owns an extensive aqueduct and reservoir network for water-supply purposes, much of it outside the city limits. By state law the aqueducts are exempt, while watershed and reservoir property, under an attorney general's interpretation, are taxable.[20] In Colorado, meanwhile, though the Denver Water Board has acquired thousands of acres of watershed across the Continental Divide from Denver—contributing to exempt-property ratios of 50 per cent or more in such Colorado counties as Park County—all such properties remain exempt.[21] In California, land—but not structures—owned by a city, county, or municipal corporation is taxed if outside that jurisdiction's borders and if it was taxable to its prior owner. Thus the San Francisco International Airport, built by the city of San Francisco in neighboring San Mateo County, is taxable by San Mateo—but only on a valuation as underwater land. The airport was built on land fill in San Francisco Bay.[22]

There is, moreover, a legitimate question as to what constitutes "public property." In Pittsburgh Allegheny County Solicitor Maurice Louik notes:

> Pennsylvania's law exempts public property used for public purposes. It certainly is clear that property owned by a government unit is public property. But what about property owned by authorities or public utilities? The legislature has provided by statute that such ownership is in effect public ownership. On the other hand . . . [in Pennsylvania] courts have construed property of public utilities as being "quasi-public" and entitled to the same tax exemption as public property.[23]

Definition of "public purpose" also can prove troublesome, particularly in view of the increasing tendency of government-owned property to be utilized for proprietary activities, sometimes under lease. "In many states," says Louik, "there is a limitation to exemption of property 'not leased or otherwise used with a view to profit.'" This or similar terminology appears in the statutes of at least thirteen states.*

Some quasi-business uses of Federal properties are taxable by law: realty of such credit and banking agencies as the Commodity Credit Corporation, Federal Credit Corporation, Federal Farm Mortgage Corporation, Federal Home Loan Bank, Federal Deposit Insurance Corporation, Federal Reserve Banks,

---

* Alabama, Arkansas, Idaho, Illinois, Iowa, Kansas, Louisiana, Maryland, North Dakota, Texas, Vermont, West Virginia, and Virginia. Michigan removes the exemption from all property leased, loaned, or otherwise used by any private proprietor for profit; California requires that exempt property not be used to directly or indirectly enhance the private gain of any individual; Maryland holds that any property rented commercially is taxable; Nebraska prohibits financial gain to either the owner or user; Virginia limits leasing for revenue or profit.[24]

Federal Savings & Loan Insurance Corporation, Reconstruction Finance Corporation (and any public corporation wholly financed and managed by it), and the National Agricultural Corporation; and real and tangible personal property of the Federal credit unions, lending agencies supervised by the Farm Credit Administration, and property acquired under laws relating to loans for veterans.[25]

But private rights to possession and use of publicly owned property—known as a "possessory interest"—have caused periodic controversy since World War II, when the Federal government plunged heavily into owning defense-plant properties and leasing them to private contractors. In 1953, Michigan, confronted with a huge potential tax loss to local jurisdictions caused by various leasebacks of government property by corporations, passed a law making taxable any public property leased or loaned to a business conducted for profit. Three challenges to the law reached the United States Supreme Court (*U.S.A. and Borg-Warner* v. *City of Detroit, Continental Motors Corp.* v. *Township of Muskegon,* and *City of Detroit* v. *the Murray Corp.*), and in 1958 it upheld the statute. The Court held, in part:

> It is well settled that the Government's Constitutional immunity does not shield private parties from whom it does business from State taxes imposed on them merely because all or part of the financial burden of the tax eventually falls on the government. . . . So far as the U.S. is concerned, as the owner of the exempt property used in this case, it seems clear that there was no attempt to levy against its property or its treasury . . . [Michigan] Public Act 189 was apparently designed to equalize the annual tax burden carried by private businesses using exempt property with that of similar businesses using non-exempt property. . . .[26]

54

*Who Defines "Government"?*

According to Michigan State economist Denzel C. Cline, valuations of $19.3 billion nationally were involved in the decisions. Of these, $11 billion in valuations belonged to the Defense Department and $8.3 billion to the Atomic Energy Commission. The Defense Department held title to 236 defense plants (valuations: $2.5 billion) used by private contractors.[27]

California, in particular, might have radically altered its property tax base as a result of the decision. As the report *Taxation of Property in California* points out:

> Possessory interests in California are widespread. They range from harbor leases in Los Angeles to Indian land in Palm Springs to National Park and Forest land in various parts of the state. . . . [In real estate they] amounted to more than $165 million in assessed value in 1963 . . . $77 million . . . in Los Angeles County.[28]

After Los Angeles County began assessing and taxing possessory interests in land, however, the California Supreme Court ruled in *General Dynamics v. County of Los Angeles* (1958) that California law—the United States Supreme Court decision notwithstanding—did not authorize such a tax. Some $60 million in disputed taxes was refunded to the contractors, and when a bill was introduced in the 1969 legislature to authorize such a tax, the Senate rejected it.

Acknowledging the importance of defense and aerospace industries because they employ so large a proportion of California workers, the authors of *Taxation of Property in California* nevertheless asked:

> Should the state, in effect, subsidize certain industries by giving tax relief . . . ? Other California industries

55

in addition to the aerospace industry are in competition
with firms in states with no personal property taxes. . . .
In many cases the value to the lessee is as great as if the
property were owned outright. In a limited way, the tax
exemption frees capital for other types of activities. To
the extent that these businesses compete with businesses
which do not enjoy this type of tax exemption, there is
inequity. . . .[29]*

Other states have been equally reticent to impose across-
the-board possessory interest taxes. The New York legislature
tried in 1959 with passage of three such measures, but Governor
Rockefeller vetoed them, explaining:

> These bills, by imposing an unexpected burden, may
> cause these firms to leave the state. . . . Even more drastic
> could be the effect of these bills on the awarding of de-
> fense contracts by the federal government.[30]

In Rhode Island, the Commission To Study Tax Exemption Laws recommended negotiation for taxation of privately
owned property on Federal land, indicating that North Kings-
town alone has a million dollars in valuations of such property,
while Newport and Middletown have almost as much.[31] As yet
there has been no follow-up.

The wondrous underpinnings of ventures typified by the
Houston Astrodome—including its property tax status—also
have raised multitudinous eyebrows. The immense domed
arena, promoted by former Houston Mayor and Judge Roy Hofheinz, was built by Harris County with proceeds of $31 million

---

* It should be noted, however, that personal property—inventories,
movable equipment, etc.—of such companies is taxed under California's possessory interest law.

56

in bond issues, then was leased to Hofheinz's Houston Sports Association for forty years at $750,000 a year. Although HSA officials reported 1966 profits of $3 million on a gross of $11 million for stadium operations, the Harris County Commissioners Court, sitting as a Board of Equalization, valued the leasehold at $1—too insignificant to be taxed. Assessor Carl Smith, however, after receiving four independent appraisers' valuations of $9.5 million to $12.4 million, assessed the leasehold at the lowest of the four, which would have produced taxes of $222,000. But HSA, by challenging the action in court, was able to avoid taxation on grounds its lease guarantees "exclusive right to possession, use, and occupation and control of the lease premises."[32]

Nor was a restaurant owner successful in a bid to buy the lease for its $1 valuation, though he reported having "put together a group of businessmen . . . very capable in the realms of higher finance" who had raised "the necessary capital," and he dispatched an earnest money check for 25 cents.[33] Indeed, Assessor Smith, as a result of attempting to fulfill his duty, at one point was threatened by an assistant county attorney with removal from office—a threat in effect recanted later with the comment that it was "just a remark."[34]

Exemption of state and local special-purpose public commissions and authorities also is attracting increasing attention, not merely over traditional questions of efficiency but also over exploitation of virtual carte blanche exemption. Because of permissive charters or statutes, for instance, one finds the Illinois Toll Highway Commission, whose right-of-way and structures are exempt, leasing out land for restaurants and service stations which, because of their location, pay no property taxes. (A challenge to this exemption was dismissed by the Illinois Supreme Court in 1965.[35]) And in Boston, the Massachusetts Port Authority operates Logan International Airport under an exemption extending even to the Logan International Hotel, leased to the Hotel Corporation of America. Thus when the Authority announced plans for a $75 million redevelopment of Boston's South Street Station area, the City Council unanimously petitioned the legislature for restrictions on Port Authority operations, including prior approval by the Mayor and Council for property acquisitions, and approval by the Boston Redevelopment Authority of all renewal plans.[36]

"As of now," a member of the assessor's staff explained, "the Authority is exempt even from filing for building permits, so we don't even know what they're building. If their plan for a $75 million South Street trade and transportation center goes through, the city would lose $60,000 in permit fees alone."[37]

Perhaps the most bizarre consequences of special-charter authority, however, have occurred in New York City with the Port of New York Authority. Established in 1921 ostensibly to administer air, water, and ground transportation terminals and related facilities in metropolitan New York City–New Jersey, the Authority has ranged far afield. As noted by Harry W. Wolkstein in an unsuccessful suit to compel payment of taxes on proprietary ventures:

> The Authority has engaged in a constantly growing list of business ventures that are in no way connected with its original statutory functions . . . a large office building for rental purposes . . . a grain elevator building in Brooklyn . . . warehouses . . . a hotel . . . truck terminals . . . a miniature golf course, a drive-in movie, bowling alleys . . . restaurants . . . to the point where its industrial activities can no longer be ignored.[38]

58

In 1962, Abraham D. Beame, then New York City con-
troller, noted that since 1959 the Port Authority had built almost $12 million worth of buildings for other than aviation pur-
poses at John F. Kennedy International Airport, then known as
Idlewild. These included a copper concern, a hotel, a box company, a bank, a large office building, and a restaurant-commis-
sary structure.[39] After taking over the Teterboro, New Jersey,
airport, the Authority doubled the airport's acreage, then introduced ancillary functions, starting with leasing of ten acres
to a manufacturer of windows, screens, and awnings (an enterprise which a New Jersey court since has ruled taxable because
of a specific agreement between the Authority and local officials).[40] The climactic project in the Port Authority's sequence
will be the World Trade Center, whose twin 110-story towers
will alter Manhattan's skyline, further congest the Wall Street
area, and disturb the region's TV transmission patterns. Com-
plementing the towers will be a six-hundred-room hotel, restaurants capable of feeding two thousand persons at a sitting,
parking for two thousand cars, and eight acres of shops. Like
certain other Authority business properties, the WTC will
make designed payments in lieu of taxes—but by no means the
equivalent of regular levies.[41]

The WTC's announced $600 million construction cost,
when added to the Port Authority's 1968–1969 New York City
assessed valuation of $428.9 million, will enable the Port Au-
thority to pass the less venturesome Triborough Bridge and
Tunnel Authority (with a city-assessed valuation of $694.8
million) in real estate valuations within the city limits. Locally,
only the $2.5 billion valuation of the New York City Transit
Authority—which operates the world's largest subway system
—then would exceed it among authorities' valuations.[42]

In Minnesota, the St. Paul Port Authority, which has impressive investments in grain elevators leased to private concerns, in 1969 lost a State Supreme Court appeal to perpetuate the elevators' exemption;[43] and in Atlanta, Chairman Charles A. Henson, Jr., of the City-County Board of Tax Assessors, obtained a legal counsel's ruling that portions of Atlanta's stadium, though owned by a Stadium Authority, can be taxed if under year-around control of the Atlanta Braves baseball or Atlanta Falcons football teams. Henson even has hinted at a tax on individual player's contracts, on the premise the players are listed on the teams' books as depreciable assets. But, he says, "We find our attorneys reluctant to tackle the problem, though we are still working to this end."[44]

In general, though, state statutes and public commissions' charters are drawn so that comparatively few challenges to the largest and best financed authorities succeed. Yet particularly where income from tolls is involved, a paucity of restrictions on commissions' functions may be damaging. For, as Columbia University economist William Vickrey told a National Seminar on Urban Transportation for Tomorrow in May 1969,

> Such revenues are very likely to be spent uncritically on expansion or improvement of the facilities, or on such ancillary activities as can, by some stretch of the language, be brought within the scope of the authority, often while adjacent municipalities are unable to finance highly urgent projects.[45]

Nearly four decades ago, property tax expert Jens Jensen wrote:

> It would appear . . . that the question of taxation of public property could hardly be dismissed by saying that, being publicly owned, it must of course be exempt.[46]

60

## Who Defines "Government"?

Were he alive now and able to behold a tax-exempt privately leased defense plant, airport, hotel, or skyscraper World Trade Center, he might regard that as egregious understatement.

# 6

# The Expanding Campus

IN EARLIER TIMES the audio signature of a college campus was the blare of a band, the roar of a football crowd, the shout of intramural softball or soccer contenders. Today it is the snarl of a bulldozer, the clank of a piledriver, the staccato of a riveter. In the decade ending in 1969 more than five hundred colleges and universities were added to the United States Office of Education's compilation of American institutions of higher education, and the number of institutions enrolling thirty thousand or more students increased sixfold.[1] With every campus born, or bucolic teachers college enlarged to multiversity magnitude, complex new exempt-to-taxable property relationships were sired.

Thus, in its growth pattern alone, American higher education would seem a certain candidate for listing as an exemption problem. But it has other qualifications as well. In the centuries since basic exemption principles for such institutions were codified, colleges and universities have developed components never envisioned by Henry VIII or Elizabeth I. What, for example, should be the exemption policy toward fraternity houses? Faculty residences? Sports stadiums? Profit-making business properties? Land held for expansion or redevelopment? Research institutes?

Indeed, consider a select few colleges and universities—perhaps two dozen—which possess what is known as "blanket charter exemptions." Dating mainly to the mid-nineteenth century, when land grants and like incentives were devised to spread higher education westward from the Atlantic states, these provisions enshrined in charters the principle of exemption for any property owned by the institution for any purpose. Thus, in Michigan, the University of Michigan's exempt portfolio includes huge Willow Run Airport, on which it netted $50,000 profit in a recent year, and Michigan State's exempt holdings encompass a large department store in Lansing.[2] In St. Louis, about one-third of Washington University's $17 million assessed valuation reportedly is profit-making blanket-charter exemption property—including much of the downtown warehouse complex in the Busch Stadium area;[3] in St. Paul, Hamline University's blanket-exemption properties include the land under the Sheraton Hotel (leased to commercial interests, which pay tax on the building leasehold but not the land);[4] and in Denver, some $3 million of Denver University's* $13.8 million assessed valuation is a blanket-exempt property not used for educational purposes.[5]

* Denver University originally was chartered as Colorado Seminary by Methodist minister John Evans, who also founded Northwestern University in the Chicago suburb of Evanston, Illinois, and obtained for it a similar blanket-exemption territorial charter.

Northwestern, which occupies two scenic lakefront campuses in Evanston and Chicago, probably has received the most publicity for its entrepreneurship. The largest of a half-dozen Illinois institutions granted blanket exemptions, it was awarded this charter-amendment concession in 1855, four years after its founding:

> That all property of whatever kind or description belonging to or owned by said corporation shall be forever free from taxation for any and all purposes.

As a result, the university owns, tax-free, a prime downtown Evanston corner on which the highest building between Chicago and Milwaukee is being constructed; Evanston's main downtown medical office center; a Kroger supermarket building; and Chicago buildings leased to Pepsi-Cola, Wilson & Company, Illinois Bell Telephone, and the National Biscuit Company. Ten such properties, most of them bought from the firms to which they subsequently were leased back, netted Northwestern $496,000 in a recent year—$176,000 of it from a bottling plant Northwestern built to Pepsi-Cola's specifications.[6] The school also owns nearly three dozen homes occupied by university staff and faculty members, and another twenty rented to non-university tenants.[7]

The Illinois Supreme Court invalidated blanket exemptions shortly after adoption of the state's 1870 constitution, declaring "it was not competent for the General Assembly to exempt from taxation property . . . which was not itself used directly in aid of the purposes for which the corporations were created, but which was held for profit."[8] But the United States Supreme Court overruled the decision. Two subsequent suits, one challenging the exemption on property acquired before the

64

1855 charter amendment and other post-1855 acquisitions, later were dismissed by the Illinois Supreme Court, though in a 1908 opinion the court agreed that in 1855 "the legislature did not foresee the enormous growth of the City of Chicago [and suburbs]."

In 1967 the Cook County assessor, in attempts to obtain revenue from commercial tenants of exempt property, proposed a leasehold "use tax" which would have affected twenty-seven Chicago properties in addition to Northwestern's, among them the Inland Steel Company's modern Loop skyscraper, built under ninety-nine-year lease on exempt Chicago Board of Education property, with a "leasehold equity value" for present tax purposes listed as zero. Potential air-rights valuations of $500 million on exempt Illinois Central Railroad lakefront right-of-way also were involved.[9] But Northwestern legal counsel Alban Weber dispatched a self-styled "Paul Revere message" to all leaseholders, urging contact with "all of the politically influential people you can" to halt "this double-tax legislation . . . since there is an immediate danger that this legislation will be passed." Marshaled by the State Senate Majority Leader from Evanston, the bill's opponents scuttled it in committee.[10]

Cooper Union in New York City also has a blanket charter exemption, this bestowed by the New York legislature in 1859 —and therein lies the reason for the Chrysler Building's exemption. Both the skyscraper and the land under it are owned by Cooper Union, which uses the income to subsidize a tuition-free program in engineering and art. Were the building (assessed at $19.8 million), taxable, $1.5 million in revenue would result. But there appears to be little likelihood of this happening. Two court challenges, carried all the way to the State Court of Appeals, have failed, and neither the New York legislature nor Cooper Union seems disposed to alter the skyscraper's status, though Cooper Union did agree in 1969 not to acquire any other business property on which it would claim exemption.[11]

Most institutions, however, receive far more modest concessions than blanket exemption. In general, these encompass classroom and administrative buildings and grounds, libraries, on-campus student housing (usually including fraternity and sorority houses if the school holds title), on-campus parking lots not used for income, and athletic facilities used for intramural and intercollegiate sports.[12]

Dormitories owned by the institution usually are exempt, even though not on campus. As Associate Law Professor Allison Dunham of Columbia University explained in a report for the Commission on Financing Higher Education: "The leading case, Yale University v. New Haven (1899) . . . makes much of the fact that college originally meant residence of the students."[13] At least ten states specifically exempt college fraternity houses, but a Kansas court has held fraternity houses taxable because they are not open to the whole student body and, hence, do not "promote the general welfare."[14] In a similar decision, the Appellate Division of the New York Supreme Court in 1965 ruled Cornell University liable for taxes on fraternity and sorority houses because "they are used substantially for the social and other personal objectives of a privately organized and self-perpetuating club."[15]

Married-student housing, because of its impact on public school enrollments, also is becoming increasingly controversial. In Cambridge, Massachusetts, when Harvard and the Massachusetts Institute of Technology built separate housing for married students, the city assessed it. The universities went to court,

66

then in the spring of 1969 decided to negotiate a twenty-five-year agreement to pay in lieu of taxes on the property at the same rate as public housing: 10 per cent of net shelter rents.[16] Princeton, in an even more generous arrangement, not only pays regular taxes on university-owned apartments in Princeton Township but adds enough to cover "the full cost of educating each school-age child living in the apartments."[17] Various other arrangements prevail elsewhere.

The issue of faculty housing has proved even more abrasive. Of this, says Dunham:

> The problem is one of concluding from all the facts whether the dominant purpose is that of a residence for the employee or furthering the objectives of the college. If it is the former the housing is taxable; if it is the latter it is exempt. . . . Factors considered relative by the courts are the inadequacy of accommodations otherwise obtainable, disciplinary and other functions of the instructor in his residence, and the historic organization of the college. . . . The president's house has been the easiest for the college officials to establish as essential to the college.[18]

Thus in 1964 the University of Pittsburgh was able to win court approval of exemption for its chancellor's thirty-six-room mansion, despite charges of ostentation in transforming so grand a dwelling into a tax-exempt residence. But the general trend has been to restrict exemptions on faculty/staff housing. Brown University, despite a blanket charter exemption in 1764 for $10,000 valuation for the university president and each professor, now requires new appointees to sign exemption waivers, thereby assuring eventual return to the tax rolls of ninety-seven professors' homes reported exempt in 1967.[19] Carleton College, though owning twenty-nine exempt homes and a faculty club housing fifty-five persons, between 1955 and 1959 sold eighteen houses in a program to persuade faculty members to purchase their own dwellings. Meanwhile, it was contributing $1,500 a year in lieu of taxes to its home city of Northfield, Minnesota.[20] And Columbia University, on discussing an option on 545 acres of land in suburban Rockland County, New York, promised local officials that, were it to build faculty homes there, the school would bear the "full share" of the cost of schools, utilities, and other municipal services.[21]

Though college football is a multimillion-dollar revenue producer, luring eighty thousand or more customers to some stadiums, Allison Dunham's 1951 study concluded that "in general the receipt of revenue from college athletics has been said to be 'incidental' to the main purpose—physical education."[22] Indeed, he found only three cases in which college stadium exemptions had been threatened or revoked by court action. In one case, Miami of Ohio won affirmation of a stadium exemption in 1932. But in 1904 Adelphi lost a similar suit on grounds it received large rental revenues, and in 1946 Rutgers' stadium was ruled taxable in a judgment stressing its seating capacity of twenty thousand, its distance from the campus proper, and the "incidental or occasional use . . . at the most twelve or thirteen Saturdays during the year."[23] On the other hand, the Cleveland Municipal Stadium, which has no collegiate affiliation, in 1950 was ruled taxable, and there have been proposals for at least partial taxation of university stadiums, pro rated according to use by non-university organizations.*

---

* In Philadelphia, for instance, the Eagles of the professional National Football League use Penn's Franklin Field, and the Philadelphia Bulldogs use Temple Stadium. In each case there is no contract for rental, but the visitors assume the responsibility for year-round maintenance. If these properties and Penn's Palestra,

Of course, where statutes provide exemption regardless of use of a property for profit, no challenge to any college-conducted activity could succeed. Hence, the University of Minnesota can draw income from a two-hundred-acre plot next to Brookdale Shopping Center in the Minneapolis environs, renting out five houses, several barns, and warehouse space, and can retain exemption—even though the houses' occupants include children who go to school and, according to Hennepin County Assessor Wayne Johnson, "the university admits to this day that it has never had any intention of developing this acreage in any way . . . to be a part of the training . . . or the educational program of the university";[25] Iowa State University can operate network station TV-WOI in Ames, Iowa, at a sizable profit without subjecting the property to taxation;[26] and some universities, even in "strict-exemption" states, can operate profit-making farms, printing plants, or research institutes without paying property taxes if, as Dunham notes, "the dominant purpose is training of staff and students and the furthering of knowledge."[27]

Each case must be examined according to applicable state statutes and the activity's relationship to the university program. Battelle Memorial Institute, operated under an arrangement allowing Ohio State University students to do research there

---

used for basketball by five colleges and universities, had been taxed on their 1967 valuation of $7.1 million, the Pennsylvania Economy League calculated, $360,000 in revenue would have been realized. Pro-rating for intramural athletics and other nonrevenue producing uses would have reduced this somewhat, the PEL added, but the amount could not be calculated without additional data.[24] At many colleges and universities receipts from sports events support other activities, and therefore the athletic program, on paper, may show no profit.

for university credit, was ruled taxable by the Ohio Supreme Court in 1947, on the ground that the Institute was used essentially for the private advantage of a few industries. On the other hand, a New Jersey court held the Stevens Institute of Technology exempt despite a showing that research was for government benefit and despite failure to demonstrate that lab experiments were part of the college curriculum, holding that "colleges must engage in research as well as teaching."[28] And a New Jersey Superior Court in 1960 held the Institute for Advanced Study exempt, though there is "no formal instruction" and "no degrees or diplomas are given." Its reasoning was that "college" is more than "a word . . . fixed forever in its meaning like a bug in amber,"[29] and that the Institute does schedule seminars, furnish students' office and secretarial help, and allow them to pursue their own research. But shortly thereafter the Division of Tax Appeals denied exemption to the Textile Research Institute, also in Princeton Township, on the grounds that "it is sponsored directly by an industry which is conducted for a profit."[30]

Nonetheless there have been suggestions that research institutes operating under negotiated contracts might pay some taxes. The Pennsylvania Economy League, for instance, after itemizing contractual research at five Philadelphia institutions, calculated that if space for this were rented in a taxable office building an average of 15 per cent of the rental would go to property taxes. A social science research project, it added, might require 4 per cent of the budget for rental, and costs for other research activities might range to 2 per cent of gross expenditures—but the average tax would be less than 1 per cent of budgets. Therefore, assuming $3 million of contractual research, property tax payments of some $300,000 might be made to the city and school districts, with the ultimate burden, or "shift," of course, falling on the contractor.[31]

The tax status of college or university land held for future development also varies greatly, depending on statutes. If ownership alone is the criterion, acquisitions for future use would be exempt; if use is decisive, only nonrevenue property used for educational purposes would qualify. Illustrating the diversity of practices, Dunham notes:

> Property developed by planting trees and shrubs and acquired to improve the appearance of the entrance to the college proper has been held exempt. On the other hand, college property has been held taxable where it appeared that the land was held to control neighborhood development.[32]

Again, the trend appears to be toward strict interpretation where statutes permit.

In some instances, college and university officials, under pressure from local state officials concerned about local tax bases, have voluntarily restricted exemptions in certain categories. In Indiana, for instance, after a State Tax Board chairman proposed a *de facto* prohibition on universities' owning or leasing income-producing properties, both Indiana and Butler Universities voluntarily surrendered exemption on property not used for educational purposes. Butler's action was to take effect after a ten-year grace period to avoid "sacrifice sales" of property. At Purdue University the policy already was to encourage gifts through the Purdue Research Foundation, which pays taxes on income property; henceforth, income property for Indiana University will be similarly channeled to a taxpaying realty corporation.[33]

71

Fordham University, after being given title to the 115-acre Lewis Calder estate in suburban Westchester County, New York, agreed to construct no academic buildings and restrict occupancy to two persons per acre, as well as make payments in lieu of taxes, in return for a zoning change permitting use of the property as a conference center;[34] Princeton, after announcing its intention to convert the taxpaying Princeton Inn into an exempt residence for newly admitted women students, agreed to phase the tax withdrawal over a ten-year period to ease its effect on the borough tax base;[35] and Northwestern University, in addition to expanding its campus on Lake Michigan fill rather than removing more Evanston property from the tax rolls, has begun a long-term program of selling exempt local income properties.[36] Indeed, as will be discussed later, the practice of payments in lieu of taxes by colleges and universities is much more widespread than usually realized, and is rapidly spreading.

More such accommodations surely are inevitable, for in some communities the tax impact of college and university property is serious. Charles Laverty, Jr., of the Cambridge, Massachusetts, Board of Assessors, probably best summarized the growing dilemma implicit in such situations when he told me: "Cambridge is what it is because of the universities. On the other hand, the city has a limited amount of land and we have to raise operating revenue from the properties that can be taxed. If the total taxable property keeps declining and the tax rate keeps going up, that certainly cannot help having negative effects on both the universities and the city. Things certainly cannot continue in their present direction for much longer."

# 7

# Welfare Exemptions: "The Indigent Rich"

In 1944 California voters vehemently debated adding a new exemption category to the constitution encompassing properties of "welfare" organizations—religious, hospital, or charitable institutions and societies presumed to exist to advance community welfare.* "In support of this amendment," the authors of *Taxation of Property in California* recalled, "proponents advanced the argument that while the loss in the tax base would cost the taxpayer possibly 1 cent per $100 of assessed value, 'additional health and welfare services resulting from the exemption would save the entire exemption cost.' They also assured the voters that 'the meaning of every phrase has been clearly defined by the taxing authorities and by the courts.' "[1] Since adoption of the amendment, welfare exemptions have

*Some properties previously discussed under university and religious exemptions would be included in this category as well.

73

proliferated—to the accompaniment of constant litigation—to the point that, in Los Angeles County alone, according to Assessor Philip E. Watson, "The welfare category makes up about one-fourth of all [nongovernmental] exemptions granted in our county, [and] it is the fastest-growing category of exemptions."[2]

California's experience is not unique. Twenty-three states have constitutional or statutory provisions to exempt most or all property used by literary, scientific, charitable, benevolent, agricultural, and religious institutions and societies and the like.[3] In most cases, these originally were applied rather strictly to libraries, hospitals, orphanages, and other religious or secular social welfare properties which, in the Elizabethan tradition, serve "humanitarian" purposes or assume a "public burden" which otherwise would fall upon government.[4] But as with other exemptions this early rationale steadily has crumbled. Indeed, says the International Association of Assessing Officers, in addition to approval of broad exemption categories, "at the instance of certain pressure groups, legislatures have listed specific organizations for exemption . . . the YMCA, YWCA, Elks, Eagles, 4-H, Red Cross, Salvation Army, Knights of Columbus, Masonic lodges, American Legion, VFW, Boy and Girl Scouts, state bar associations, the DAR . . . local organizations . . . such as the Polish Army Veterans in Delaware and the Confederate Soldiers Home in Mississippi."[5]

Politics aside, the logic underlying such exemptions frequently is difficult to ascertain. In Pennsylvania, for instance, the Elks, Moose, Eagles, Masons, and several kindred organizations are taxable, but the American Legion and Veterans of Foreign Wars are exempt.[6] In Virginia, real and personal property of "benevolent institutions" is exempt "if the property is

74

used exclusively for lodge and other organizational activities."[7] In Georgia, property of a chamber of commerce is taxable,[8] but Louisiana exempts "property of nonprofit organizations with assets of more than $250,000 devoted to the promotion of trade, travel, and commerce."[9] Louisiana also exempts "property owned by athletic or physical culture groups of a specified nature . . . carnival organizations . . . agricultural fair associations conducted as civic enterprises."[10] In Minnesota, under 1946 and 1967 attorney general rulings, even dwellings of public school teachers and administrators can be exempt if owned by the local school board and certified by the board as "teacherages" needed to help attract staff or facilitate the staff's performance of its duties. As a result of this practice, originated in the Depression and extended during housing shortages following World War II, Minnesota's Department of Education estimated in 1968 that "about one-fourth of the 452 districts operating graded elementary and secondary schools have school-district-owned residences."[11] College-level instructors in Minnesota, meanwhile, receive no such statewide beneficence.

In New York, statutes exempt property of "a membership corporation used to provide housing and auxiliary facilities for faculty members, students, employees, nurses, interns, resident physicians, researchers and their immediate families in attendance or employed at colleges, universities, educational institutions, child care institutions, hospitals, and medical research institutes."[12] Consequently, notes the Syracuse Governmental Research Bureau in the report *A View from the Center:*

> Researchers and faculty members of educational institutions, regardless of personal income, can form a membership corporation, build residences for themselves, and be completely exempt from property taxes. Their fel-

75

low academicians who build their own homes receive no tax exemptions.[13]

There also is an exemption for property "owned by a minister, priest, or rabbi or his unremarried widow, up to $1,500 of assessed valuation," adds the report, resulting in this contradiction:

> Clergyman A buys his own house and receives a reduction of $1,500 in his assessment. Clergyman B lives in a house owned by his church or synagogue. His assessment is nothing.[14]

In Iowa, whose exemption statute speaks only broadly of "literary, scientific, charitable, benevolent, agricultural, and religious institutions and societies," Des Moines City Assessor Andrew S. Regis made an informal survey of exemption policies toward chamber of commerce, fraternal, and labor union property in Iowa counties and cities. He discovered these inconsistencies:

### Chambers of Commerce

> Of forty-one counties whose chambers own property, thirty-three exempt and eight tax personal property; two exempt and four tax real property.
> Of twenty-one cities, fifteen exempt and six tax personal property; two exempt and two tax real property.

### Labor Unions

> Of six counties having labor unions which own property, three exempt and three tax personal property; two exempt and one tax real property.
> Of twenty cities where unions own property, ten exempt and ten tax personal property; six exempt and eleven tax real property. (No real property was union-owned in three cities.)

# Welfare Exemptions

## Fraternal Organizations

Eagles—exempted by twenty assessors (ten partially), taxed by nine.

Elks—exempted by thirteen assessors (eight partially), taxed by six.

Moose—exempted by eighteen assessors (eight partially), taxed by six.[15]

Similar anomalies exist in almost every state. The report *Real Estate Tax Exemptions in Nebraska*, for example, states:

> It would appear that the flood of tax exemptions given to private institutions in Nebraska has stemmed from the 1921 case involving the Masonic Lodge in Lancaster County (Lincoln) wherein the court began to give a broad interpretation to "charitable." This was accelerated in 1932 with another Masonic Lodge case. . . . Furthermore, the opinions of the Attorney General during this latter period, particularly concerning Ak-Sar-Ben and the veterans organizations, have also exempted considerable property from taxation.
>
> The Nebraska Supreme Court, however, has never ruled on tax exemptions for Ak-Sar-Ben, nor on veterans organizations. Nor has it ruled on the nature of veterans organizations. . . . Exemptions are given to various other properties which are questionable. . . . These include women's clubs, union halls, and ethnic social clubs.
>
> The meandering course followed by the courts and the Attorneys General is a confusing one for tax assessors. . . .[16]

In Colorado, a legislative report notes that fraternal organizations formed for charitable purposes are eligible for exemption under Tax Commission rulings, but clubs "organized for social purposes" are not:

77

For instance, if the bylaws of an organization emphasize charity, and social activities are of secondary importance—Elks, Masonic lodges, etc.—the organization may qualify for exemption. On the other hand, if the social aspects are of uppermost importance, the exempt status is denied. . . .

In at least four situations, the Tax Commission has denied exemptions to social clubs—the Polish Club and Slavic Club, for example. . . . A review of the tax exempt records of the city and county of Denver reveal that the Denver Press Club and the Denver Women's Press Club currently are exempt. . . . Those exemptions have not been reviewed by the Commission.[17]

The Denver Press Club's exemption was particularly intriguing in view of this statement in the *Colorado Revised Statutes, 1963:*

The property of the Denver Press Club, a social, nonprofit organization, is not exempt from taxation under this section because its charitable activities were insufficient to classify it as a charitable organization.[18]

In Pennsylvania, Allegheny County twice prevailed against challenges to attempts to tax civic/social organizations, one known as the Bower Hill Civic League, the other the Richland Civic Club. In the Bower Hill case, the Superior Court of Pennsylvania ruled:

A judicial desire to be liberal towards institutions which are doing praiseworthy public work has sometimes led the courts to invest the word "charity" . . . with a meaning not warranted either lexicologically or by a consideration of the ideology of the constitutional provision invoked.

78

## Welfare Exemptions

The league was founded not as a benevolent or eleemosynary organization but as one to coordinate various civic groups in the community; and it is not bestowing any charitable bequests upon anyone except to the extent that it permits nonprofit organizations to share its quarters without charge, at the same time demanding of others able to pay a rental sufficient to more than defray its expenses. . . . There are many civic, social service, and fraternal nonprofit groups that devote much of their time, and efforts, and money in bestowing charitable assistance to others. However, such projects do not make organizations "purely" (wholly) charities so as to entitle them to exemption. . . .[19]

In the Richland Hill Civic Club case, the Superior Court added:

In the present case there is more charity bestowed in the form of cash contributions to various local organizations than in Bower Hill. However, it is not our understanding of the law that a group of citizens may secure the benefit of tax exemption by bestowing charity in a manner they may privately determine to be proper. . . . Commendable as its efforts and projects may be, we must conclude that its property is not exempt from taxation.[20]

Colorado and Michigan—among others—require that certain properties be indigenously owned to qualify for exemption. Colorado's Tax Commission ruled as much in denying exemption to a geology summer camp for students of an out-of-state university, an action affirmed by the Colorado Supreme Court. Said the court:

While it is the policy of society to encourage education, benevolence, and charity, we do not believe it to be

79

a proper function of the state to go outside of some borders and devote its resources to the support of education, religion, and charity for the benefit of the human race. Such would be a direct diversion of the state's resources at the expense of its resident taxpayers.[21]

The question of the extent to which exemption should be extended to activities tending to compete with taxpaying properties also has proved nettlesome. In Portland, Oregon, after hotel operators complained about a YMCA exemption for rooms and eating accommodations open to the public—even to a government contract for housing and feeding draftees—Multnomah County Finance Director Herbert A. Perry placed the property on the tax roll.[22] But in Missouri and California, among other places, YMCA hotel and dormitory accommodations have been held by courts to be exempt, though the California Supreme Court allowed taxation of a YMCA restaurant, barber shop, and tailor shop as "largely commercial in character, and properly classifiable as business ventures . . . in competition with like enterprises maintained in the community."[23] Oregon, among other states, also allows taxation of hospital gift and beauty shops and like facilities open to the public, pro-rated as to percentage of the total hospital building valuation; but in St. Louis, Assessor Joseph C. Sansone was prohibited by the State Tax Commission from assessing portion of a luxury tower wing of Barnes Hospital. Sansone had contended that several floors of the wing were leased to doctors for private practice and that use of a rooftop restaurant and sleeping rooms intended for patients' friends and relatives was being offered to persons presumably unable to obtain reservations in commercial establishments.[24] But Missouri has an "all-or-nothing" exemption law that forbids dual assessment of properties by taxable and exempt segments. Proprietary (profit-making) hospitals, however, are entirely taxable in California, Georgia, Pennsylvania, and elsewhere.[25]

Some exempt organizations also have demonstrated a penchant for seemingly inordinately large properties. Hennepin County Assessor Wayne Johnson, for example, told a Minnesota legislative subcommittee of "a widespread growth of day camps" that "are taking up a large amount of undeveloped acreage" and claiming exemption on the basis that all the acreage is used for day-camp purposes. "The YMCA in Edina, for instance, actually uses about twenty acres of a hundred-acre site," he said.[26] Indeed, so tempting are the opportunities for entrepreneurship under welfare exemptions that Alfred Willoughby, executive director of the National Civic Association, recalls a wry conversation with the late Charles Edison, then the Association's president, after a nonprofit organization had announced purchase of a pickle factory.

"Would you like to own a toll bridge?" asked Edison.

"You're kidding."

"I'm not. I know where we can buy a toll bridge."

"Over my dead body!"[27]

With welfare exemptions, as with other exemption questions, a root problem is definitions. What is charity? What serves public in contrast to private interests? What property is essential and what is incidental to fulfilling a charitable purpose? As a Minneapolis *Star* study of tax exemptions asked, "Is just being a 'nice guy' enough to get you on the property-tax free list?"[28]

Perhaps nowhwere is the centrality of these questions better illustrated than in a fast-spreading controversy over retirement homes. Accelerated by passage of Federal legislation

allowing 100 per cent mortgages with forty-year repayment provisions on housing for the elderly, multiple-unit retirement
homes have expanded rapidly throughout the country—many
under the aegis of church groups, to whom the most favorable
terms are available. "Many leading churchmen—and periodicals
such as the *Christian Century* . . . argue that acceptance of
subsidies constitutes a violation of the Constitutional separation
of church and state," contends Lyle E. Schaller, director of the
Regional Church Planning Office of Cleveland.[29] Nonetheless,
several hundred church-sponsored retirement complexes have
been built in recent years, and more are planned particularly in
appealing-climate areas such as California, Colorado, the North-
west, and Florida.

"Retirement," in a sizable share of such complexes, means
anything but spartan living. One such home, in Oregon, requires up to $23,000 as an "entry fee," plus monthly charges;[30]
another, in Illinois, asks $25,000 or more as a "founder's fee,"
plus monthly charges;[31] still another, in Wisconsin, wants
$15,000 for entry, plus monthly fees.[32] More than half the
$61.7 million assessed (as contrasted to market) valuation of
life-care homes in California could be attributed to such luxury
or semi-luxury properties in 1969, a California Senate committee was told;[33] and Colorado in 1966 estimated fixed assets of
such homes in excess of $25 million of assessed (less than half
of cash) valuation, with occupancy fees "suggesting that little
consideration is given to the destitute."[34]

In 1966, Colorado's Committee on Tax Exempt Property
was told, one exempt high-rise retirement home's residents in
Denver included "personnel from the University of Colorado
Medical School . . . First National Bank, the Post Office Department, and Denver Convention and Visitors Bureau Em-

ployees."[35] At another exempt Denver high-rise, a witness reported, "inquiry . . . indicates dentists and doctors, supervisors from the telephone company . . . an assistant vice president . . . are currently residing at this property . . . the sign located at the front . . . advertises 'high-rise luxury living.' Inquiry by prospective tenants indicates that occupancy may be gained by individuals as young as forty-five years old as this building has a 74 per cent occupancy."[36]

A realtor reporting on a Presbyterian high-rise retirement home in Pueblo, Colorado, declared that of fifty-nine tenants listed, 28.8 per cent were employed or have financial means "well above the average of property owners that are paying real property taxes," and another exempt high-rise's residents included "the owner of a surgical supply house and the president of one of the region's largest photo-finishing plants and camera store chains."[37] A newspaper reporter, checking the parking lot of another exempt Colorado retirement home, observed Cadillacs and other expensive autos in residents' parking spaces.[38]

Should such properties be exempt?

In Wisconsin, a circuit court in 1967 sustained Milwaukee Tax Commissioner Vincent Schmit's assessment of $1.3 million Bradford Terrace, which required entry fees up to $15,000 and monthly payments up to $250, but in February 1969 the State Supreme Court reversed the ruling, 4 to 3.[39] In Kansas, a similar ruling evolved from a 1965 case involving Topeka Presbyterian Manor.[40] California courts, in a series of decisions, also have held such homes exempt, including cases involving high-rise apartments[41] and, in 1969, detached-dwelling complexes in Lancaster and Palmdale.[42] The court decision in the latter case is instructive:

The County argues that the property is not exempt because the sole and exclusive use is for private residential purposes, a non-charitable use, that the tenants were totally self-sufficient and not in need of some of the services which they could provide themselves. Public policy governing tax exemption requires, in principle at least, that the exemption tend to reduce governmental financial burdens. As there is no government obligation to provide housing for financially self-sufficient persons over age 60, the tax exemption is of no benefit to government, and there is no object of charity. . . . And further with particular respect to the Palmdale property, the County emphasizes that of the 141 homes, 85 were occupied by tenants under age 40. . . .

Nevertheless in the opinion of this court the plaintiff has sustained its burden of proof that it has satisfied all of the requirements of tax exemption. Plaintiff was not organized nor operated for profit; no part of its earnings inure to the benefit of any private shareholder or individual; the home was not used or operated so as to benefit anyone through distribution or profits . . . ; it was not used for fraternal or lodge purposes. . . .

To adopt the County's view would lead to the absurd result that if a few vacancies existed on the tax date it could not be said that the entire property was used for a charitable purpose, and that unless all of the homes were occupied by qualified persons the entire project would be denied tax exemption.[43]

In most other states, however, the tendency has been to tax such homes. Arizona exempts only homes "for relief of the indigent or afflicted"; in Ohio, full medical and personal care is required for exemption, and no more than 95 per cent of costs can be recovered from residents; in Virginia, housing for the aged must be a hospital to be exempt.[44]

Taxability of retirement homes in Oregon has been upheld in court decisions involving Willamette View Manor and Oregon Methodist Homes, Inc. (1959) and Friendsview Manor (Quaker) (1967);[45] in Illinois, the Methodist Old Peoples' Home (formerly the Pick-Georgian Hotel) in Evanston (1968);[46] and in Minnesota, Madonna Towers (Oblate Fathers) in Rochester (1969).[47] Montana and Florida courts also have held such homes taxable, but subsequent legislative action has restored their exemption.[48] In Colorado, meanwhile, the opposite occurred: the legislature, after court and Tax Commission rulings exempting retirement homes, in 1967 passed a law subjecting them to taxation.[49] And in Maryland, the legislature has authorized local jurisdictions to negotiate payments in lieu of taxes from sponsors of retirement homes.[50]

Where exemption is allowed, controversy remains lively. In California, a legislative study committee declared: "There is no compelling social obligation on the part of the public to subsidize housing and services for those aged persons who can afford to pay."[51] It recommended fixing a maximum exemption of $1,000 per resident of all retirement homes. In Florida, the Brandenton *Herald* editorialized: "For churches to accept— much less claim—the right to operate luxury-class retirement buildings tax-free, leeching up on the poor of the community, is neither charity nor Christianity. It's blasphemy!"[52] Nonetheless, in many jurisdictions permissive definitions of charity or loosely phrased exemption statutes failing to require "purely" charitable purposes for exemption appear, in the words of a California report, to allow "the definition of a charity to include almost any public good . . . [for] the rich as well as the poor."[53]

The Advisory Commission on Intergovernmental Relations summarizes the welfare exemption situation this way:

Over the years all kinds of organizations that are affected with a public interest, or have been able to persuade state legislatures that they have the status and therefore have received exemption from paying property taxes, have been steadily expanding. It seems to have become progressively easier for almost any organization that engages in some activity of social or cultural significance to make the tax-free list—and once on the list its subsidy tends to be permanent.

This, in effect, adds up to a large, concealed government subsidy for numerous classes of nonprofit institutions and organizations ranging down from those whose services clearly are of a public nature to those whose activities may be socially desirable but also may be intermingled with professional and business interest or even subsidiary to such interests.[54]

In too many instances of welfare exemptions, one is reminded of the universal truth written by the Missouri State Supreme Court in denying exemption to the Benevolent & Protective Order of Elks many years ago:

Charity is not a promiscuous mixer. Here she modestly stands outside or goes away and waits; waits until the plaintiff has finished using the spacious and comfortable rooms for the pleasures of its members; waits until the curtain has fallen upon the last scene of the vaudeville performance on the stage; until the dancers are tired and have gone home; until the billiard rooms have been deserted to the markers; until the plaintiff has paid the cost of its own entertainment and goes out and finds her and hands her whatever it may have left in its own pocket. She gets not the use of the premises but what remains of income to the owners after they have used it in carrying out the injunction of their organic law, by promoting their own welfare, enhancing their own happiness, and cultivating their own good fellowship among themselves.[55]

86

# 8

# Dwellings Without Taxes: Homeowners/Veterans/ Aged

Only in fantasy would most homeowners postulate a situation in which nonresidential property owners pay real estate taxes while they do not. Yet, thanks to a provision known as "homestead exemption," this now is at least theoretically possible in eleven states.[1]* Merely by owning and occupying a home, one can be exempt from real estate levies on a designated maximum valuation—which in some instances amounts to total property tax forgiveness. But this is only the beginning of the tax concessions bestowed on certain homeowners. Veterans, widows, the handicapped, the aged—these and other subgroups of the homeowning populace are granted special tax treatment in about two-thirds of our states. For them, the homeowner's "impossible dream" is happily fulfilled.

* They are: Colorado, Florida, Georgia, Hawaii, Iowa, Louisiana, Mississippi, North Dakota, Oklahoma, Washington, and West Virginia.

Consider first the ordinary homeowner's, or homestead, exemption. Introduced and then rejected in the Dakotas and Wisconsin between 1917 and 1923, it was designed to encourage home ownership, especially in rural areas, by alleviating the tax load, with assumed special impact in recessions. Then came the Depression and a flurry of homestead exemptions or tax preference measures in at least thirty legislatures.[2] Michigan and New Mexico rejected the exemption in referenda; North Carolina and Utah adopted constitutional amendments that were never implemented; and Arkansas, South Dakota, and Wyoming terminated the exemption by formal vote or disuse, Wyoming most recently (1955).[3] In other states where it was adopted, the exemption remains in use—albeit to the occasional detriment of local tranquility.

In Florida, for instance, where the law provides exemption on a homestead's first $5,000 of assessed valuation, an imbroglio over the exemption placed Miami's experiment with a metropolitan government in temporary jeopardy in the early sixties. As one provision of the Dade County Metro charter adopted in 1957, a reassessment of all property was to be made by January 1, 1961, raising the then-prevailing fractional assessment level of 50 per cent to 100 per cent, or "full cash valuation." Of course, in practice the fractional assessment made the $5,000 statutory exemption applicable to double that valuation— $10,000 true market value. Consequently, when the new assessments were announced, thirty thousand previously exempt homeowners were added to the rolls, resulting in a petition for a referendum to abolish the county manager form of government. The controversy was resolved only by the county manager's unilateral downward revision of the assessments, followed by a referendum altering the reassessment provision to require

88

merely "a just valuation." Whereupon the county manager, under a cloud for "botching of the tax situation," was fired.[4]

In 1962, according to one study, forty-one Florida counties were assessing real property at ratios below 60 per cent of market value, and thirty-four below 50 per cent, perpetuating the higher effective exemption than provided in Florida law,[5] and approximately one-third of all locally assessed real property in the state was covered by the exemption.[6] Taxes thus forgiven, according to one calculation, exceed $150 million a year.[7] Indeed, when President Nixon purchased his vacation home in Key Biscayne for $127,700, *The New York Times* noted that it was assessed at only $56,500; should he be living there January 1 and wish to declare the house his principal residence, the $5,000 homestead exemption could be applied to reduce his $1,126 tax bill by at least $110.[8]

Other states' homestead exemption ceilings range downward from $5,000 in Mississippi. Since none assesses at full cash value, however, the effective exemption ceiling, as in Florida, actually is greater than at first apparent—with a *de facto* maximum of $25,000 in Mississippi, where the assessment ratio averages 25 per cent of market value. Therefore, according to the Census Bureau, 44.5 per cent of locally assessed real property is covered by the exemption in Mississippi, and more than 30 per cent in Georgia, Louisiana, and Florida.[9] In aggregate, the Census calculates, $9 billion in assessed valuation received homestead exemptions in 1966.[10] Iowa, Louisiana, and Mississippi, through credits or direct payments, reimburse local governments for revenue thus lost.[11] In 1968 this placed Louisiana in the singular position of expecting to pay out more for homestead exemption reimbursements ($53 million) than was collected in residential property taxes ($24 million).[12]

Special exemptions for veterans have an even lengthier history, dating at least to ancient Rome, when members of Caesar's legions were granted tax concessions on their return from foreign expeditions.[13] New York, among other states, granted veterans exemptions as early as the Civil War,[14] though exemption often was restricted to men with disabilities. From the start, the exemption was surrounded by controversy. In California, for instance, the first veterans exemption (1911), applying only to survivors of the Civil, Spanish-American, and Indian wars, narrowly won adoption—106,554 to 96,891. The principal argument in its favor, according to *Taxation of Property in California*, was not that it would "reward" military service but that it might help "bring new citizens to the sparsely settled West."[15]

Today, the Advisory Commission on Intergovernmental Relations reports, "some kind of property tax exemption for veterans" is provided in about thirty-two states,* "though the categories and conditions are infinitely varied." It continues:

> Exemptions based solely on service are granted to all veterans in ten states and to veterans of wars prior to World War I in five others; but in six of these states, only if the value of the veterans' property (and in Idaho's, income) does not exceed specified amounts. The majority of these states also provide *larger exemptions based on* disability and the other states provide exemptions entirely on this basis. . . . Ten states in all have . . . property qualifications, with ceilings ranging from $3,600 to $8,000. . . .

* Behrens, in *Municipal Finance*, lists thirty-three: Alabama, Arizona, Arkansas, California, Connecticut, Florida, Georgia, Hawaii, Idaho, Indiana, Iowa, Louisiana, Maine, Maryland, Massachusetts, Michigan, Minnesota, Montana, Nevada, New Hampshire, New Jersey, New Mexico, New York, North Carolina, North Dakota, Oklahoma, Oregon, Rhode Island, South Carolina, Tennessee, Utah, Vermont, and Wyoming.

> In over one half of the states the exemption applies to all classes of property, in most of the others to the veteran's homestead or homestead and personal property....
>
> Most exemptions extend over the life of the veteran, quite commonly extended to his widow and minor children, and sometimes to his father or widowed mother....[16]

Louisiana limits the exemption to a maximum of 160 acres of property, and New York restricts the exemption to $5,000 in valuation of property bought with "proceeds from pension, insurance, or other government benefits."[17] In practice, the State Board of Equalization has determined, mustering-out pay and readjustment and severance allowances also constitute "eligible funds," though enlistment allowance, flying compensation, and leave bonds do not.[18] Most states compel filing of an annual application for the exemption,[19] but the comprehensiveness of information required and efforts to verify it vary.

Hence, in California, where veterans exemptions swelled into the largest component of private exempt valuations in the fifties, little was done to enforce property-net-worth ceilings ($5,000 for single, $10,000 for married veterans) until the early sixties. At that time, Los Angeles County Assessor Philip Watson began requiring an annual affidavit listing real estate, cars, boats, aircraft, and the like, and making the applications available as public records for inspection by any taxpayer. The result —something akin to a French farce in which bedrooms, closets, hallways, and stairwells suddenly disgorge hidden culprits—was a one-year decrease in applications in the county from 496,000 to 309,773, and a decline in exemptions granted from 456,000 to 262,417, with a net tax recovery of $10 million.[20] The comprehensive application, open to public inspection once filed, now is standard practice in the state.[21]

Again, a precise tabulation is unavailable, but the United States Census notes that eleven states reported some $2.1 billion of property tax exemptions for veterans in 1966, most of it applicable to real property.[22] As with other homestead exemptions, the value of the veterans exemption also varies with the base to which it is applied—assessed valuation yielding higher effective exemptions than a true cash-value basis.

Fourteen states provide exemptions for homesteads of the elderly, but here, too, provisions are disparate. In some states, Oregon for one, tax deferral is combined with exemption; in others, such as Wisconsin and New Jersey, the exemption takes the form of a tax credit; and in still others, notably Connecticut, tax concession is made through freezing the assessment as of a given date.[23] In Maryland, Rhode Island, and New York, the option of exemption rests with local government; and in Wisconsin the exemption (or credit) is extended to elderly renters as well as homeowners. The minimum qualifying age also varies —one must be at least sixty in Hawaii, for example, and at least seventy in Massachusetts.[24]

So, too, do income and assessment ceilings differ—with $2,000 to $5,000 the typical maximum income allowable for exemption claimants (under varying definitions of income); and with the exempt assessed valuation range generally from $1,000 to $5,000, except in Florida. There the state's new constitution permits the legislature to double the extant $5,000 homestead exemption for persons aged sixty-five or older. Should the legislature implement this provision, in Pinellas County (St. Petersburg-Clearwater), where 120,000 of the 450,000 residents are sixty-five or older, an estimated 100,000 homeowners would pay no property tax at all.[25]

One survey revealed that exemptions for the elderly already cost Indiana some $60 million in taxes annually; and Hawaii and New Jersey some $10 million each.[26] Moreover, in several states the totals recently have taken sharp upward swings. Massachusetts, for instance, reported $17.2 million in tax losses from the exemption in 1965, and $28.7 million in 1968, with another increase of some $14 million expected due to a 1969 law allowing up to $1,920 in Federal, state, or local pensions to be credited against property tax assessments.[27]

Two of every three families in the over-sixty-five age group own their own homes. Yet, as one elderly widow told an interviewer, they have increasing difficulty "squeezing more taxes" out of a fixed income.[28] Hence, pressure for even greater expansion of exemptions for the elderly is likely to intensify before it wanes.

To what extent have the various homestead exemptions achieved their purpose?

Professor Wylie Kirkpatrick, writing in *Municipal Finance*, drew these conclusions about general homestead exemptions:

> The most plausible reason for [the] exemption is that the lessening of homestead taxes may induce the spread of home ownership. . . . The argument should be displaced by comparing the Census housing reports for 1930 before exemption and for 1950 after long experience with exemption. Owner-occupied homes as a percentage of all occupied housing in exemption states were 42.0 per cent in 1930 and 52.7 per cent in 1950, a gain of one-fourth in proportion. In all other states corresponding proportions were 47.6 per cent and 55.4 per cent, a

93

gain of one-sixth. Owner-occupied homes per thousand population in exemption states were ninety-nine in 1930 and 146 in 1950, a growth of 47 per cent. By the same measure the ratios rose from 116 to 157, an increase of 35 per cent. . . .

The inference is not that failure to exempt promotes home ownership but that underlying economic forces caused an upsurge in home ownership throughout the nation. The South, starting with less, had more to gain than the North.[29]

The Advisory Commission on Intergovernmental Relations was even more critical:

The policy of homestead exemption involves a substantial amount of injustice. It starts out by awarding a special bonus to one class of property in the form of an increase in its capital value and then provides a continuing subsidy to this class at the expense of the tenant and the business class. Rented properties occupied by low-income families help to pay the taxes from which homeowners—all homeowners, not just small homeowners—are freed, and business interests suffer hardship unless they are able to shift the tax increases to their customers and clients. Since all of the states assess property at some fraction of full value, moreover, the value of homestead exemptions is much greater than the law appears to indicate. . . .

Homestead exemption no doubt has offered some stimulus to home ownership, but other stimuli that are not unjust and not disruptive of local government have been able to make good progress in the states that have shunned this policy. . . .[30]

Of veterans' homestead exemptions, John O. Behrens, former assistant director of the International Association of Assessing Officers, notes:

94

Processing for eligibility can be a time-consuming, costly activity. . . . A considerable amount of processing time and effort may yield no revenue. . . . The temptation is great to "modify" assessments downward if any conceivable flaws can be discerned, in order that resulting figures will enable the veterans' owners to get below the ceiling. . . . There is naturally a reluctance to prosecute even the small minority of fraudulent claimants. . . . Universally they represent a recognition of a veteran's service to his nation, yet seventeen states do not use them.[31]

An Iowa Taxation Study Committee adds:

Veterans comprise a very substantial segment of the taxpaying population. [Yet] less than one-half of the estimated number of veterans in Iowa derive tax benefits from the military service exemption. . . . It is quite illogical to defend the military service exemption on the ground that it provides for veterans *as a group*. Quite clearly it does not. Rather it benefits some veterans while it increases the tax bills of a larger number of veterans, and all nonveterans.[32]

The Advisory Commission on Intergovernmental Relations concludes:

Property tax exemption is the wrong way to finance veterans' continuing bonus and disability payments. . . . If these benefits to veterans are socially desirable they should not be contingent on property ownership. . . . Veterans exemptions, like homestead exemptions, generate pressure for underassessments. . . . The assessor has to check the eligibility of veterans and their heirs . . . and the complications continue through the record-keeping, collection, and accounting procedures.

All of the foregoing defects could be eliminated by

95

replacing the granting of benefits to veterans through tax
exemption with a stated administered benefit program
based on merit and need instead of property ownership,
and financed by general state revenues or by the levy of
the state property tax.[33]

Regarding exemptions for the elderly, the Advisory Commission states:

> Some aged homeowners undoubtedly present a spe-
> cial welfare problem but that property tax exemption is
> the best solution is questionable. . . . If this method of
> subsidy for the property-owning aged is chosen, it should
> at least: (1) have an accurately defined rather than a
> nebulous value; (2) be easily administerable; (3) be as
> equitable as possible for those who have to pay for it; and
> (4) be clearly identified as a cost of government. The re-
> cently adopted exemption systems fail to meet these spec-
> ifications.[34]

"The case for granting some property tax relief for some of
the aged poor seems persuasive," three economists concluded
in a National Tax Journal report on the subject. They point out:

> There may be recipients of small fixed incomes de-
> pleted by inflation. . . . Their demand for housing may be
> peculiarly inelastic because of inertia and sentimental
> attachments to family property. . . . This makes them es-
> pecially vulnerable to rising property taxes. Thus it is a
> constant concern and they respond with avid opposition
> to every new bond issue and boost in the general prop-
> erty tax rate, however meritorious. . . . There is support
> for the critics' view that it is the property tax and not
> the income tax which provides the onerous pinch for the
> elderly.

96

But then they add:

> Erosion of the property tax base is not a negligible concern. . . . Relief should be pinpointed for those who are clearly experiencing inordinate burdens.[35]

In short, here, too, as the Advisory Commission on Intergovernmental Relations has written, symptoms of malaise in both conception and execution of the exemption machinery are so conspicuous that, beyond doubt, an entire "re-examination of this device is needed."[36]

# 9

# "Incentive Exemptions"

In GREENVILLE, ALABAMA, about forty miles south-west of Montgomery, travelers can stay at the sixty-unit Holiday Inn motel as guests, in effect, of the city. Rates quoted in a recent brochure were $8 to $10 a night for one person; $12 for two. The motel pays no real estate tax. The same is true for the Holiday Inn in Boaz, Alabama, and for several other motels in the state.[1] Under the Lawless and Cater Acts, Alabama counties and cities may "acquire property, build factories, and buy machinery and equipment" to be leased to corporations. These leases usually extend thirty to forty years, with no *ad valorem* or other tax payments made on the properties—for they are owned by the city or the county. Hence, the tax "holiday" for some Holiday Inns.

"Some of the largest industrial plants in Alabama," says a state legislative committee, "are owned lock, stock, and barrel by the cities and counties and no *ad valorem* taxes are paid on this property."[2] By the end of 1966, the committee calculated, valuation of all such property owned by municipalities and Cater Act industrial development boards in Alabama exceeded $357 million. The next year this valuation made a quantum jump when the town of Scottsboro sold a $97 million bond issue (tax-exempt) to finance a plant for lease to the Revere Copper and Brass Company, providing a windfall estimated at $970,000 for Revere and its 7,800 stockholders.[3]

About one-third of the states, mostly in the South and New England, have authorized such real estate exemptions for new industry, according to the Advisory Commission on Intergovernmental Relations.[4] Most *ad valorem* tax exemptions are made for from five to ten years; some are longer. In some instances, state statutes enumerate the types of industries eligible for exemption. Alabama's law, for example, encompasses, among others:

> Calcium cynamide aluminum or aluminum product plants for ten years after beginning of construction; ten-year exemption from date of completion for the following industries, factories, or plants—spinning, knitting, and weaving of cloth and yarn, pulp, pulp products, gold, graphite, manganese, salt, sulphur and tin mining, ship and airplane building, glass, light wood or metal products, ceramics, enameling, silica processing, farm implements, milk products, creameries, milk cooling stations, trade or commercial articles, or any other industry located within five miles of a rehabilitation colony.[5]

In Maryland, a study committee reported these local-option variations:

> Allegheny County grants ten-year exemptions for real and personal property of new industry. . . . Carolina

99

County exempts from county and municipal taxes new industry valued over $50,000, and . . . additions to established industry valued over $25,000. . . . Calvert County exempts for ten years 100 per cent of the value of plant and equipment of many new manufacturers. . . . Cecil County grants an exemption through 1971 of new manufacturing business with capital investment of at least $75,000. . . . In St. Mary's County the real property of any new manufacturer employing more than seventy-five people is exempt from county and local taxation for a period of ten years.[6]

A Tennessee survey found that seventy-one cities and fifteen counties in the state in 1966 owned some type of industrial building leased to a private corporation, and that 1967 industrial bond sales in the state exceeded $80 million—including a $46 million issue in Union City for Goodyear. It explained:

Most [new] plants pay some local property tax, but not as much as the cost of increased services—additional streets, roads, water and sewer lines, fire and police protection. Plants financed with industrial bonds do not pay property taxes on the land and buildings because they are owned by the local government. Many corporations, however, voluntarily agree to pay some amount of money to the county and city. Rentals to the county or city . . . often are regarded as an in-lieu payment.[7]

Delaware, to encourage native timber industry, extends exemption to "any landowner who intends to establish a commercial forest plantation" if the owner applies to the State Forestry Commission for listing in this exempt category—and if the property has "sufficient forest growth of suitable character and physical distribution as to give reasonable assurance that a stand

100

of merchantable timber will develop therefrom."[8] Exemption then becomes contingent on passing periodic inspection by the state forester.

No valuation totals for industrial property-tax exemptions are available, but exempt industrial development bond issues are known to have risen from $100 million in 1962 to some $2 billion in 1968, causing an estimated annual revenue loss to the United States Treasury of $50 million.[9] Since January 1969, exemption of state or local governmental industrial bonds has been limited to $5 million in face valuation, except for special properties such as sports arenas, convention facilities, and airports, which are not restricted.[10]

Several states also offer "incentive" exemptions for urban redevelopment.* Massachusetts, for instance, allows any three or more persons to form a redevelopment corporation to "rehabilitate" and "reconstruct," and property involved is exempt from taxes and special assessments for forty years, though there is a 5 per cent excise tax on gross income, plus taxes of $10 per $1,000 of the property's assessed valuation. New Jersey provides exemptions of up to twenty-five years for urban renewal project improvements, but imposes an annual service charge of 15 per cent of a corporation's annual gross revenue, or 2 per cent of the project cost if gross revenue cannot readily be ascertained. Missouri law allows urban redevelopment corporations twenty-five-year partial exemption, with assessment only of land for the first ten years, then for the next fifteen years assessment of both land and improvements at half value, with an annual

---

* They include Massachusetts, New Jersey, Missouri, Hawaii, New York, Indiana, Michigan, Minnesota, Nebraska, and California. Wisconsin for a time allowed an assessment freeze, but it was ruled unconstitutional.

101

earnings limitation of 8 per cent per year of the project cost. And Hawaii exempts urban redevelopment projects from taxes until 1972.[11]

New York State, in keeping with the dimensions of its urban problems, has one of the most multifaceted exemption/ abatement frameworks, encompassing area redevelopment, individual building rehabilitation, and limited-dividend corporations for new-apartment construction. Municipalities may enact ordinances exempting improvements for up to twelve years after completion of an alteration, except that in New York City and Buffalo alterations must have been started after 1962 and been completed in two years, or before 1970. For as long as twelve years, up to 8.3 per cent of property taxes may be abated on the cost of alterations and improvements, but the total may not exceed taxes payable for the year; land taxes may be abated for thirteen to twenty years at a percentage up to the cost of alterations.[12] Thus in New York City in one recent year property owners received $8 million in tax relief on improvement of some five thousand apartments, many in Manhattan's West Side renewal area.[13] New York's legislature in 1968 also authorized cities with a population of 125,000 or more, and their home counties, to grant ten-year exemption on property of certain businesses in census tracts where median family income is in the lowest quarter for these cities. The exemption applies to any increase in value from investment certified by the New York State Urban Job Incentive Board.[14]

Dozens of large apartment buildings have been constructed in New York City under a "Mitchell-Lama Act" which allows the city or state to provide forty-year mortgages for 90 per cent of development cost, plus exemption from 80 per cent of real estate taxes for thirty years. Indeed, Mitchell-Lama is the basis for construction of one of the world's largest apartment complexes, Co-op City, sponsored by a nonprofit organization of forty labor unions. When completed, the $300 million development, on 300 acres of filled marshland in the Bronx, will house 50,000 people in thirty-five towers and town houses; also included will be six schools, a library, a fire station, and several shopping centers.[15] The property's exemption will cover 50 per cent of real estate taxes for the life of its 90 per cent mortgage.[16]

In Boston, the $100 million Prudential Center in Back Bay was built under a complicated agreement for deferred assessment during construction and partial exemption later. Assessment was on the land only pending construction above plaza level, then taxes were increased on a graduated scale for seven years, allowing time for every component of the project to begin earning full revenue. Taxes are pegged to guarantee Prudential a 7 per cent annual return on net income, leaving about $3 million a year for taxes—in effect, according to one analyst, providing Prudential "practically an annuity."[17]

New York State's statute, for one, also offers an exemption for development of railroad property, providing that "the aggregate amount of taxes levied on qualified real property owned by railroad development corporations shall not exceed the aggregate taxes payable on the property for the year in which the corporation acquired the property."[18] In addition, railroad property in any zone defined as a "commuter area" and "used exclusively for passenger service" receives an exemption tied to the earnings ratio. If the ratio is 2.5 per cent or less, the passenger railroad property is totally exempt.[19]

Another form of exemption—preferential assessment or partial tax abatement for "urban fringe farmland"—has evolved to deal with one cause of urban sprawl: sudden waves of land sales by farmers unable to pay the high taxes that accompany urbanization's appreciating property values. Maryland passed the first such law in 1955, providing that land "used in agriculture" be assessed according to its agricultural value, regardless of market factors. After this statute was ruled in violation of legally required uniformity of assessment, a constitutional amendment in 1960 legitimized it.[20] Since then, similar laws have been enacted in several other states, including Arkansas, California, Connecticut, Florida, Indiana, Iowa, Minnesota, and Oregon.[21]

Already Maryland's law has partially undermined the tax base of urbanized counties, resulting in an average tax reduction of 53 per cent on properties to which preferential assessment was applied.[22] Had there been no preferential assessment, gains in the 1965 tax base of urban counties would have ranged from an estimated $13 million in Baltimore County to $83 million in Montgomery County, which borders Washington, D.C. Prince Georges County, also in metropolitan Washington, lost $58.9 million of potential tax base; Anne Arundel County (Annapolis), $23 million.[23] Moreover, Frederick D. Stocker, Ohio State University professor of business research, has pointed out several serious deficiencies in the law:

> No provision is made for restricting the application to owner-operated farms, or to what might be thought of as "bonafide" farms. Nor is there any provision for capturing any of the tax loss at such time as the land may be developed or sold to a developer. Consequently, there are opportunities, perhaps not intended by the framers of the law, for developers and speculators to buy and hold tracts of underdeveloped land, while hiring a nearby farmer to cut hay or pasture a cow or two.[24]

*"Incentive Exemptions"*

Oregon and New Jersey, among other states, have tried to remedy such shortcomings in part by providing for partial recapture of taxes when preferentially assessed farmland is sold—two years' taxes at the full assessed rate in New Jersey, five years' full assessment in Oregon. "One advantage of [this] deferral concept—to the extent that it is not compromised by a short time limit on the recapture of back taxes," says Professor Stocker, "is that as applied to properties in a transition zone, it really gives nothing away. The full tax is payable . . . or eventually collected, perhaps with interest."[25]

There are also incentive exemptions for property used for air and water pollution control. Wisconsin in 1953 exempted for five years all equipment installed to abate or eliminate air and water pollution, and provided accelerated amortization of industrial waste treatment facilities. Virginia followed with accelerated amortization; and in 1955 North Carolina granted perpetual exemption to such facilities, while New Hampshire bestowed a twenty-five-year exemption. Since then, most states have enacted at least partial exemption for air or water pollution control equipment.[26] By the end of 1966, exempt valuation of such facilities in Ohio alone exceeded $80 million, seven-eighths of it in fifteen counties.[27]

Other incentive exemptions range from preservation of historic or architecturally valuable buildings—designated structures in New Orleans' Vieux Carre, for instance, or distinctive mansions of Newport, Rhode Island—to construction of fallout shelters.* To what extent do these various incentive exemptions ac-

* At least a dozen states enacted total or partial exemptions for shelters in the early sixties, some requiring use solely as a shelter, as well as certification of compliance with specified standards, to

complish their desired ends? Some clearly fail abysmally. In Delaware in the thirties, for instance, fifteen-year property-tax exemptions were provided for motion picture companies' land, buildings, and equipment, including offices, warehouses, trackage, and locations. But, as a state report conceded, "this attractive inducement to encourage the establishment of the cinema industry in Delaware . . . has obviously missed its mark."[30]

Other incentive exemptions are more difficult to evaluate. Many communities and several states appear reasonably convinced of the benefit of industrial exemptions. Yet, studies of their impact on Louisiana, for one, cast strong doubts on these assumptions. William D. Ross, in the Louisiana Business Bulletin, calculated that the value of industrial investments (apart from any increase in income accruing from them) based on the property tax program for 1946–1950 was less than the value of the tax revenue lost. "In other words," he said, "if the Louisiana government, instead of granting tax exemptions, had collected this tax revenue and invested it themselves in new plants and equipment, they would have created more jobs than were created by the exemption program."[31] A 1967 study substantiated this finding in Louisiana:

> The cost of exemptions granted in 1966 was $30.1 million and the value to recipients only $13 million . . . the present value [of exemptions] to corporate recipients was only $13 million [but if a] cash grant [had been] made for the construction of a plant with a depreciable life for tax purposes of thirty years, the present value would have been $22.6 million [nearly twice the percent-

qualify for exemption.[28] In practice, fallout shelters elicited so little interest that for all of New York City, only $12,100 in valuation was listed as exempt in 1968–1969.[29]

age of total investment outlay]. . . . The property tax exemption is an extremely inefficient subsidy.[32]

"The role of property taxes in industrial location decisions is generally of minor importance," observed a 1967 National Tax Association report based on a survey of ninety corporate, state and governmental, and taxpayer association officials. It added:

> Corporation officials and others indicate that industry can obtain a "favorable" or competitive assessment almost anywhere they may locate through the bargaining and negotiation which are inherent in the property valuation procedure. . . . Industry officials do not generally approve of the practice of real estate tax exemptions for new industries. This may weaken the local tax base, and it is also discriminatory.[33]

The Advisory Commission on Intergovernmental Relations declares:

> The immediate effect of such subsidies is to benefit the recipient; however, they also harm competitors, place a burden on the taxpayers who have to carry the tax from which the beneficiary has been freed, and promote interstate tax warfare that endangers the development of fair and adequate tax systems generally. There is some doubt, moreover, that there is sufficient long-term benefit to the economy of the state to justify the cost imposed on the taxpayers and the possible hardships to nonsubsidized industry. . . .
> Authorizing local governments to grant industry tax exemptions is unsound policy.[34]

Where industrial exemptions persist, they at least usually have the virtue of initiation by local option—though admittedly voters or their elected representatives may be unaware of the

107

negative economic factors, including the long-term effect on their community's tax base. Nor may they have considered that the exemptions' capacity to lure industry rather than merely award bonuses for foregone decisions may diminish as the exemptions become more universal. And, as one corporate executive put it, the subsidy may tend to attract industry that is "marginal in operation" to "an area for which it is not suited by other factors," boding ill in "even the smallest economic depression."[35]

Urban renewal exemptions involve many variables, but there is some evidence that in the long run they pay. New York City's Lincoln Center cultural complex, for instance, though removing potentially valuable land from the tax rolls, has led to improvements in land use in a thirty-seven-block area, producing more than $20 million in new taxes by 1969, with the prospect of an increase to $30 million by 1972.[36] Stuyvesant Town, a thirty-five-building project granted a twenty-five-year reduced assessment in the late forties, cost the city $2.6 million in tax losses in 1960, but improvement of the East Side neighborhood yielded an additional $1 million in taxes, and by 1974–1975, when the temporary exemption expires, the city will gain an additional $2.5 million a year at 1960 assessed valuations and tax rates.[37]

Nonetheless, the negative impact of such exemptions mounts. Incentive exemptions in New York City alone in 1968–1969 totaled $913.4 million in assessed valuation, excluding public housing. This exempt valuation by category included: limited dividend housing, $80.3 million; redevelopment, $215.9 million; limited profit housing, $290.1 million; railroad exemptions, $268.1 million; alterations, $58.8 million.[38]

Core cities' tax bases are so restricted in growth potential (partly due to mandated exemptions), while their operating and capital investment costs are so heavy, that there is a convincing case that temporary incentive exemptions are indispensable to rebuilding, at least until more ambitious Federal and state assistance programs materialize. Indeed, such exemptions appear almost imperative as palliatives for a property tax system which, as Jerome P. Pickard of the Urban Land Institute has said, "gives reductions for poor conditions, rewards crumby buildings, and penalizes good ones."[39] Moreover, such exemptions, again, usually have the virtue of local initiation, as opposed to mandating from above without compensation.

It remains true, however, that like other exemptions of even the most worthy stripe, urban renewal or anti-pollution or commuter railroad exemptions must be used sparingly, for the shortest possible durations, under assiduously defined conditions. If not, they may constitute a mortgage on the community's future tax base carrying as little hope of redemption as the innocent-appearing but insidious currency of the loan shark.

# 10

# The Differential Burden

IN DEFENSE OF exempt properties, Harvard University President Charles W. Eliot once said that it is tax-exempt institutions that make a community worth living in. One even hears quantitative arguments that exempt properties "pay." To a degree, obviously, both the qualitative and quantitative arguments are sound. Parks, museums, libraries, hospitals, public schools, and similar exempt properties do enrich a community environment in ways that cannot always be quantified, and an exempt property that fosters jobs, retail sales revenue, and increased property values can cause measurable net revenue gains. Nevertheless, in evaluating exempt properties' economic effects, several points must be considered.

One is that, the conventional wisdom notwithstanding, certain types of property development do not "pay their way." Among these are all but relatively high-priced single-family homes. A Monroe County (Rochester), New York, survey, for example, quoted a Hofstra College Bureau of Business and Community Research finding that "residential property receives $1.20 in local governmental services for each tax dollar paid, whereas nonresidential property receives between 33 and 44 cents in services per tax dollar paid." It added:

> The presence of factories and shopping centers can increase some costs disproportionately, under certain circumstances (traffic control, fire protection, etc.). . . . But . . . the school levy is usually more than half the total of the property tax levy, and business property produces a "school tax profit."[1]

Homer Hoyt Associates, of Washington, D.C., refined this residential cost index further in a survey of Fairfax County, Virginia:

> A house selling for $10,000, assessed for $3,200 with the lot, with the average number of children, would pay $82.09 in taxes and cost the county $120.67. . . . On the other hand, a house selling for $20,000 and assessed for $7,000 would yield a surplus of $58.88 a year. A $25,000 house (market value), . . . $84.53 . . . a $30,000 house, $135.83, and a $40,000 house, $187.13. In addition to yielding a profit on real estate taxes, the higher income family would also pay more in personal property taxes. . . . Apartments yield a slight surplus above cost. . . .[2]

Hoyt made similar findings in surveys of Montgomery and Prince Georges counties in Maryland and in Evanston, Illinois. "One cause of snob zoning [requiring at least two-acre lots]," he says, "is that you have to build an expensive house on two acres. This is more apt to yield a surplus."[3]

Hence, if a government office complex or military installation is planned for a community, one cannot necessarily assume that an attendant increase in home construction for employees will "pay out." The cost of residential services its employees may require, plus the cost of services to the exempt property combined with its shrinkage of the tax rolls, may result in a diseconomy. In fact, as Herbert F. Moore of the Greater Trenton Chamber of Commerce told a New Jersey legislative hearing into the effects of state properties on Trenton, even the assumed direct benefits of an increased local payroll may be partly illusory:

> Unquestionably, Trenton depends in large measure upon the payroll of the State of New Jersey, but that argument does not hold the same amount of weight today as it did twenty, thirty, or forty years ago, because we have a very highly mobile population. The fact that the State pays Mary Jones as secretary $100 a week doesn't mean that she spends that $100 or any part of it in Trenton.[4]

Trenton Councilman Gerard Naples added:

> There is a certain amount of prestige to the State buildings. . . . But in the last fifteen years you have seen the flight [of] businesses and individuals, largely because of the tremendous taxes, cost of acquisition within the city, etc. It is reaching the point where people who would on their lunch hour patronize these businesses may not have too many businesses to patronize. . . . Actually, I think that some day this is going to result in the municipalities actually fighting the erection of State property. . . .[5]

Moreover, some exempt properties are exceptionally high consumers of local governmental services. In Ewing Township, New Jersey, for instance, a study showed that 19.5 per cent of all larceny-theft reports originated at Trenton State College. Police issued parking decals for 1,526 day and 1,227 night students at the college; they performed 300 checks for applicants to the college; they were required for extra duty for traffic control at athletic and social events; several fires at the college necessitated time-consuming arson investigations by police and firemen—and this was only part of the special services required.[6] Similarly, in Chapel Hill, North Carolina, according to a legislative study, the police force is "twice the size of departments in towns with an equivalent civilian population but without an equivalent number of students," and "the net cost of police protection to the town is about $100,000, or almost one-sixth of the budget."[7] In Raleigh, according to the same study, "State installations are scattered all over the city . . . [which] is spending more than $600,000 a year for police protection [and] the city's major employer is not contributing toward this cost, as the employer who makes textiles or electronic devices must contribute."[8] In general, it concluded as to the impact of state agencies on the local tax base:

> It is doubtful that the indirect additions to the property tax base by reason of higher salaries or wages paid by the State equal the average valuation of a private firm employing the same number of persons.
> The indirect addition to the tax base resulting from such things as home ownership or additional commercial activity tend to lag behind the more immediate payments which would accrue from a taxable industry.
> The higher the proportion of State employment to total employment in a community and/or the higher the amount of land devoted to State purposes, the greater the apparent impact on the tax base. If a large propor-

113

tion of land in a county is owned by the State (e.g., forests or parks) the fewer the possibilities [sic] for development of taxable property.

The principal impact of government ownership of property . . . is *removal* of formerly taxable property from the tax base.[9]

As Jens Jensen has written, the relative concentration of exempt property is indeed "material." For without a critical mass of taxable property no community can finance essential local services for which the property tax still is the principal assigned source. As Mayor Kevin White has said of Boston: "What do you do with a city that is 50 per cent nontaxable, that must derive 80 per cent of its taxes from the land, that can't raise any other revenues, whose population swells by a third every day due to commuters, and that has a student population of more than 100,000 that doesn't pay a dime in taxes and pushes rents sky high?"[10]

Yet, as has already been suggested, the distribution of exempt property is demonstrably uneven. In general, it tends to be concentrated in and around:

1. *Capitals and regional governmental centers.* Note the 52.3 per cent of total valuation exempt in Washington, D.C.; 50 per cent in Boston; 50.2 per cent in Albany; 41 per cent in Harrisburg, etc.

2. *Educational centers.* Again, Boston; or Athens, Ohio, with 50.7 per cent of the valuation exempt; Oberlin, Ohio, 45.3 per cent; Montpelier, Vermont—also a capital—37.9 per cent.

3. *Metropolitan core cities.* Again, Washington, New York City, and Boston, plus San Francisco, Milwaukee, Buffalo, Pittsburgh, and others.

114

4. *Large parks and preserves.* Note the plight of Teton County, Wyoming, with 98 per cent of its area exempt due to Grand Teton National Park. Exempt status also covers half or more of the areas of other jurisdictions in which national or state parks are located in the West, or in northern Wisconsin, Michigan, and Minnesota.

Compounding the effect of large parks is the fact that major trading centers may be miles away—Denver, for example, for Federal preserves high in the Rockies; or Minneapolis and Duluth for upper Minnesota counties in the Boundary Waters Canoe Area. In addition, there usually is a seasonal aspect to tourist traffic in parks and preserves, and few localities are in the fortuitous position of clean and prosperous Cody, Wyoming, in Park County (Yellowstone Park). There, although half of the county's area is in Federal jurisdiction and tourism is essentially a summer business, a burgeoning oil industry helps stabilize county revenues—some 70 per cent of which now are derived from petroleum firms. "If there were no oil revenues," says Park County Assessor Louis Prante, "we would be back where we were fifty or sixty years ago, getting along on a mill levy higher than a cat's back and with no money for anything we need to do."[11]

Because of myriad variables, there is no simple formula for calculating the point at which exempt property begins to become a burden. In urban areas, public officials and taxpayer groups usually become restive when the exempt-to-taxable ratio exceeds 20 per cent; in rural counties, 30 per cent. Again, the payroll or taxpaying commercial activity stimulated by exempt institutions, as well as the services they must be furnished, are germane. So is the size of the constituency served by an exempt property. For an individual exempt property tends to be a burden when it serves only a small segment of a community at a relatively high per capita tax cost, or when it serves a far larger constituency than the local populace. In economic terminology, the cost of the exemption then has been shifted.

For metropolitan core cities, already enmeshed in a negative equation of increasing expenses coupled with static or diminishing tax sources, this can be particularly debilitating. In the first place, population density itself is costly. As Selma J. Mushkin points out:

> The public services required by a population small in size living and working the way rural people do are very different from those required by an enlarged population in a crowded metropolis. In a rural setting we dig our own well, put in our own septic tank, burn our trash, build and maintain our access road, have ample living space for older members of the family, and use our own shotgun for protection. We cannot do these things in a crowded city without creating a hazard for our neighbors or threatening the well being of members of our own family. . . . Water and air, for example, once free goods, now have a price—the price of waste treatment works and air and water pollution control measures.[12]

Further, as Mayor Thomas J. Whelan of Jersey City explains:

> It is the misfortune of most central cities to be old. Fire protection is a tremendous financial burden, a burden almost unknown to the new horizontal suburbs. What sort of a suburb knows anything about cost of providing recreation for children who have never had a backyard, whose only playground is the street, whose only toy is a broken bottle?[13]

Milwaukee Tax Commissioner Vincent Schmit adds:

### The Differential Burden

> The city . . . by reason of its zoning, has become a haven for the elderly and poorer strata of society. It has accepted its burden of providing housing and services for the masses of poor. Communities outside the city, by zoning and other devices, have effectively eliminated the poor. . . .[14]

Yet it is the city that must provide much of its region's central transportation network, higher educational and cultural institutions, medical centers, and Federal/state office complexes—all of which are tax-exempt and therefore entail reduction of the city's (but usually not the suburbs') tax base. Hence, when the New York State Conference of Large City Boards of Education compared the effective tax base of the state's six major cities with that of the state as a whole, it found that 33.03 per cent of the six cities' real property valuation was exempt, in contrast to a statewide average of 16 per cent.[15] In large but necessarily imprecise measure, the burden of providing services represented by the exempt property has been shifted to the central cities. As William O. Winter stated in an analysis in *Municipal Finance*, in effect "the city taxpayers are subsidizing the people in the remainder of the institutional service area."[16]

Indeed, according to a report to Milwaukee Mayor Henry Maier, the city-provided subsidy to suburbs is far greater than generally acknowledged. Consider:

> In the area of cultural activity it can be said that those who benefit the most contribute the least. . . .
> In 1966 the suburban units of government in Milwaukee County received $2.3 million from the State in highway aid and highway privilege taxes. Assuming that at least 50 per cent of driving by suburbanites is on

117

city streets, the city then should be entitled to 50 per cent of the revenue derived from suburban autos. . . .

The assumption . . . is that persons living in poverty are the responsibility of all. . . . Suburbanites in part, at least, escape this responsibility. . . . They escape that portion of local property taxes which is needed to provide the extra services required by persons in poverty . . . an additional $9 million per year . . . raised largely through property taxes. . . .

The high level of efficiency and readiness of the Milwaukee Fire Department undoubtedly permits suburban communities to maintain smaller departments than would be the case if the Milwaukee Department were not in existence. . . .

Suburban police are trained at the Milwaukee Police Training School without compensation to the city. . . .

The Milwaukee Port promotes economic growth throughout the metropolitan area to the benefit of suburban communities as well as Milwaukee. . . .

There are numerous other benefits that could be examined in detail and, in some instances, quantified. Among these are benefits derived from the City Department of Public Works, the City Water Department, the City Safety Commission, auditorium convention hall, civic celebrations and functions, and the tax-exempt properties for churches, cemeteries, boys clubs, YWCA and YMCA, women's clubs, governmental offices, and expressways. . . .[17]

The fiscal advantages of perpetuating this arrangement, of course, are not lost on suburban residents. In 1966, when the University of Wisconsin at Milwaukee announced plans to acquire a ten-acre site in the suburb of Shorewood, the village board opposed the move and the village manager suggested that expansion be within Milwaukee's city limits. "Every inch of land taken off the tax rolls hurts us," added the village attorney.

Whereupon the university reversed itself and announced it would expand only within the city of Milwaukee—at a potential cost to Milwaukee of $6.3 million in taxable property.[18] Again, due to the more-than-local nature of a locally exempt property, one municipality's taxpayers were subsidizing those of other communities, in this case localities with a notably greater per capita ability to pay.

Increasingly, as the impact of exempt property becomes more apparent, individual institutions are being asked to make special non-tax payments to help lighten the burden. In fact, in a 1969 survey by the American Council on Education, 52 of 301 colleges and universities—or 17 per cent of those responding to the questionnaire—indicated that they make payments in lieu of taxes to local governments.[19] In a similar survey made especially for this book, 53 of 99 home cities of higher educational institutions—or 54 per cent of those responding—reported receipt of some form of "in-lieu payments."[20] (See Appendix.)

Some such arrangements are formalized so as to be legally binding. Since 1928, for instance, Harvard, MIT, and Radcliffe have had signed agreements with Cambridge, Massachusetts, for designated in-lieu payments on certain properties. For all properties acquired since 1928, payments are made at current rates on the assessed value of the land (but not buildings) at the time of acquisition. In addition, when MIT bought the Lever Building, it agreed to help cushion the impact on the tax base by paying full taxes for two years and half taxes for another two years. Under the agreements, renegotiable every twenty years, MIT in 1969 remitted to Cambridge more than $200,000 in in-lieu payments; Harvard, more than $145,000; and Radcliffe, about $11,000. In 1969 Cambridge and the universities also concluded a twenty-five-year agreement to tax married students' dormitories at 12.5 per cent of gross income.[21]

"It is politically expedient to be against the universities," says Charles Laverty, Jr., of the Cambridge Board of Assessors. "On the other hand, Cambridge is what it is because of the universities, and we feel we have to work together. We have always had a friendly relationship administratively."[22]

In 1909, Princeton University made a donation equal to 10 per cent of the taxes raised by the Borough (city) of Princeton, New Jersey, for schools and local government, and since 1914 the university has subscribed to a "gentleman's agreement" to donate a flat sum annually. Full taxes are paid on faculty housing, the stadium, the university theater, and some five thousand off-street parking spaces; and, in addition to having donated land for and shared construction costs of an incinerator plant, the university shares operating costs, pro-rated according to tonnage of materials delivered to the plant. The university also shares with the borough and with Princeton Township the cost of the local sewage system, at a rate based on metered water consumption compared to volume of sewage passing through the plant. And the university pays the township the full cost of educating school-age children living in its apartment developments.[23]

In Chapel Hill, North Carolina, where the University of North Carolina once had more resources than the town, the school built and still operates the water, electrical, and telephone system; it has paid half the cost of two sewage disposal plants and all but one fire truck bought by the city; and it makes an annual payment, based on an agreed formula tied to enrollment ($4.9636 per student, or $42,000 in a recent year).[24] Other cities receiving payments under verbal agreements or written contracts include College Park, Maryland (from the University of Maryland); Coral Gables, Florida (University of Florida); New Brunswick New Jersey (Rutgers—the State University); Middletown, Connecticut (Wesleyan University); Norman, Oklahoma (University of Oklahoma); and East Lansing (Michigan State University) and Ann Arbor, Michigan (University of Michigan).[25] There also are innumerable arrangements for sharing the cost of or donating certain capital improvements from which a college or university derives direct benefits. (See Appendix.)

In the case of state universities, legislative approval usually is involved, but agreements with private institutions are made directly with local authorities—often as a result of intrepid political maneuvering. In Evanston, Illinois, Northwestern University for years resisted city officials' importunings for in-lieu payments of some sort, pointing to the university's role in establishing the city, past donations of land for streets and parks, the university's importance to the city economy, and the financial pressures inherent in providing quality higher education. City officials, though sympathetic, nonetheless believed that some adjustment in tax status was justifiable. "The university, while making admittedly important contributions to the community, had received a century of free services from the community," City Manager Wayne Anderson explained. "A great deal of our land was off the tax rolls. We felt we had to do something."

In Spring 1968, when the university applied for a zoning permit to build two ten-story dormitories—each housing 250 graduate students—the city made its move. Current police and fire costs, Anderson calculated, are $36 per capita, and any new housing would add to the burdens on both firemen and police.

On the other hand, he computed, sales tax collected from students' purchases in Evanston amount to $700 per student per year, or some $5 million. Thus $30 per student seemed a fair net cost calculation—or $15,000 for the new dormitories' total population. Were Northwestern to contract to pay half this amount to the city annually, Anderson informed the university, a zoning permit could be granted for the first building.

There the matter stood for months. NU then informed Anderson of its wish, "as a gesture of appreciation for the fire and police protection afforded us by the city over the years," to buy the city a $30,000 fire truck and, upon conclusion of litigation over another aspect of its tax exemption, to "make every effort to reach some satisfactory agreement about . . . the dilemma resulting from the university's unusual charter privileges and the needs of the city." Henceforth, says Anderson, city permission for new building by any higher education institution in Evanston will be contingent on a comparable *quid pro quo*.[26]

Yale University, too, has been requested to make substantial in-lieu payments—$9 million over a three-year period, according to New Haven Mayor Richard G. Lee. That total, he says, is "less than half the amount it would cost the university were its property not tax exempt."[27] In a reply to the request, Yale President Kingman Brewster declared, "Offhand I can think of no way in which we would be legally empowered to make a grant to the city government,"[28] and there the matter rested at this writing.

Among other private-exempt institutions, the Ford Foundation and Twentieth Century Fund in New York City have voluntarily instituted in-lieu payments to the city. Ford, which occupies an architecturally distinguished glass-wall building assessed at $18 million, has made a five-year, $5 million pledge to an independent fund for the city's use—a total approximately equivalent to potential tax revenue on its property.[29] Twentieth Century, housed in a handsome brownstone in Manhattan's East 70s, pays $10,000 a year, also the approximate equivalent of a full tax bill.[30] The Andrew W. Mellon Foundation, meanwhile, never has claimed exemption from the estimated $9,000 in annual taxes on the Park Avenue building it occupies.[31] (Foundations that lease quarters—including the sponsor of this study—of course pay full property taxes, in effect, through rent paid to commercial landlords).

There also are sporadic instances of in-lieu payments by religious institutions. After its General Assembly had passed a resolution endorsing in-lieu payments in 1967, the United Presbyterian Church in the U.S.A. made an initial $10,000 donation to the city of Philadelphia on behalf of its Witherspoon Building and Krisheim Study Center there.[32] In Minneapolis, the Augsburg Publishing House of the American Lutheran Church made a $6,700 in-lieu payment after winning a court test of its exemption,[33] and Unitarian, Presbyterian, Methodist, Baptist, and other Protestant churches in Cleveland, Washington, D.C., Montclair, New Jersey, Des Moines and Ames, Iowa, Medford, Oregon, and elsewhere also have made voluntary payments.[34] Still, from available sources it appears that no more than $50,000 is so contributed by all religious institutions in a given year—scarcely a groundswell.

At least twenty states have programs for in-lieu payments to localities in which state conservation lands are located,[35] and eighteen provide for sharing revenue from state forest lands with local jurisdictions in which they are located.[36] A few states also share revenues from property other than park and forest lands. (California, for instance, shares rentals from state highway lands.)[37] Connecticut and Massachusetts, among others, make "grants" or in-lieu payments to localities for specified types of state properties, ranging from state prison farms to military grounds.[38] New Jersey and New York make in-lieu payments to localities in which the Palisades Interstate Park Commission owns land (though in New Jersey such property must total 10 per cent or more of a municipality's area to qualify).[39] New Jersey makes in-lieu payments to municipalities in which more than 9 per cent of the area is in state-owned public use,[40] and Vermont in 1968 passed a law allowing taxation of any state-owned property in excess of 10 per cent of a town's total valuation.[41] On the whole, however, state in-lieu payment programs are exceedingly small and inconsistent.

The Federal government, according to the Public Land Law Review Commission, has twenty-eight revenue-sharing and in-lieu payment programs in force. Eleven programs involve the public lands; others, school districts near military installations ("impacted educational area grants"); communities with Federal projects such as those of the Tennessee Valley Authority or St. Lawrence Seaway; or national forests and wildlife refuges and the like. (See Appendix.) But payments to states and counties for the decade ending in 1966 totaled only some $1 billion, according to the PLLRC, while state and local revenue needs increased at twice that rate. Moreover, the PLLRC study showed, "the current payment system is not related to the economic value of the public lands," nor is there a correlation "between the property taxes levied in a state and the payments received from public lands in that state."[42] Federally supported public housing authority programs, while requiring payments to local governments, are in the same category of inconsistency—10 per cent of net shelter rents, as provided by law, neither covers the cost of essential services nor bears appreciable relationship to market factors.

Dozens of witnesses at Public Land Law Review Commission hearings throughout the country urged an expanded Federal program of in-lieu payments.[43] New York City Finance Administrator Fioravante G. Perrotta, for one, has questioned why New York City taxpayers should have to bear the exemption burden of United Nations properties and consulates as sessed at some $88 million when participation in the UN, and accommodation of the foreign consulates it attracts, are primarily in the national, not local, interest.[44] District of Columbia officials continue to pose similar questions about large exempt holdings there.

Hubert H. Humphrey, while a senator, was chairman of a subcommittee which tried to remedy this situation by proposing a larger, more carefully focused in-lieu payments program, but none of the proposals reached the floor for a vote.[45] And the minority report of the Joint Economic Committee of Congress in 1969 stated:

> Federal payments should be made to local governments of some in-lieu of real property taxes on federal property and foreign property in the form of embassies, consulates, and missions. This is only basic equity. . . . This change would also serve to impose a greater degree of discipline on the federal government in its acquisition and retention of land for federal purposes.[46]

The majority of the committee totally ignored the subject, though, and the majority of Congress still seems constrained to do the same. Until this attitude is changed, Federal governmental properties will remain one of the most pervasive causes of the differential burden of exemptions.

# 11

# Formula for Change

THE PROPERTY TAX long has been favorite whipping boy for critics of our revenue system. Whole volumes have been devoted to chronicling its many faults, and conferences, symposia, and commissions have solemnly marshaled facts to prove that the tax is obsolete, unjust, and resistant to reform and should therefore be abolished. Still, the property tax not only persists but in this country raises nearly nine-tenths of all local governmental revenue and almost half of all local general revenue from all sources, including state governmental grants.[1]

Similarly, some authorities have suggested that outright abolition is the only real cure for the failings of the property-tax exemption system. A spokesman for the Pennsylvania League of Cities, describing the result of contemplated piece-meal reform of Pennsylvania's exemption structure, declared:

We started with the assumption that there should be some exemptions—for churches or charitable institutions, for example—but we soon found ourselves right back where we are at the present time. And finally our position evolved very clearly, and it can be stated basically this way: If we want our local government to provide public services at a level which we have a right to expect, then all of us must resign ourselves to paying our fair share of local taxes.[2]

However, the idea of rescinding all exemptions, like the notion of abolishing the property-tax system of which they are a part, appears to be theoretically appealing rather than politically feasible. For complete abolition to occur, individuals and organizations now favored with tax advantages would have to be seized by a magnanimous urge to renounce their advantages, and fifty state legislatures and their multitudinous subdistricts would have to spontaneously embrace bold progressivism. Time and accumulating evidence of the unworkability of present procedures ultimately might bring about such changes. Reorganization to increase the size of taxing districts also might solve many problems of differential impact of exemptions—eventually. But for the short run, the most relevant question is, What meaningful reforms might be realized within the present broad exemption structure?

*Of first importance to reform: Requirements for more comprehensive and accurate exemption data, regularly reviewed and published.*

The Advisory Commission on Intergovernmental Relations, for one, has said:

> In order that the taxpayers may be kept informed,
> each state should require a regular assessment of all such
> tax-exempt property, compilation of the totals for each
> type of exemption by taxing districts, computation of
> percentages of the assessed valuation thus exempt in
> each taxing district, and publication of the findings. Such
> publication should also present summary information on
> the function, scope, and nature of exempted activities.[3]

The Congress of Cities, in a National Municipal Policy
Program adopted in New Orleans in 1968, employed substantially the same language, saying:

> [There must be] regular assessment by the state and
> local governments of tax-exempt real property, compila-
> tion of the totals for each type of exemption by taxing
> districts, computation of the percentages of assessed val-
> uation thus exempt in each taxing district, and publica-
> tion of the findings.[4]

"Knowledge is the beginning point of change," says Allen
D. Manvel, former associate director of the National Commission on Urban Problems.[5] "I think it's a fundamental thing,"
agrees Vernon Scott, president of the National Tax Equality
Association. "It seems incredible to me that an advanced country wouldn't even know the valuation of the property off the
tax rolls."[6]

In 1969 New Jersey began a complete exemption inventory, using county tax board records of existing exemption. Listings are being computerized, and assessors will be asked to
update valuations and, for the first time, note for each listing the
state provision under which the property was granted exemption.
"We expect when the listings are returned, a good many of

those exemptions are going to disappear," says William Kingsley, acting director of the New Jersey Division of Taxation. Because part of the clerical work is being handled by the state's Department of Community Affairs as a training project, he estimates relatively little additional expense is involved.[7]

Larger states might find the task more complicated. In California, for example, one tax official estimates that a complete inventory of private exempt valuations alone would cost $2.5 million—assuming 50,000 man-days of work for valuation of nearly 25,000 properties.[8] But, a League of Nebraska Municipalities report noted, approximate valuations might be obtained much less expensively, even where localities lack exempt-property inventories:

> The Secretary of State does . . . require an annual report from each nonprofit corporation, and although the law does not require that the tax-exempt status or the amount of, or a description of, the real estate held be reported, the Secretary might be able to do so. Precedent for such action by the Secretary may be found in the fact that the Secretary now requires the listing of capital stock by nonprofit corporations, although the law does not require that such be included in the annual report.[9]

Progress at the local level also is possible without major expenditures. Richmond, Virginia, began compiling exemption data in 1955 without extra staff or budget because, Assessor Richard A. Chandler says, "The citizens should know that they're supporting with 26 per cent of their tax dollars [Richmond's exempt-to-taxable valuation ratio]. If you don't know, how can you control it? You have to find time."[10] And in fast-growing Orange County, California, Assessor Andrew Hinshaw in 1968 compiled land valuations for all Federal properties in his jurisdiction. Over the next three years he will compile valuations for all buildings and other improvements on the properties.

"We will be able to obtain from local jurisdictions the original cost of construction," he says, "and adjust for changes in the construction dollar and depreciation. It will be relatively simple to keep the new construction current. I think it's important to know the mix of valuations which are taxable and those which are not taxable. If we're going to have an efficient operation, we must know the valuation of everything in the country."[11]

*As a second component of reform, state exemption provisions should be clarified.*

As we have seen, vagueness or ambiguity in state constitutional or statutory provisions have led to fascinating loopholes. What, for example, does the legislature mean by "charitable" —help only for those physically or financially unable to help themselves? Or an act of generosity even to a millionaire? To qualify for exemption as "charitable," must a property be devoted "wholly" to "purely" charitable purposes? If not, is complete exemption to be granted though only a proportion of time and resources are devoted to purely charitable activities?

Is exemption contingent on both ownership and use for exempt purposes? Must property owners apply for exemption and substantiate statements in their application? Is reapplication required periodically—again with substantiating statements about current usage? Are exempt properties (including governmental) and their valuations listed on the assessment rolls? Is the listing separate from that for taxable properties and therefore readily accessible? Are acreage and/or valuation maximums specified for certain exempt uses, including land that may be held for expansion? Is it specified that property leased out or otherwise used to produce revenue is taxable? Can new categories of exempt properties be added by simple vote of the legislature, or is there the added check of requiring a constitutional amendment?

The Virginia constitution, one of the most strict in defining exemptions, prohibits the general assembly from enacting "any local, special, or private law" to exempt property. The assembly may only restrict, not extend, exemptions—except, as one legal official noted, that it may add organizations "similar in fact to the American Legion or the historical societies" enumerated in Section 183, paragraph G, of the state constitution. These organizations include the Association for the Preservation of Virginia Antiquities, the Mount Vernon Ladies Association, the Virginia Historical Society, and the Thomas Jefferson Memorial Association.

Therefore, when a 1962 bill adding a historical society to the list was amended to encompass fraternal orders of police and firemen, the Virginia Elks Boys Camp, and the Boys Club of Richmond, the governor simply vetoed the bill as unconstitutional; the general assembly then passed a new bill without amendments—and without appreciably lengthening the list of exemptions. Similarly, when bills to exempt the Virginia Home for Incurables (a hospital-asylum treated in an entirely separate provision) were amended to cover the American Cancer Society, Virginia Heart Association, Virginia Tuberculosis Association, and several other groups, the governor again used his veto power, and legislators once more removed the amendments in order to adhere to the constitution.[12]

The Minnesota legislature in 1969 decided to ask voters to approve similar safeguards in a constitutional amendment to be acted on in 1970. It provides that "the legislature may by law more narrowly define the property exempt . . . other than churches, houses of worship, and property solely used for educational purposes by academies, colleges, universities, and seminaries of learning."[13] "When our subcommittee began to discuss these things, I was called a tool of the devil and about every other name you can imagine," says State Representative Ernest A. Lindstrom, who represents a conservative Republican suburban district, "but we kept calling in groups to testify and kept the matter in the papers, and now the pendulum is starting to swing the other way. In my opinion, the public wants the exemption situation brought under control, and this can be a first step."[14]

Oregon State Senator Vernon Cook, a leader in efforts to curb exemptions in that state, agrees. "It boils down to the fact that an organized minority with a good battle cry is able to come to the legislature and get its property removed from the tax rolls, even though the legislature should know better," he says. "They could never survive a referendum. The property tax is a pretty fair tax if it is not undermined by exemption. If it's shot too full of holes, then it's bad."[15]

*A third essential reform: Intergovernmental payments in lieu of taxes.*

More than a hundred years ago, Britain first considered formal arrangements for in-lieu payments on Crown property. At the instigation of Sir James Elphinstone, Liberal-Conservative from Portsmouth, a select committee was appointed to

133

study the question, and though its report recommending payments was tabled, the proposals were revived by William Gladstone in 1873. Indeed, he and fellow reformers suggested abolition of all statutory exemptions on charitable, educational, scientific, and some religious property—a notion so controversial that it resulted in a second tabling of payments on Crown property. Finally, in 1874, a bill was passed allowing the chancellor of the exchequer to negotiate in-lieu payments, on the principle that, as the chancellor declared in a subsequent memorandum, "property occupied for the public service should contribute to the local rates [taxes] equally with other property in the parishes in which it is located." In no instance, he added, "will we contribute less than was payable on the assessment of the property at the time the Government acquired it . . . [and] these regulations will apply to Government property in Scotland and Ireland as well as to that in England."[16] Today, almost half the payments are for defense properties; the second-largest amount is for post offices; and designated payments are made even for properties occupied by the Houses of Parliament.[17]

In Canada, meanwhile, Federal governmental grants in lieu of taxes have been made on certain properties since 1950, and at least seven provinces make in-lieu grants to local governments: Ontario, Quebec, New Brunswick, Nova Scotia, Manitoba, Alberta, and British Columbia. Provincial rates vary, and there are major exclusions at both the Federal and provincial level: large institutions such as defense plants, hospitals, and penitentiaries, for instance. But all Crown corporations are required to make full payments as if taxable—among them, the St. Lawrence Seaway Authority, Bank of Canada, Canadian Broadcasting Corporation, and National Harbors Board.[18] Consequently, for all its shortcomings the system seems considerably advanced over United States practices.

In the opinion of Ronald B. Welch, assistant executive secretary for property taxes, California State Board of Equalization, local as well as state and national governmental agencies should be required to make such payments. "The immunity of a local government from its own taxes or those of another local government is usually rationalized on the ground that it doesn't pay to transfer money from one pocket to another," he says. "Often, however, the pockets are in different pants. For example, there would be little point in imposing county taxes on the county jail, but a good argument could be made for imposing city taxes on a county jail that is in the city."[19]

How might such payments be calculated?

"About one-half of property tax revenues are devoted to education, and perhaps another 20 per cent to health, welfare, and other 'human services,'" economist Dick Netzer estimates. "The remainder is used to finance what can be characterized as services to property . . . and general local government overhead."[20] Hence a starting point for calculating in-lieu payments might be one-third of the bill normally due on a given assessed valuation.

Interestingly, the relative accuracy of this estimate was substantiated by the Pennsylvania Economy League in an extensive breakdown of the cost of services to property in Philadelphia. One-third of the cost of law enforcement, 90 per cent of fire protection and civil defense, and 90 per cent of street functions were allocated to direct benefit to property; and general city administrative costs, including debt service, were pro-rated among various budget categories as proportions of total expenditures. The result was a finding that 30 per cent of the general budget represented direct benefits to property. Therefore, the Economy League noted, were an in-lieu payments program to be initiated, this figure could be applied directly to assessed valuations (subject, of course, to adjustments for other payments described below).[21]

*Fourth: Exempt organizations should be required to pay direct charges for specific community services.*

Instituting a broad program of payments in lieu of taxes requires clearing certain political obstacles. There is, first of all, the problem of multiplicity of exempt organizations. Policies of governmental agencies may be changed by Congress, a state legislature, a county board, or a city council, but no single body speaks for all private exempt organizations. Moreover, except for a few large institutions of high visibility and vulnerability to bargaining on such matters as zoning (universities, for instance), nongovernmental exempt organizations tend to be immune to all but appeals to goodwill—scarcely a potent weapon, if the negligible sums now volunteered as in-lieu payments are taken as evidence. In effect, then, revenue aid through in-lieu payments is determined not by the governmental body desperate for the revenue, but is left to the discretion of organizations receiving free services that constitute a drain on available revenue.

A partial solution, therefore, appears to be imposition of non-exempt charges for services provided directly to property. As Doctor Herbert J. G. Bab, Los Angeles economic consultant, explained, "Tax-exempt property has to pay for the use of water, gas, electric current, and power, if these services are provided by private utility companies"; why, then, should exempt-property owners expect to receive other direct services free?[22]

Denver and Colorado Springs now charge exempt and tax-paying property owners alike a water and sewerage charge.[23] Nashville has instituted an across-the-board sewer service charge at one and a half times metered water bills.[24] Milwaukee in 1969 adopted a sewer service charge against all exempt institutions except elementary and secondary public and parochial schools.[25] And Pittsburgh, in a slight variation on this approach, imposed an "institution tax" affecting, among other exempt properties, hospitals, nursing homes, colleges, universities, veterans' posts, recreational centers, and other organizations that charge fees to the public. Nicknamed the "sick tax" by opponents, it is levied at a rate of $6 per $1,000 of assessed valuation and at passage was expected to raise at least $2.2 million a year.[26] At this writing, New York City, among other municipalities, was contemplating charges to exempt properties for water, sewer service, and refuse collection—all of which at even modest levels could raise $25 million or more annually.[27] And Virginia's electorate was to vote in 1970 on a constitutional amendment to allow localities to impose service charges on exempt groups.[28]

According to a number of authorities, this is the wave of the future in municipal financing. The National Commission on Urban Problems, for instance, states:

> The Commission urges that local governments re-examine intensively their existing practices with regard to service and benefit charges and make adjustments to put appropriate services on a self-sustaining basis. We also urge the state governments to encourage and assist local governments in such efforts.[29]

And a conference report of the National League of Cities and United States Conference of Mayors declares:

> We are unanimous in urging more cities to make more use of service charges. . . . All water should be metered at rates high enough to cover the cost. Parking meter rates should be at least as high as off-street charges. Industries should be charged the full cost of purification. Cities should charge property owners more for garbage collection than it would for them to install and operate garbage incinerators equipped with water washers and electrostatic filters.[30]

Indeed, says Columbia University economist William Vickrey, variable charges for, say, use of designated expressways in rush hours even could be employed to reduce traffic congestion, or for other regulatory purposes. "A typical result of congestion tolls," he explains, "would be that motorists would find that for a price they can move about at speeds that are totally impossible at present."[31]

Certainly, in the short run, user or service charges are the most promising device for easing part of the financial pressure of serving exempt properties without becoming embroiled in the debilitating controversy that might attend more ambitious reform. For, as John Shannon, assistant director of the Advisory Commission on Intergovernmental Relations, observes: "If you liberate the financing of the great share of services and put it on a user-charge basis, you are automatically setting up tax-exempt properties to participate."[32]

As a fifth element of reform, states should be required to reimburse local governments for mandated partial exemptions.

138

*Formula for Change*

In 1969, New York City Finance Administrator Fioravante G. Perrotta asked the New York legislature to rescind requirements that various nongovernmental "welfare" properties be exempt from local taxes, and instead give the city local option on such exemptions. "We lose four to five million dollars a year on such properties as private clubs for actresses, explorers, and colonial dames," Perrotta explained, adding that in his opinion the local citizens on whom the added burden fell—not the state government, whose tax base was unaffected—should determine whether such organizations were "worthy of exemption."[33] Failing that, Perrotta declared, the state at least should reimburse localities for such required exemptions.

Neither of these pleas was heeded, and probably neither soon will be—regardless of by whom or to whom they next are made—for legislators appear to favor the image of uniform state-wide exemption provisions. State reimbursement for *partial* exemptions, however, is another matter. As noted in Chapter 8, several states already compensate localities for revenue forfeited due to exemptions for homeowners, veterans, the elderly, urban-fringe farmers, and the like. Ideally, such exemptions should be repealed. As the National Commission on Urban Problems says:

> The question here is not with the methods but with the use of these methods. . . . Like many other legalized tax loopholes, any social benefits they may yield generally are provided at grossly excessive cost and with that cost substantially lost from public view. Sounder public policy would involve open regular subsidies. . . .[34]

No such millennium now being in view, the best alternative would be for state legislators, upon "generously" giving

139

away local governments' tax potential in the form of partial exemptions, to recompense those same localities for the tax losses thus involuntarily incurred.

*Sixth: State and local tax officials should begin to regard their duties as more than ministerial.*

Time after time in my travels I was impressed by the progress that could be stimulated by a single vigorous tax official. In Des Moines, for example, short, stocky, voluble Andrew S. Regis was appointed assessor in 1966, after more than two decades as a deputy, and he immediately embarked on a campaign to arrest a spiraling exemption trend. Aided by a retired judge who served as volunteer special counsel, he challenged exemptions previously granted the Chamber of Commerce, fraternal organizations, labor union halls, the YMCA, YWCA, retirement homes, and business schools. In most cases, he was upheld in court, and in two years he reported having restored some $2 million in real estate valuation to city tax rolls. He also was instrumental in persuading the Iowa legislature to pass a law requiring assessors to list and value all nongovernmental exempt property; for this he was praised by leading Des Moines citizens, the local press, and even out-of-state tax officials, who credit his example for helping make possible progress in their jurisdictions.[35]

The late Bruce D. Gillis, while South Dakota state tax commissioner, for instance, in reviewing events which led to that state's first exempt-property inventory, said:

> The inspiration I received was in observing my good friend Andy Regis . . . make his courageous fight in his city to put so much of this questionable exempt property

140

before his Boards of Review and the courts. . . . This great effort inspired me to go before the South Dakota legislature and ask for the passage of a bill which would enable me and the assessors of the state to emulate, at least to some degree, that work which he has done.[36]

In Richmond, Virginia, wry, wiry Assessor Richard Chandler also has invested enormous effort in trying to control exemptions, including undertaking a survey of other capital cities' exemption and in-lieu payment procedures (see Appendix) which then was made available to other assessing officials. Chandler's campaign has restored to the tax rolls university property leased to professors, fraternities, and commercial firms; state property leased to a restaurant, a bank, and a hotel; and dozens of miscellaneous properties.[37] Also appointive, he, too, has won frequent praise for his attention to exemptions—as have local assessing officials elsewhere. They include John G. Arthur of Baltimore, Kenneth Back of Washington, D.C., Vincent Schmit of Milwaukee, Norman Register of Dallas, Carl Smith of Houston, Kenneth R. Kunes of Phoenix, Philip Watson of Los Angeles, Michael Licht of Denver, and Charles A. Henson, Jr., of Atlanta.

At the state level, Ronald B. Welch of the California State Board of Equalization has proved to be one of the most authoritative though unassuming voices for improved exemption procedures—and California's generally progressive, steadily improving exemption practices reflect his quiet competence. In Colorado, the persistence of State Senator Ruth Stockton was in large part responsible for continuing investigations by a Tax-Exempt Property Committee which have led, among other changes, to taxation of previously exempt retirement homes. Mrs. Rex Oberhansley, a Utah state representative, has been instrumental in obtaining a preliminary hearing into exemption problems in Utah; Representative Ernest Lindstrom has spurred the Minnesota legislature to action on the previously mentioned constitutional amendment proposal and other reforms; and Oregon State Senator Vernon Cook and State Representative Donald Stathos have been prominent in that state's re-examination of the question of at least partial taxation of churches and other exempt institutions.

Despite the presumed delicacy of the subject, in only one place I visited—Rhode Island—did I find that any official seeking exemption reforms had been penalized for it by the electorate. There, Irving G. Bilgor, a state senator who headed a Commission To Study Tax Exemption Laws, was defeated for reelection in 1968. On one radio call-in program in particular, says Bilgor, it was evident that a commission recommendation to tax church-owned revenue property was being advanced as "proof" that he was "anti-church." But other factors contributed to his defeat, he concedes.[38]

Given only one known casualty among advocates of exemption reform—and that due to ambiguous causes—it well may be that tax officials not only are overestimating the hazards of raising the issue but also are missing an opportunity for both community service and professional esteem. Admittedly, in some instances their powers in this area are severely circumscribed. If so, who but the official himself is in a better position to educate the press and public about needed changes? Especially when taxpayer groups become interested in the problem and become allies of reform-seeking officials—as in New York City, Philadelphia, and other localities—a critical nucleus of public backing for open dialogue can be created. In this effort, organizations such as the Council on State Governments and the International Association of Assessing Officers, and their subdivisions, can assume a leading role.

*Seventh: Officials of both governmental and private exempt organizations should be required to use property more efficiently.*

One of the most serious criticisms of real estate tax exemptions is that it fosters inefficient use of property. Or, as property-tax expert Dick Netzer put it: "Failing to pay taxes leads to extravagant uses of land."[39] A favorite example is the Department of Defense. There, according to a 1969 report of the Joint Economic Committee of the Congress, "The Subcommittee on Economy in Government has documented the existence of inadequate property accounting records, deficient inventory practices, absence of financial control, and other serious departures from good property management."[40]

Other governmental agencies are comparably culpable—including state agencies. In 1969, for instance, Maryland Governor Marvin Mandell revealed that the valuation of excess parcels of land owned by the State Roads Commission "could run into millions of dollars," and he urged that the commission "get it on the tax rolls."[41] Bishop Fulton J. Sheen, as noted in Chapter 4, has said, "There never should be a new church built here [in his Rochester diocese] that costs more than, say, one million dollars."[42] Officials of other exempt organizations, both public and private, also have expressed concern about overbuilding.

Required payments in lieu of taxes obviously would help discourage profligate property usage by imposing a penalty, albeit modest, on excess holdings. More than that, awareness of

143

alternate use value needs to be cultivated, particularly for the almost innumerable excess parcels of government land. According to a United States Bureau of Outdoor Recreation survey, nearly 12,000 acres of surplus Federal government land in twenty-one states have recreation potential; were they to be made available cheaply to state and local governments, as proposed in a bill in the United States Senate in 1969, a giant step could be taken toward meeting immense needs for open-space and recreation sites.[43] Denver also has inquired about the future availability of the 25,000-acre Rocky Mountain Arsenal as a possible site for a new jetport—which projections show will be needed by 1980.[44] Other parcels of Federal land could be put to equally productive public use if not required for military, conservation, or other positive purposes.

At the local level, urban school sites always are expensive, and tax losses from exemption of valuable sites add to the cost. In New York, however, an agency known as the New York City Educational Construction Fund has begun combining school construction with sale of air rights for commercial usage, obviating both large investments in school buildings and sites, and complete loss of revenue from land parcels so allocated. The school is paid for by leasing of air rights to an apartment developer (the school and the apartment high-rise above it have separate entrances) who then is granted exemption on the property until the debt for the school is retired—in fifteen to twenty years. At that time the income-producing property is returned to the tax rolls.[45]

Whether owned by government, universities, churches, foundations, or other exempt organizations, property needlessly kept off the tax rolls is doubly costly to society—in the tax loss and in the resources thus diverted to investment in the prop-

144

erty. The sooner society becomes cognizant of that fact and orders its tax relationships accordingly, the healthier will be the climate for both society and its individual institutions.

The question of how one acquires and retains a place on the "free list"—of which property avoids local taxes—is far more, then, than an economic issue. It also reflects social and political considerations basic to the long-term vigor of our society. Bearing that in mind, we would be well advised to pay vastly greater attention to it in the future than we have in the past.

# Notes

CHAPTER 1

1. Harold B. Meyers, "Tax-Exempt Property: Another Crushing Burden for the Cities," *Fortune*, 79 (May, 1969), 76–79.
2. Editorial, Milwaukee *Journal*, January 2, 1969.
3. See, for example, *Newsweek*, July 14, 1969; *U.S. News & World Report*, July 10, 1967; *The Wall Street Journal*, October 29, 1963, November 16, 1966, and September 11, 1967; *The New York Times*, April 14 and 18, 1968, July 2, 1968, August 21, 1968, and November 25, 1969, *CBS Reports*, June 18, 1968; Minneapolis *Star*, January 2–5, 1967.
4. See, for example, Editorial, *Nation's Cities*, March, 1969; "Statement of the National Association of County Officials in Support of Payments in Lieu of Taxes," a report prepared by the National Association of County Officials, January, 1956; "Tax Losses from Property Tax Exemption," a report prepared by the National Education Association, 1954; Eugene P. Conser, in a speech delivered before the National Association of Real Estate Boards, St. Louis, Mo., October 13, 1968.
5. "Tax Losses from Property Tax Exemption."
6. Conser, speech cited in note 4.
7. Advisory Commission on Intergovernmental Relations (hereinafter

147

cited as ACIR), *The Role of the States in Strengthening the Property Tax* (Washington, D.C.: Government Printing Office, 1963).

8. Roy M. Goodman, in a speech delivered before the Municipal Forum of Washington, D.C., April 17, 1968.

9. Research interview.

10. Minutes, Minnesota Exempt Property Subcommittee of Legislature, January 12, 1968.

11. Report of the California Advisory Commission on Tax Reform, March, 1969.

12. "Maryland Tax Study," a report prepared by the Bureau of Business and Economic Research in conjunction with the University of Maryland, College Park, Md., 1965.

13. Legislative Council of Iowa, *Study of Property Tax Exemptions Under Provisions of the Code of Iowa* (Iowa City, 1955).

14. Research interview.

15. Research interview.

16. *Walz v. Tax Commission of the City of New York.*

CHAPTER 2

1. Meyers, "Tax-Exempt Property."

2. Letter to author.

3. Martin A. Larson and C. Stanley Lowell, *The Churches: Their Riches, Revenues, and Immunities* (New York–Washington, D.C.: Robert B. Luce, Inc., 1969). Revised ed. (1969) published under title, *Praise the Lord for Tax Exemption.*

4. *Ibid.*

5. Those compiling regular reports include California, Colorado, Connecticut, District of Columbia, Hawaii, Maryland, Massachusetts, Minnesota, New Jersey, New York, and Ohio.

6. *Study of Property Tax Exemptions* (Iowa).

7. Letter to author.

8. Research interviews, Colorado State Tax Commission staff.

9. Reports of the California State Board of Equilization, published annually.

10. Author's estimate of governmental property ratios, from state records.

11. National Bureau of Economic Research, *Measuring the Nation's Wealth* (Washington, D.C.: Government Printing Office, 1966).

12. General Services Administration, *Inventory Report on Real Property Owned by the United States Throughout the World* and *Inventory Report on Real Property Leased to the United States Throughout the World* (Washington, D.C.: Government Printing Office, 1968).
13. *Ibid.*
14. Letter to author.
15. Research interview.
16. Larson and Lowell, *The Churches.*
17. Research interview.
18. Pennsylvania Economy League (hereinafter cited as PEL), *The Problem of Tax-Exempt Property in Philadelphia* (Philadelphia; PEL [Eastern Division], 1966).
19. Author's research, from city records.

Chapter 3

1. Larson and Lowell, *The Churches.*
2. *Ibid.*
3. *Ibid.*
4. Leo Pfeffer, *Church, State, and Freedom* (rev. ed.; Boston: Beacon Press, 1967).
5. Amos G. Warner, *American Charities and Social Work* (4th ed.; New York: Thomas Y. Crowell Co., 1908).
6. Pfeffer, *Church, State, and Freedom.*
7. Philip Adler, *Historical Origin of the Exemption from Taxation of Charitable Institutions* (White Plains, N.Y.: Westchester County Chamber of Commerce, 1922).
8. Pfeffer, *Church, State, and Freedom;* Roland H. Bainton, *The Reformation of the Sixteenth Century* (Boston: Beacon Press, 1952).
9. Warner, *American Charities.*
10. *Ibid.*
11. Jens P. Jensen, *Property Taxation in the United States* (Chicago: University of Chicago Press, 1931).
12. Adler, *Historical Origin of Exemption.*
13. Warner, *American Charities.*
14. Adler, *Historical Origin of Exemption.*
15. D. B. Robertson, *Should Churches Be Taxed?* (Philadelphia: Westminster Press, 1968).

16. Jensen, *Property Taxation.*
17. Allen Nevins and Henry Steele Commager, *A Pocket History of the United States* (New York: Washington Square Press, 1960).
18. Robertson, *Should Churches Be Taxed?*
19. *Ibid.*
20. *Ibid.*
21. *Ibid.*
22. Fred L. Israel (ed.), *The State of the Union Messages of the Presidents, 1790–1966* (New York: Chelsea House-Robert Hector, 1966), Vol II.
23. Reuben E. Gross, "Relationship of Church and State," *Wilson Library Bulletin*, March, 1967.
24. Robertson, *Should Churches Be Taxed?*
25. Jensen, *Property Taxation.*
26. *Local Finance* (Albany: Temporary Constitutional Convention, State of New York, 1967).

## CHAPTER 4

1. George R. LaNoue, *Public Funds for Parochial Schools?* (New York: National Council of Churches of Christ in the U.S.A., 1963).
2. J. Lloyd Mecham, *Church and State in Latin America* (Chapel Hill, N.C.: University of North Carolina Press, 1934).
3. Robertson, *Should Churches Be Taxed?*
4. As quoted in *The New York Times*, June 20, 1969; report of Court decision, May 5, 1970.
5. Andrew D. Tanner, *The Question of Tax Exemption for Churches* (New York: National Conference of Christians and Jews, 1963).
6. *Ibid.*
7. *Ibid.*
8. Author's survey, from state laws.
9. Report of Commission To Study Tax Exemption Laws, State of Rhode Island, 1968.
10. Minneapolis *Star*, January 2–5, 1967.
11. Editorial, *Church-State*, July–August, 1969.
12. Research interview, Dallas assessor.
13. Florida statutes.
14. Quoted from a speech delivered in 1961.

15. Research interview, Eugene Maynard, State of Illinois Department of Revenue.

16. Lester Kinsolving, syndicated column as printed in Chicago *Sun-Times*, March 29, 1969.

17. Research interview.

18. Research interview, Thomas Rutter, Allegheny County Law Office.

19. *The Wall Street Journal*, July 9, 1968.

20. Research interview.

21. From the Court brief, 1962 ruling, State Supreme Court, Nashville, Tenn.

22. Minneapolis *Star*, January 2–5, 1967.

23. San Francisco *Chronicle*, November 2, 1961; Mendicino County assessor's testimony before State hearing.

24. *Malad Second Ward of the Church of Jesus Christ of Latter Day Saints v. State Tax Commission of Idaho*, State Supreme Court, April term, 1954.

25. Oregon Tax Commission ruling, June 2, 1961.

26. Jensen, *Property Taxation*.

27. Editorial, *Church-State*.

28. Personal communication, Nicholas Kitsos to author; from the Court brief, 1959 ruling, State Supreme Court, Chicago, Ill.

29. Kitsos to author.

30. *The Wall Street Journal*, October 29, 1963; Alfred Balk, "God Is Rich," *Harper's*, October, 1969; *The New York Times*, January 24, 1969.

31. Minneapolis *Star*, January 2–5, 1967.

32. *Ibid.*

33. Assembly Interim Committee on Revenue and Taxation (hereinafter cited as AIC), *Taxation of Property in California* (Sacramento: California State Legislature, 1964).

34. Hartford *Times*, November 13, 1967.

35. *Time*, August 16, 1968.

36. Larson and Lowell, *The Churches*.

37. *Newsweek*, July 14, 1969.

38. Prospectus, First Baptist Church, Gulfport, Miss., November 1, 1966.

39. *Yearbook of American Churches* (New York: National Council of Churches of Christ in the U.S.A., published annually).

40. Neil Morgan, "Utah: How Much Money Hath the Mormon Church?" *Esquire*, August, 1962.

41. Seymour Freedgood, "Mormonism: Rich, Vital, and Unique," *Fortune*, April, 1964.

42. Morgan, "Utah: How Much Money?"

43. *The Wall Street Journal*, December 31, 1968.

44. Neil Morgan, "Temple Square in Salt Lake City," a pamphlet distributed by the Mormon church.

45. As quoted in *Christianity Today*, August 3, 1959.

46. As quoted in Buffalo *Courier-Express*, July 12, 1968.

47. Larson and Lowell, *The Churches*.

48. Research interview.

49. Research interview.

50. *CBS Reports*, June 18, 1968.

51. *The New York Times*, May 3, 1969.

52. *The New York Times*, June 11, 1969.

53. *Time*, September 22, 1967.

54. Cleveland Heights *Sun-Press*, July 25, 1968, and November 7, 1968.

55. Editorial, Phoenix *Gazette*, March 20, 1969.

56. Minutes, Taxation Committee, Oregon House of Representatives, 1969.

57. Los Angeles *Times*, August 17, 1968.

CHAPTER 5

1. Walter W. Heller, in a speech delivered before the National Tax Association, 1961.

2. Records of the Public Land Law Review Commission (hereinafter cited as PLLR).

3. Author's estimate, from city records.

4. Walter W. Heller.

5. Hearing, Tax Study Commission, New Jersey State League of Municipalities, June, 1968.

6. Research interview.

7. Allen D. Manvel, "Land Use in 106 Large Cities," Research Report #12, National Commission on Urban Problems, Washington, D.C., 1968.

8. "Revenue Sharing and Payments in Lieu of Taxes on the Public

Land," a report prepared by EBS Management Consultants, Inc., for PLLR, July, 1968.

9. *Harvard Business Review*, May–June, 1968.

10. Statement, National Association of County Officials, 1936.

11. *Ibid.*

12. *Ibid.*

13. Report of the Finance Office, Washington, D.C.

14. Research interview.

15. Revised statutes, District of Columbia.

16. Jensen, *Property Taxation*.

17. Marion Clawson, "Should Public Lands Pay Taxes?" *American Forests*, March, 1965.

18. *Ibid.*

19. "The Proposed Sleeping Bear Dunes National Seashore," a study prepared by Michigan State University for the National Park Service, 1967.

20. "Real Estate Tax Exemption in New York City, A Design for Reform," a report prepared by the Citizens Budget Commission, Inc., New York, April, 1967.

21. Letter, Colorado State Tax Commission to author.

22. AIC, *Taxation of Property in California*.

23. Research interview.

24. Maurice Louik's research, from state records.

25. Kentucky Legislative Research Commission, 1958.

26. From the U.S. Supreme Court opinion, cases cited in text, 1958.

27. Sidney Glaser, Proceedings of the Seventh Annual Conference of Assessing Officers, Rutgers University, New Brunswick, N.J., 1960.

28. AIC, *Taxation of Property in California*.

29. *Ibid.*

30. Veto message to the legislature, 1959.

31. Report of Commission to Study Tax Exemption Laws.

32. *Houston Chronicle*, November 9, 1966.

33. *Houston Post*, May 12, 1967.

34. *Houston Chronicle*, December 19, 1966.

35. Letter, State Revenue Commission to author.

36. *Christian Science Monitor*, March 5, 1969.

37. Research interview.

38. Statement, September 22, 1959.
39. *The New York Times*, November 30, 1962.
40. *The New York Times*, November 3, 1962.
41. Data given by City Finance Office staff to author.
42. Annual Report of the Tax Commission, 1968–1969.
43. Letter, Hennepin County assessor to author.
44. Research interview.
45. William Vickrey, in a speech delivered before the National Seminar on Urban Transportation for Tomorrow, May, 1969.
46. Jensen, *Property Taxation*.

CHAPTER 6

1. U.S. Office of Education, *Opening Fall Enrollment in Higher Education* (Washington, D.C.: Government Printing Office, 1968).
2. Robert Purnell, in a speech to the Michigan Tax Commission, 1966.
3. Research interview, Joseph Sansone, city assessor, St. Louis, Mo.
4. Research interview, E. R. Welhaven, Ramsey County assessor.
5. Research interview, Michael Licht, deputy assessor, City and County of Denver, Colo.
6. Chicago *Daily News*, August 12, 1967.
7. Data received from the city manager's office, Evanston, Ill.
8. *Northwestern University v. the People, ex. rel. Henry Miller.*
9. Cook County assessor's estimates.
10. Chicago *Daily News*, August 12, 1967.
11. *The New York Times*, December 30, 1968; research interview, city finance administrator.
12. PEL, *Problem of Tax-Exempt Property*.
13. Allison Dunham, "Property Tax Exemptions of College and Universities," a report prepared for the Commission on Financing Higher Education, 1951.
14. *Ibid.*
15. PEL, *Problem of Tax-Exempt Property*.
16. Records of the Cambridge Board of Assessors.
17. *Princeton University Newsletter*, May 26, 1969.
18. Dunham, "Property Tax Exemptions of Colleges."
19. Data received from the Providence, R.I., assessor's office.
20. Minutes, Minnesota Exempt Property Subcommittee, April 19, 1969.

21. *The New York Times*, May 14, 1968.
22. Dunham, "Property Tax Exemptions of Colleges."
23. *Ibid.*
24. PEL, *Problem of Tax-Exempt Property.*
25. Minutes, Minnesota Exempt Property Subcommittee, January, 1968.
26. Research interview, Andrew Regis, city assessor, Des Moines, Iowa.
27. Dunham, "Property Tax Exemptions of Colleges."
28. *Ibid.*
29. Thomas J. McCann, New Jersey Local Property Tax Bureau, to Assessors Conference, Rutgers University, New Brunswick, N.J., 1960.
30. *Ibid.*
31. PEL, *Problem of Tax-Exempt Property.*
32. Dunham, "Property Tax Exemptions of Colleges."
33. United Press International dispatch, 1963.
34. *The New York Times*, September 3, 1967.
35. *Princeton University Newsletter*, May 26, 1969.
36. Research interview, Charles Rohr, assessor, Evanston, Ill.

## CHAPTER 7

1. AIC, *Taxation of Property in California.*
2. Testimony to legislature, 1964.
3. *Assessors News Letter*, International Association of Assessing Officers, Chicago, Ill., September, 1967.
4. PEL, *Problem of Tax-Exempt Property.*
5. *Assessors News Letter*, September, 1967.
6. Data received from the Allegheny County, Pa., assessor's office.
7. William O. Winter, "Tax Exemption of Institutional Property," *Municipal Finance*, February, 1960.
8. Research interview, Charles A. Henson, Jr., chairman, Joint City-Council Board of Tax Assessors.
9. Report of the Bureau of Governmental Research, New Orleans, La., 1963–1964.
10. *Ibid.*
11. Minutes, Minnesota Exempt Property Subcommittee, May, 10, 1968.
12. Syracuse Governmental Research Bureau, *A View from the Center* (Syracuse, N.Y.: n.p., 1967).
13. *Ibid.*

14. *Ibid.*
15. Report of the city assessor, Des Moines, Iowa.
16. Ellen Sim Dewey, *Real Estate Tax Exemption in Nebraska* (Lincoln: League of Nebraska Municipalities in cooperation with the Department of Political Science, University of Nebraska, 1962).
17. "Property Tax Exemptions in Colorado," a report of the Colorado Legislative Council, November, 1966.
18. *Denver Press Club v. Collins* (1932), 92C74, 18P, 2d451.
19. Court opinions, Superior Court of Pennsylvania, April term, 1965.
20. *Ibid.*
21. "Property Tax Exemptions in Colorado."
22. Research interview.
23. *YMCA of St. Louis v. Assessor; YMCA of Los Angeles v. Los Angeles County.*
24. Research interview, Joseph C. Sansone.
25. Research interviews with assessors.
26. Minutes, Minnesota Exempt Property Subcommittee, January, 1968.
27. Research interview.
28. Minneapolis *Star*, January 2–5, 1967.
29. *Christian Century*, October 16, 1963.
30. Research interview, Herbert A. Perry.
31. Research interview, City Manager Wayne Anderson.
32. Milwaukee *Journal*, August 31, 1967.
33. Willis L. Culver, in a staff report to the Senate Committee on Revenue and Taxation, Sacramento, Calif., February, 1969.
34. "Property Tax Exemptions in Colorado."
35. Minutes, Colorado Committee on Tax Exempt Property, June 7, 1966.
36. *Ibid.*
37. *Ibid.*
38. *Ibid.*
39. Milwaukee *Journal*, February 4, 1969.
40. Letter, Kansas State Chamber of Commerce to author.
41. *Fredericka Home v. San Diego County*, 1950; *Fifield Manor v. County of Los Angeles*, 1961.
42. *Martin Luther Homes v. Los Angles County.*
43. Arizona statutes.

44. Survey conducted by Ronald Welch, California State Board of Equalization.
45. Court decisions, Oregon.
46. Court decisions, Illinois.
47. Court decisions, Minnesota.
48. Court brief, Evanston, Ill.
49. Court decisions, Colorado.
50. Letter, Department of Assessment to Montgomery County, Md.
51. Report to California legislature.
52. Brandenton *Herald*, February 23, 1969.
53. AIC, *Taxation of Property in California*.
54. ACIR, *The Role of the States*.
55. *St. Louis Lodge #9 v. Koln*, 1914; quoted in Walter J. Norbet, Jr., "Exemption of Property from Local Taxation in Delaware," 1960.

## CHAPTER 8

1. ACIR, *The Role of the States*.
2. *Ibid*.
3. Wylie Kirkpatrick, "Homestead Exemption Reexamined," *Municipal Finance*, February, 1960.
4. "The Burden of Ad Valorem Real Property Taxes Under Varying Assessment Ratios: A Case Study," a pamphlet prepared by the Public Administration Clearing Service of the University of Florida, 1965.
5. *Ibid*.
6. ACIR, *The Role of the States*.
7. National Tax Association, 1962.
8. *The New York Times*, December 21, 1968.
9. ACIR, *The Role of the States*.
10. U.S. Bureau of the Census, *Taxable Property Values* (Washington, D.C.: Government Printing Office, 1967).
11. Kirkpatrick, "Homestead Exemption Reexamined."
12. *Esquire*, June, 1968.
13. Jensen, *Property Taxation*.
14. Research interview, Thomas McGrath, New York State Board of Equalization and Assessment.
15. AIC, *Taxation of Property in California*.
16. ACIR, *The Role of the States*.

17. John O. Behrens, "Property Tax Exemption for Veterans," *Municipal Finance*, February, 1960.

18. Research interview, Thomas McGrath.

19. AIC, *Taxation of Property in California*.

20. Los Angeles *Times*, February, 1965.

21. Research interview, Ronald Welch.

22. U.S. Bureau of the Census, *Taxable Property Values*.

23. *National Tax Journal*, September, 1966.

24. Margaret Greenfield, *Property Tax Exemptions for Senior Citizens* (Berkeley: Institute of Governmental Studies, University of California, 1966).

25. Study material, Pennsylvania legislative task force on homestead exemptions for the aged.

26. Greenfield, *Exemptions for Senior Citizens*.

27. Research interview, Donald Wood, commissioner, Department of Corporations and Taxation.

28. Greenfield, *Exemptions for Senior Citizens*.

29. Kirkpatrick, "Homestead Exemption Reexamined."

30. ACIR, *The Role of the States*.

31. Behrens, "Property Tax Exemptions for Veterans."

32. *Study of Property Tax Exemptions* (Iowa).

33. ACIR, *The Role of the States*.

34. *Ibid.*

35. *National Tax Journal*.

36. ACIR, *The Role of the States*.

### Chapter 9

1. Alabama State Planning and Industrial Board, Montgomery, Ala.

2. Report of the Joint Interim Committee on Ad Valorem Taxation of the State of Alabama, 1968.

3. Des Moines *Tribune*, December 23, 1967.

4. ACIR, *The Role of the States*.

5. Report of Joint Interim Committee, State of Alabama.

6. "Maryland Tax Study."

7. *Municipal Finance*, May, 1968.

8. "Exemption of Property from Local Taxation in Delaware," 1960.

9. *National Observer*, December 23, 1968.

10. *Business Week*, December 28, 1968.

11. Illinois Legislative Council, Springfield, Ill.
12. *Ibid.*
13. *The New York Times*, June 5, 1966.
14. *Assessors News Letter*, September, 1968.
15. *The New York Times* magazine, January 24, 1969.
16. Research interview, New York City Office of Finance.
17. William M. Timmins, "The Prudential Center Agreement: A Case Study in Property Tax Concession," *Assessors Journal*, July, 1967.
18. State of New York Outline of Exemptions, December, 1967.
19. *Ibid.*
20. Frederick D. Stocker, *Property Tax: Problems and Potential* (Princeton, N.J.: Tax Institute of America, 1967).
21. *Farm Land Assessment Practices in the United States* (Washington, D.C.: International Association of Assessing Officers, 1966).
22. Peter W. Hause, *Opposing Views on Taxation of Land Near Cities* (Washington, D.C.: U.S. Department of Agriculture Economic Research Service, 1968).
23. Peter W. Hause, *Differential Assessment of Farm Land Near Cities . . . Experience in Maryland Through 1965* (Washington, D.C.: USDA, 1967).
24. Stocker, *Property Tax.*
25. *Ibid.*
26. Data taken from a 1965 speech by J. K. Hunter, Ohio Department of Taxation.
27. *Journal of the Air Pollution Control Association*, September, 1966.
28. *Federal Tax Administrators Bulletin*, December 15, 1961.
29. Annual Report of the Tax Commission, City of New York, 1968–1969.
30. "Exemption of Property from Local Taxation in Delaware."
31. William D. Ross, *Louisiana Business Bulletin*, December, 1953.
32. William Stober and Laurence Falk, "Property Tax Exemption: An Inefficient Subsidy to Industry," *National Tax Journal*, December, 1967.
33. *A Report of the Committee on Intergovernmental Fiscal Relations: Property Taxation and Interstate Competition for Industry* (New York: National Tax Association, 1967).
34. ACIR, *The Role of the States.*
35. Quoted from a 1965 speech by T. M. Wellspring, Truckline Gas Company.

36. *The New York Times*, January 14, 1969.
37. "Tax Exemption for Housing: A Case Study," a pamphlet prepared by the Citizens Budget Commission, New York, September 26, 1960.
38. Annual Report of the Tax Commission.
39. Stocker, *Property Tax*.

CHAPTER 10

1. *The Real Property Tax* (Rochester, N.Y.: Rochester Bureau of Municipal Research, 1968).
2. "Economic Survey of the Land Uses of Fairfax County, Virginia," a report prepared by Homer Hoyt Associates, June, 1954.
3. Research interview.
4. Testimony at a public hearing before the Commission to Study the Adequacy of Existing Laws Pertaining to Taxation of State-owned Lands in Municipalities, Trenton, N.J., June 6, 1968.
5. *Ibid.*
6. *Ibid.*
7. Report of the Commission to Study the Impact of State Sovereignty upon Financing, Chapel Hill, N.C.
8. *Ibid.*
9. *Ibid.*
10. Research interview.
11. Research interview.
12. Selma J. Mushkin and Robert F. Adams, "Emerging Patterns of Federalism," *National Tax Journal*, September, 1966.
13. Testimony at a hearing before the Assembly Committee on Taxation, June 26, 1968.
14. Report for Joint Survey on Tax Exemptions, Milwaukee, Wisc., 1968.
15. An Analysis of the Educational and Financial Needs of the Large Cities in New York State with Recommendations for Legislative Action," Albany, N.Y., October, 1967.
16. Winter, "Tax Exemptions of Institutional Property."
17. Report from the tax commissioner, Milwaukee, Wisc., 1967.
18. *Ibid.*
19. Survey, American Council on Education, Washington, D.C., 1967.
20. Author's survey.

21. Assessment and Tax Summary, Cambridge Board of Assessors, 1969.
22. Research interview.
23. *Princeton University Newsletter*, May 26, 1969.
24. Report of the Commission to Study the Impact of State Sovereignty upon Financing, Chapel Hill, N.C.
25. *City-University Cooperative Relationships*, a survey published by the International City Managers Association, November, 1964.
26. Research interview, City Manager Wayne Anderson.
27. *The New York Times*, April 1, 1969.
28. *The New York Times*, April, 13, 1969.
29. *The New York Times*, May 8, 1968.
30. *The New York Times*, December 7, 1967.
31. Letter to author.
32. Philadelphia *Bulletin*, May 5, 1967.
33. *The Wall Street Journal*, September 11, 1967.
34. *Church-State*, various issues, 1963–1969.
35. Minutes, Committee on Tax Exempt Property, Colorado, Appendix C.
36. PLLR Commission study.
37. *Ibid.*
38. Peter A. Boone, *Payments in Lieu of Taxes in Connecticut* (Hartford: Department of Finance, 1954); research interview, Donald Wood.
39. New Jersey hearings on adequacy of laws pertaining to taxation of state-owned lands, cited in note 4.
40. *Ibid.*
41. Department of Taxes.
42. PLLR Commission study.
43. Hearings, PLLR.
44. Research interview.
45. Report accompanying S910, 1959.
46. From the Committee report.

CHAPTER 11

1. Robert D. Calkins in Dick Netzer (ed.), *The Economics of the Property Tax* (Washington, D.C.: The Brookings Institution, 1966).
2. Quoted from a 1968 speech by William B. Harral, assistant executive director, Pennsylvania League of Cities.

3. ACIR, *The Role of the States.*

4. Congress of Cities Conference report, National Municipal Policy Program, New Orleans, La., 1968.

5. Research interview.

6. Research interview.

7. Research interview.

8. Research interview, Ronald B. Welch.

9. "Real Estate Exemptions in Nebraska."

10. Research interview.

11. Research interview.

12. James Eichner, assistant city attorney of Richmond, in a speech delivered before the Virginia Assessors Institute, Richmond, Va., 1962.

13. From the proposed amendment to the Minnesota constitution.

14. Research interview.

15. Research interview.

16. Douglas H. Clark, "Grants in Lieu of Taxes on Crown Property: An Historical Note," *Canadian Journal of Economics and Political Science,* May, 1955.

17. *Ibid.*

18. Douglas H. Clark, letter to author.

19. Ronald B. Welch, in a speech delivered before the Governmental Finance Section, Commonwealth Club of San Francisco, 1965.

20. Netzer (ed.), *The Economics of the Property Tax.*

21. PEL, *Problem of Tax-Exempt Property.*

22. Herbert J. G. Bab, "Land Service Taxes Can Help To Overcome the Crisis of the Cities," unpublished paper.

23. Research interview, Elmer A. Johnson, budget and management director, City and County of Denver, Colo.

24. Report, Legislative Council Committee, Nashville, Tenn.

25. Milwaukee *Journal,* April 16, 1969.

26. *The New York Times,* January 6, 1969.

27. *The New York Times,* June 10, 1968.

28. Associated Press dispatch, May, 18, 1969.

29. "Building the American City," a report prepared by the National Commission on Urban Problems, December, 1968.

30. Conference Report, "Financing Our Urban Needs," *Nation's Cities,* March, 1969.

31. William Vickrey, in a speech delivered before the National Seminar

Notes

on Urban Transportation for Tomorrow, May, 1969.
32. Research interview.
33. *The New York Times,* January 31, 1969.
34. "Building the American City."
35. Research interviews.
36. Bruce D. Gillis, *Assessment Administration* (Washington, D.C. International Association of Assessing Officers, 1967).
37. Research interview.
38. Research interview.
39. Research interview.
40. Report of the Joint Economic Committee of the Congress, April, 1, 1969.
41. Associated Press dispatch, March 19, 1969.
42. Quoted from a speech.
43. *The New York Times,* June 17, 1969.
44. Denver *Post,* August 21, 1968.
45. *Business Week,* April 26, 1969.

163

# Appendix

## 1. Survey of State Exemption Practices*

1.  Is an application required in your state before a real property tax exemption can be granted?

    For organizations:
    Initially only (19): Ala., Calif. (some), Colo., Conn., Del., D.C., Hawaii, Ill., Kan., Md., Mich., Miss., O., Okla., Ore., S.C., S.D., Tex., Wash.
    Regular intervals (21): Ariz., Calif. (most), Colo., Conn., D.C., Fla., Ida., Ind., Ia., Kan., Mass., Minn., Neb., Nev., N.H., N.J., N.D., S.D., Tex., Vt., Wyo.

    For individuals:
    Initially only (8): Ala., Conn., Ga., Ida., Me., Md., N.J., N.Y.

> * This survey was carried out by the International Association of Assessing Officers in cooperation with the author. Questionnaires were sent to tax officials of the fifty states and the District of Columbia. Only Louisiana, New Mexico, and Rhode Island failed to respond. Some respondents omitted answering some questions because they felt technicalities in the law made it too difficult to generalize. Responses below are summaries, omitting comments or qualifications for the sake of brevity. Because of this, and because answers are unverified as received, they should be regarded as general guidelines only.

Regular intervals (18): Alas., Ariz., Calif., Fla., Ida., Ind., Ia., Mass., Mich., Neb., Nev., N.H., N.J., N.Y., N.D., Ore., Wash., Wyo.

2. It is required that nongovernmental tax-exempt real property be listed?

    In the regular tax rolls? Yes (19): Ala., Ariz., Ark., Calif., Colo., Del., D.C., Fla., Hawaii, Ida., Ill., Ind., Md., Minn., Miss., Nev., Okla., S.C., Wash.

    In a special tax-exempt property roll? Yes (16): Del., Ia., Kan., Ky., Me., Mass., N.H., N.J., N.Y., N.C., N.D., O., Okla., S.D., Vt., Wash.

3. Is a valuation placed on the property?

    By the assessor? Yes (30): Ala., Ariz., Ark., Conn , Del., D.C., Fla., Hawaii, Ida., Ill., Ind., Ia., Kan., Me., Md., Mass., Minn., Nev., N.H., N.J., N.Y., N.C., N.D., O., Okla., Ore., Pa., S.C., Wash., Wyo.

    By the claimant? Yes (3): Colo., O., S.D.

4. Is the total tax-exempt real property valuation compiled?

    By local jurisdictions only? Yes (23): Ariz., Ark., Calif., Conn., Del., Fla., Ida., Ind., Kan., Md., Mo., Nev., N.H., N.J., N.Y., N.C., N.D., Okla., Pa., S.C., S.D., Va., Wash.

    On a statewide basis? Yes (12): Calif., Colo., Hawaii, Ia., Me., Md., Mass., Minn., N.J., N.Y., O., S.D.

5. Is governmental real property which is immune from taxation handled the same as above?

    For listing in the rolls? Yes (28): Alas., Ariz., Ark., Conn., Del., D.C., Fla., Ga., Ia., Kan., Ky., Me., Md., Mass., Mich., Miss., Mont., N.Y., N.C., O., Okla., Pa., S.C., Tenn., Utah, Vt., Wis., Wyo.

    For valuations placed on it? Yes (21): Ariz., Ark., Del., Fla., Ga., Ia., Kan., Ky., Me., Md., Mass., Mich., Miss., Mont., Nev., N.Y., N.C., O., Ore., Pa., Wis.

    For compilation of valuations? Yes (23): Ariz., Del., Fla., Ga., Ia., Kan., Ky., Me., Md., Mass., Mich., Miss., Mo., Mont., N.J., N.Y., N.C., O., Ore., Pa., S.D., Va., Wis.

6. Has a legislative analysis of or report on the general structure of tax-exemption statutes and practices in your state ever been:

    Compiled? Yes (10): Colo. (1966), Conn. (1967), Fla. (1968), Hawaii (1961), Ia. (1969), Minn. (1969), N.J. (1969), Va. (1968), Wash. (1969), Wyo. (1953–1954).

    Approved and is now in progress? Yes (7): D.C. (annually), Mich. (1969), N.J. (1969), N.D. (prior to 1971), Vt. ("informal"— 1970), Wis.

166

*Appendix*

7. Is there a state constitutional or statutory real property exemption in your state?

   For the elderly? Yes (10): Conn., Ga., Hawaii, Ind., Mass., N.J., N.Y., N.D., Ore., Wash.

   For veterans? Yes (22): Ariz., Calif., Conn., Fla., Ga., Hawaii, Ind., Ia., Me., Md., Mass., Nev., N.H., N.J., N.Y., N.C., N.D., Ore., Tenn., Utah, Vt., Wyo.

   For the blind? Yes (13): Conn., Fla., Ga., Hawaii, Ind., Me., Md., Mass., Nev., N.H., N.J., N.D., Utah.

   For industrial development? Yes (9): Ala., Alas., Hawaii, Ky., Mass., Miss., N.J., N.D., Ore.

   For urban redevelopment? Yes (8): Alas., Hawaii, Ill., Mass., N.Y., N.C., N.D., Okla.

   For leaseholders of government land? Yes (4): Ark., Hawaii, Mass., Ore.

8. In the "education" category, does the exemption extend to property owned by the institution but used:

   For fraternity or sorority house on campus? Yes (25): Ala., Alas., Ark., Colo., Fla., Ga., Ida., Ill., Ind., Ia., Ky., Md., Miss., Mont., Neb., Nev., N.J., N.C., N.D., Okla., Ore., Tex., Vt., Wash., Wyo.

   For fraternity or sorority house off campus? Yes (20): Ala., Colo., Fla., Ga., Ida., Ill., Ind., Ia., Ky., Me., Miss., Neb., Nev., N.C., N.D., Okla., Tex., Vt., Wash., Wyo.

   For married student housing? Yes (30): Alas., Ariz., Ark., Calif., Colo., D.C., Fla., Ga., Hawaii, Ida., Ill., Ia., Ky., Me., Md., Mass., Minn., Miss., Neb., N.C., N.D., Okla., S.D., Tenn., Vt., Va., Wash., W.Va., Wis., Wyo.

   For faculty housing? Yes (28): Alas., Ariz., Ark., Colo., Conn., Fla., Ga., Hawaii, Ill., Ia., Kan., Ky., Me., Md., Mass., Minn., Miss., Mo., Neb., N.J., N.C., O., Okla., S.D., Vt., Va., Wash., Wis.

   For dormitories? Yes (37): Alas., Ariz., Ark., Calif., Colo., Conn., D.C., Fla., Ga., Hawaii, Ill., Ind., Ia., Kan., Ky., Md., Mass., Minn., Miss., Mo., Neb., N.J., N.Y., N.C., N.D., O., Okla., Ore., S.D., Tenn., Tex., Vt., Va., Wash., W.Va., Wis., Wyo.

   For future expansion, but now earning income? Yes (11): Ala., Fla., Ga., Ia., Ky., Neb., N.C., N.D., O., Okla., S.D.

   For commercial income property not directly involved in its primary educational activities? Yes (7): Ala., Fla., Ga., Ia., Ky., O., Okla.

   For business colleges? Yes (18): Ala., Ariz., Colo., Ga., Ida., Ia., Ky., Me., Mo., Neb., N.Y., Okla., S.D., Tex., Vt., Wash., W.Va., Wyo.

9. For "religious," does the exemption extend to property owned by religious institutions and used:

For ministers residence? Yes (39): Ala., Alas., Colo., Conn., Del., D.C., Fla., Ga., Hawaii, Ida., Ill., Ind., Ia., Kan., Ky., Me., Md., Mass., Minn., Miss., Mo., Mont., Neb., Nev., N.H., N.J., N.Y., N.C., N.D., S.C., S.D., Tenn., Tex., Vt., Va., Wash., W.Va., Wis., Wyo.

For parking facilities? Yes (43): Ala., Alas., Ariz., Calif., Colo., Conn., Del., D.C., Fla., Ga., Hawaii, Ida., Ill., Ind., Ia., Kan., Me., Md., Mass., Minn., Mo., Mont., Neb., Nev., N.H., N.J., N.Y., N.C., N.D., O., Okla., Ore., S.C., S.D., Tenn., Utah, Vt., Va., Wash., W.Va., Wis., Wyo.

For printing and publishing? Yes (12): Ala., Alas., Calif., D.C., Ga., Minn., Miss., N.Y., N.C., N.D., Tenn., Wis.

For publication sales? Yes (8): Calif., D.C., Ga., Minn., N.Y., N.C., N.D., Wis.

For future expansion space not now in use for religious purposes? Yes (4): Fla., Ia., N.C., Wash.

For income purposes to be used for religious and charitable activities? Yes (8): Conn., Del., Ga., Mass., Miss., Neb., N.C., S.D.

For schools? Yes (36): Ala., Alas., Ariz., Ark., Calif., Colo., Conn., Del., D.C., Fla., Ga., Hawaii, Ida., Ill., Ind., Kan., Me., Md., Mass., Miss., Mo., Mont., Neb., N.J., N.Y., N.C., Okla., Ore., S.D., Tex., Vt., Va., Wash., W.Va., Wis., Wyo.

10. For cemeteries, does the exemption extend:

    To organizations chartered for profit? Yes (15): Alas., Colo., Del., Ga., Ill., Kan., Mo., N.H., N.Y., N.D., Ore., S.D., Vt., Wis., Wyo.

    To land held for future expansion? Yes (16): Ala., Ariz., Calif., Conn., Del., Ga., Mass., N.J., N.Y., Okla., Ore., S.D., Vt., W.Va., Wis., Wyo.

11. For "medical and hospital," does the exemption extend:

    To organizations chartered for profit? Yes (3): Ala., Alas., Vt.

    To detached building for doctors' private practice? Yes (2): Okla., Va.

    To retail or restaurant facilities open to the public? Yes (17): Alas., Del., Ga., Ind., Ky., Mass., Minn., Miss., Mo., N.H., N.J., N.C., Okla., Vt., Va., Wash., Wis.

    To land for future expansion? Yes (11): Del., Ga., Ia., Ky., Md., Mass., Miss., N.C., Okla., Wash., Wyo.

12. Among fraternal/social/professional/civic organizations, does the exemption extend:

    To veterans groups? Yes (31): Ala., Alas., Calif., Colo., Conn., Del., D.C., Fla., Ida., Ind., Ia., Kan., Me., Md., Mass., Miss., Neb., Nev., N.H., N.J., N.M., N.Y., N.C., N.D., S.D., Tenn., Tex., Vt., Va., Wash., Wyo.

168

To fraternal organizations? Yes (20): Ala., Colo., Fla., Ida., Ind., Ia., Me., Md., Miss., Neb., Nev., N.C., N.D., Okla., Ore., S.D., Tex., Vt., Wis., Wyo.

To labor associations? Yes (10): Fla., Hawaii, Ida., Ind., Miss., N.D., S.D., Tenn., Va., Wis.

To professionals? Yes (7): Del., D.C., Fla., Miss., N.D., Va., Wis.

To civic groups? Yes (10): Colo., Del., D.C., Fla., Ga., Md., Miss., Nev., N.D., Wis.

To literary and scientific organizations? Yes (16): Ala., Calif., Colo., Conn., Del., D.C., Fla., Ind., Ia., Minn., Miss., Nev., N.Y., N.D., Tenn., Wis.

To chambers of commerce? Yes (6): Fla., Ga., Me., Miss., N.D., Tex.

To agricultural organizations? Yes (13): Ariz., Fla., Ga., Ill., Kan., Me., Mass., Minn., Miss., Mo., Neb., N.D., Vt., Wis.

To press clubs? Yes (1) N.D.

To YMCAs, YWCAs? Yes (34): Ala., Alas., Calif., Colo., Conn., Del., Fla., Ga., Ida., Ind., Ia., Kan., Me., Md., Mass., Minn., Miss., Mo., Nev., N.H., N.J., N.Y., N.C., N.D., O., Ore., S.D., Tenn., Tex. Vt., Va., Wash., Wis., Wyo.

To athletic and physical culture clubs? Yes (3): Calif., Colo., N.D.

To foundations? Yes (10): Calif., Colo., D.C., Ind., Ia., Minn., Miss., N.C., N.D., Wis.

To retirement homes? Yes (17): Ala., Calif., Colo., Del., D.C., Ill., Ind., Ia., Kan., Minn., Miss., N.D., O., Va., Wash., Wis., Wyo.

13. Are there service-charge or payment-in-lieu-of-taxes arrangements in your state?

For state-authorized public housing authorities? Yes (16): Ark., Colo., Conn., D.C., Ill., Md., Mass., Minn., Mo., N.J., Okla., Pa., Tex., Utah, Va., Wash.

For fish and game preserves? Yes (13): Ark., Conn., Mass., Minn., Miss., Nev., N.D., Pa., S.D., Utah, Vt., Wash., Wis.

For state parks? Yes (8): Conn., Mass., Miss., N.H., Pa., Vt., Va., Wis.

For state forest and timber lands? Yes (12): Ark., Conn., Me., Mass., Miss., Mo., N.H., Ore., Pa., Vt., Va., Wis.

For port authorities? Yes (3): Ark., Miss., N.Y.

14. What percentage of state and local revenue collected in your state derives from the property tax?

Ala. (local), 35%; Ark., 27%; Colo., 51.8%; D.C., 38%; Md., 40%; Mass., 60%; Minn., 45%; Mont., 60%; Neb., 80%; Nev., 26.6%; N.J., 58.3%; Ill., N.Y., O., Okla., Ore., Pa., S.D., Tex., Vt., Va., Wash., Wis., Wyo., 50%; Ind., Tenn., 70%; Utah, 43%.

## 2. Survey of University Payments to Local Governments*

| | Pop. 0–50,000 | Pop. 50–100,000 | Over 100,000 | Total |
|---|---|---|---|---|
| Responses: | 48 | 16 | 35 | 99 |
| 1. Does the city receive any payments from the institution for municipal services? Yes: | 34 | 9 | 10 | 53 |
| 2. Has the university ever contributed to capital improvement projects? Yes: | 16 | 6 | 8 | 30 |
| 3. Is the city negotiating or are there plans to negotiate for some form of payments in lieu of taxes? Yes: | 16 | 2 | 3 | 21 |
| 4. Is it required that tax-exempt real property be listed in the regular rolls or a special roll? Yes: | 17 | 10 | 25 | 52 |
| 5. Does the institution have a "blanket" exemption covering property used for any purpose? Yes: | 8 | 5 | 14 | 27 |
| 6. Does the university's real property tax exemption extend to: | | | | |
| Fraternity/sorority houses? Yes: | 21 | 6 | 17 | 44 |
| Married student housing? Yes: | 29 | 10 | 20 | 59 |
| Faculty housing? Yes: | 23 | 6 | 17 | 46 |
| Dormitories? Yes: | 43 | 13 | 29 | 85 |
| Property for expansion, now earning income? Yes: | 16 | 7 | 12 | 35 |
| Commercial income property not directly involved in educational activities? Yes: | 14 | 7 | 10 | 31 |
| Hospital or similar facility used by the public but administered by the institution? Yes: | 13 | 5 | 11 | 39 |

\* Questionnaires were sent by the author to tax or assessment officials in all cities which are sites of degree-granting universities. Answers are unverified, as received.

### Details of Payments

Ann Arbor, Mich. (University of Michigan): Formal agreement, based on estimate of services provided and an agreed-upon payment formula. For fire services, payments as of 1969 were $236,504 of $1,313,912 in services provided; police, $381,084 of $2,117,134; sewers, $180,789 of $1,369,297; water, $240,737 of $1,854,819. For capital improvements,

Appendix

in 1969 $237,478 was paid toward a $1,141,709 street location, and $212,000 toward a $651,760 swimming pool and rink project.

Salem, Ore. (Willamette University): In 1962 the city was paid $342,600 toward a $350,200 urban renewal project.

West Lafayette, Ind. (Purdue University): For several years the school paid $15,000 to $40,000 for fire protection; it now provides its own. For sewage treatment, it pays regular rates; for street lighting adjacent to campus, 50% of total cost; for city landfill, $10,000.

Toledo, O. (University of Toledo): In 1967–1968 the school paid $697,000 toward $2,292,000 in costs for ten university area street improvements.

Seattle, Wash. (University of Washington): The school is authorized by the legislature to make $60,000 in annual payments to the city.

East Lansing, Mich. (Michigan State University): By agreement, based on actual costs, as of 1969 the school paid $221,830 (50%) of $443,660 in fire protection costs and $18,550 (50%) of $37,100 in landfill costs. For capital improvements, in 1956 it paid $100,000 (100%) for a fire station serving the campus; in 1964, $130,000 (50%) of the costs of a bridge; and in 1965, $1.25 (50%) of the cost of a sewage treatment plant.

Laramie, Wyo. (University of Wyoming): The school voluntarily pays $8,000 toward fire protection costs and has a separate campus police department.

University Park, Tex. (Southern Methodist University): The school pays $500 a month for garbage removal and in 1968–1969 paid $4,250 toward police costs.

Arkedelphia, Ark. (Henderson State College): Payments are made by state "turnback" of funds, based on percentage of students to total population, and application of the same ratio to the total city budget for services.

Cambridge, Mass. (Harvard University, MIT, Radcliffe University): By formal agreement, payments in lieu of taxes are made on land acquired since 1928; in addition there are such special arrangements as Harvard's paying $4 million for an underpass through Harvard Square and turning it over to the city.

Macomb, Ill. (Western Illinois University): The school has paid some $27,000 annually for fire protection since 1965.

Ames, Ia. (Iowa State University): By formal agreement, based on estimates of service costs, the school pays some $50,000 annually for fire protection. Recent contributions for capital improvements have included $74,000 toward a $155,000 fire station in 1966.

Middletown, Conn. (Wesleyan University): In 1968–1969 the school paid some $10,000 for fire protection, $7,500 for police protection, and miscellaneous other costs.

Cedar Falls, Ia. (University of Northern Iowa): In 1968–1969 the school paid $44,618 for fire protection and $900 for police service.

171

Ithaca, N.Y. (Cornell University): In 1968–1969 the school voluntarily paid $25,000 for fire protection. It also pays one-third of the deficit of the transit system, or some $7,000 a year.

Newark, Del. (University of Delaware): In 1968–1969 the school paid $53,565 for police protection, and shares of engineering, inspection, fire hydrants, and other costs.

Moscow, Ida. (University of Idaho): In 1968–1969, by formal agreement, the school paid $10,000 for fire protection, $6,000 for police, and shares of capital costs for projects in the university area.

Princeton, N.J. (Princeton University): Full taxes are paid on university-owned faculty housing, Palmer Stadium, McCarter Theater, Baker Rink, and Lake Carnegie, and the university shares the costs of an incinerator and sewerage facilities.

Bowling Green, O. (Bowling Green State University): In 1968–1969 the school paid $10,000 for fire protection.

Carbondale, Ill. (Southern Illinois University): The university pays $75,000 (50%) of fire protection costs.

Morgantown, W.Va. (West Virginia University): The school in 1968–1969 paid $165,000 for fire protection, based on the valuation of its exempt property.

Iowa City, Ia. (University of Iowa): In 1968–1969 the school paid $70,000 for fire protection, based on ratio of its buildings' square footage to the city's total. In 1968 it paid 25% ($70,000) of the cost of a branch fire station.

## 3. Survey of Tax and Tax-related Payments by Colleges and Universities to Local Governments, 1969*

| Number of Institutions Which Now | Public | Private Non-Sectarian | Private Church-Related | Total Private |
|---|---|---|---|---|
| Pay taxes | 5 | 25 | 21 | (46) |
| Make other payments | 21 | 21 | 9 | (30) |
| Provide services | 20 | 9 | 6 | (15) |

| Number of Institutions Which Now | University | 4 Year College | 2 Year College |
|---|---|---|---|
| Pay taxes | 9 | 37 | 6 |
| Make other payments | 24 | 11 | 2 |
| Provide services | 20 | 11 | 2 |

* In May 1969 the Office of Research of the American Council on Education mailed a short questionnaire to 407 institutions that had participated in longitudinal studies of entering freshmen. Of the total, 318 (78%) were returned in time for the tabulations. Of 259 respondents who identified the size of the community in which they are located, 68% were in communities of less than 100,000; 25% in those up to one million; and the remaining 7% in larger cities. These are excerpts of the results.

In rank order of frequency, special purposes for which payments or equivalents were made by 105 responding institutions:

| Per Cent | Service |
|---|---|
| 50 | Sanitary |
| 40 | General fund |
| 37 | Fire |
| 18 | Police |
| 14 | Street maintenance |
| 11 | School fund |
| 7 | Utilities |
| 4 | Hospital fund |
| 3 | Flood control |

In rank order of frequency, 94 respondents who answered a question as to the basis of payments:

| Per Cent | Basis of Payment |
|---|---|
| 38 | Estimated cost of services provided by local government |

| | |
|---|---|
| 32 | Fixed proportion of assessed value on tax-exempt property |
| 20 | Fixed contribution based on some arbitrary assumption |
| 15 | Locally determined real estate law |
| 14 | Fixed proportion of revenues from nonacademic auxiliary enterprises |
| 5 | Fixed per capita (per student) rate per annum |
| 1 | Fixed proportion of total annual revenues |

On reactions to payments for services, only 9% of the respondents indicated that they were taking legal or other action to avoid, resist, or eliminate some form of tax payments (or equivalent). Of those making payments or providing services, 40% were "very satisfied" with the arrangements, 50% were "moderately satisfied," and only 10% were "very dissatisfied."

## 4. Payments Agreement Between Harvard University and Cambridge, Mass. (1948–1968)*

Agreement made this 26th day of August 1948, between the President and Fellows of Harvard College and the City of Cambridge.

1. This Agreement supersedes all previous agreements and understandings between the parties hereto concerning claims by the President and Fellows of Harvard College for exemption of real estate from taxation and payments by the President and Fellows of Harvard College to the City in lieu of taxes on real estate exempted from taxation; and the President and Fellows of Harvard College may at any time claim exemption from taxation as to any real estate owned by it on July 1, 1928, and as to which it is entitled to exemption.

2. As to each parcel of real estate in Cambridge acquired by the President and Fellows of Harvard College after July 1, 1928, with respect of which exemption from taxation has been claimed, the President and Fellows of Harvard College will pay to the City in each year until the expiration of twenty years from the effective date of such exemption a sum of money equal to a tax which would result at the tax rate then current upon the assessed value of the land alone in the year of its acquisition by the President and Fellows of Harvard College.

3. As to each parcel of real estate in Cambridge acquired by the President and Fellows of Harvard College after July 1, 1928 (including any such real estate acquired by the President and Fellows of Harvard College hereafter), with respect of which exemption from taxation has

* The second 20-year agreement of its type, this has been superseded by a new 20-year agreement effective in 1968.

174

*Appendix*

not yet been claimed but is claimed prior to July 1, 1968, the President and Fellows of Harvard College will pay to the City in each year until the expiration of twenty years from the effective date of such exemption a sum of money equal to a tax which would result at the tax rate then current upon the assessed value of the land in the year of its acquisition by the President and Fellows of Harvard College.

4. This Agreement shall terminate if and when the City of Cambridge is merged in the municipal government of Greater Boston or a substantial change is made in the laws of taxation so that the exemption of such property ceases to fall solely upon the revenue of the City.

IN WITNESS WHEREOF each of the parties hereto has caused this Agreement to be executed and its corporate seal to be hereto affixed by its proper officer thereunto duly authorized the day and year first above written.

PRESIDENT AND FELLOWS OF HARVARD COLLEGE
By /s/ Henry A. Wood, Jr.
_____
Deputy Treasurer

CITY OF CAMBRIDGE
By /s/ John B. Atkinson
_____
City Manager

APPROVED AS TO FORM:
/s/ John A. Daly
_____
CITY SOLICITOR

# 5. Accrued Payments to States Under Revenue Sharing and Payments in Lieu of Taxes Programs on Nonsection 10 Lands by Program, 1957–1966

(in thousands of dollars)

| | (1) 1957 | (2) 1958 | (3) 1959 | (4) 1960 | (5) 1961 | (6) 1962 | (7) 1963 | (8) 1964 | (9) 1965 | (10) 1966 |
|---|---|---|---|---|---|---|---|---|---|---|
| **Revenue Sharing Programs** | | | | | | | | | | |
| Department of Agriculture | | | | | | | | | | |
| National Grasslands (USDA) | 558.1 | 459.8 | 452.5 | 391.5 | 416.9 | 389.3 | 455.4 | 448.9 | 429.0 | 451.4 |
| Department of the Interior | | | | | | | | | | |
| O&C Railroad Grant Lands | 9,805.7 | 11,635.5 | 14,761.9 | 16,258.6 | 14,454.7 | 15,400.1 | 15,031.3 | 21,136.0 | 20,037.9 | 20,965.3 |
| State Selected Mineral Lands | 0 | 0 | 0 | 0 | 0 | 0 | 8.3 | 14.0 | 19.5 | 15.2 |
| National Grasslands (BLM) | 0 | 0 | 107.9 | 97.4 | 86.3 | 92.3 | 130.8 | 111.8 | 114.8 | 114.8 |
| Department of the Army | | | | | | | | | | |
| OCE, Civil Projects (Flood Control)[a] | 1,530.8 | 1,472.0 | 1,454.3 | 1,492.2 | 1,611.8 | 1,613.8 | 1,718.8 | 1,702.7 | 1,959.3 | 2,421.5 |
| Federal Power Commission | 33.0 | 43.9 | 49.5 | 58.6 | 54.8 | 54.2 | 58.4 | 98.0 | 124.1 | 70.6 |
| **Payments in Lieu of Tax Programs** | | | | | | | | | | |
| Atomic Energy Commission | 33.9 | 39.4 | 44.5 | 44.7 | 46.7 | 44.6 | 46.0 | 45.6 | 67.1 | 68.9 |
| Department of the Interior | | | | | | | | | | |
| Trinity River Basin Project | 0 | 0.7 | 3.4 | 7.8 | 9.6 | 9.7 | 9.8 | 9.8 | 9.7 | 9.5 |
| Columbia Basin Project | 19.6 | 14.6 | 12.8 | 12.0 | 10.4 | 14.2 | 12.2 | 11.0 | 10.4 | 9.6 |
| Grand Teton National Park | 26.5 | 27.2 | 29.1 | 30.1 | 29.3 | 28.6 | 27.3 | 26.0 | 24.8 | 23.6 |
| Coos Bay Wagon Road | 60.0 | 67.0 | 87.6 | 72.6 | 82.4 | 90.0 | 705.6 | 188.9 | 223.6 | 182.2 |
| General Services Administration | | | | | | | | | | |
| Surplus Property (Former RFC) | 772.0 | 516.2 | 471.1 | 457.4 | 340.6 | 264.7 | 622.8 | 576.6 | 579.9 | 585.4 |

# 5 (cont.)

*(in thousands of dollars)*

| | (1) 1957 | (2) 1958 | (3) 1959 | (4) 1960 | (5) 1961 | (6) 1962 | (7) 1963 | (8) 1964 | (9) 1965 | (10) 1966 |
|---|---|---|---|---|---|---|---|---|---|---|
| Department of Defense | | | | | | | | | | |
| Former RFC (Army) | 382.7 | 174.2 | NA | NA | 463.3 | 332.6 | 347.7 | 441.7 | 471.6 | 469.3 |
| Former RFC (Navy) | 2,658.5 | 634.3 | NA | NA | 1,347.0 | 797.0 | 1,106.6 | 913.4 | 1,033.3 | 836.0 |
| Former RFC (Air Force) | 2,560.9 | 515.2 | NA | NA | 2,420.2 | 1,532.3 | 1,399.2 | 1,269.0 | 1,685.0 | 1,595.6 |
| Tennessee Valley Authority | 4,718.4 | 5,249.7 | 5,884.6 | 6,299.9 | 6,472.5 | 6,737.9 | 7,323.4 | 8,212.6 | 9,048.3 | 10,437.1 |
| Department of Transportation | | | | | | | | | | |
| St. Lawrence Seaway | 10.7 | 12.2 | 13.0 | 11.0 | 7.0 | 7.3 | 7.6 | 7.3 | 7.1 | 6.7 |
| Totals | 23,170.8 | 20,861.9 | 23,372.2 | 25,233.8 | 27,854.1 | 27,408.6 | 29,011.2 | 35,213.3 | 35,845.4 | 38,262.7 |

[a] OCE:Flood Control program payments include payments on Section 10 lands which are not segregable.

*Source of data:* Compiled from special and published reports of agencies, including Public Land Statistics, 1957–66, Bureau of Land Management and Annual Report(s) of the Secretary of the Treasury, 1957–66.

*Source of table:* "Revenue Sharing and Payments in Lieu of Taxes on the Public Land," EBS Management Consultants, Inc., Washington, for the Public Land Law Review Commission, July, 1968.

## 6. Federal Revenue Sharing and Payments in Lieu of Taxes (PILT) Statutes

| Statute | Date Enacted | Type and Acreage of Land or Program Affected by Statute[a] | Type of Statute (RS or PILT (%)) | Deductions Made Before Computation of Payments |
|---|---|---|---|---|
| Statutes providing for admission of new states into Union (Digest LA) | 1802–1958 | Public domain land (241,775) | 5% of net proceeds from sale of public lands shared with States in which land located | 20% of price received deducted for administrative costs |
| 35 Stat. 251, 16 U.S.C. 500 National Forest Revenues Act (Digest LB) | 1908 | National Forest lands (both public domain and acquired) (131,139,900) | RS—25% of all monies realized from National Forests | None[1] |
| 36 Stat. 557, Arizona and New Mexico Enabling Act (Digest LC) | 1910 | Designated school section lands located in National Forests in Arizona and New Mexico | RS—calculated % of National Forest revenue is placed in school fund | None[1] |
| 39 Stat. 219, 43 U.S.C. 1181f–1181j Revested Oregon and California RR Grant Lands (Digest LD) | 1916[2] | Revested Oregon and California Railroad Grant Lands (2,563,700) | RS 50%—Counties 25%—access roads and improvements 25%—administration | Cost of access roads up to the first 25% received by the county |
| 40 Stat. 1179, Reconveyed Coos Bay Wagon Road Grant Lands (Digest LE) | 1919[3] | Reconveyed Coos Bay Wagon Road Grant Lands (74,500) | PILT—Current taxes are paid out of first 75% of receipts[4] | Cost of appraisal |

# Appendix

| Political Subdivision Receiving Payments | Date of Payments According to Statute | Restrictions Placed on the Use of Payments | Administering Agency | Price/Value At Which Share Is Calculated | Method of Assessment of Land for PILT |
|---|---|---|---|---|---|
| States | None given (end of fiscal year) | Generally for public schools and roads | Dept. of the Interior (Bureau of Reclamation, BLM) | Fair market value | Standard real estate appraisal methods |
| States for distribution to the counties | End of fiscal year | Benefit of schools and roads of county within which forest is located | Dept. of Agriculture (Forest Service) | "Stumpage" value of timber; market value of other products | — |
| Arizona and New Mexico | End of fiscal year | Proceeds go into common school funds of Arizona and New Mexico | Dept. of the Interior (BLM) | Stumpage value of timber | — |
| The 18 counties in which the O&C lands are located | End of fiscal year | 25% is used for access roads and improvements; residue is returned to the counties | Dept. of the Interior (BLM) | Gross proceeds from the sale of timber and other forest products | — |
| The 2 counties in which the Coos bay lands are located | End of fiscal year | Must be used for schools, roads, highways, bridges and port districts | Dept. of the Interior (BLM) | Local tax rates applied to appraised value of lands. Lands appraised every 10 years | Land is assessed by a committee of three 1. county rep. 2. Interior rep. 3. nonaligned third party |

179

## 6 (cont.)

| Statute | Date Enacted | Type and Acreage of Land or Program Affected by Statute[a] | Type of Statute (RS or PILT (%)) | Deductions Made Before Computation of Payments |
|---|---|---|---|---|
| 41 Stat. 437, 30 U.S.C. § 191 Mineral Leasing Act (Digest LF) | 1920 | Public domain land including National Forests but excluding National Parks (62,184,000) | 52½% Reclamation Fund 37½% States 10% U.S. Treasury Alaska—90% to State 10% to Treasury for expenses of administration | None |
| 41 Stat. 1063, 16 U.S.C. § 810 Federal Power Act (Digest LG) | 1920 | Public lands used for power purposes (70,600) | RS 37½% States 50% Reclamation Fund 12½%—U.S. | Administrative costs, designated in individual leases |
| 45 Stat. 1057, 43 U.S.C. § 617 Boulder Canyon Project (Digest LH) | 1928 | Boulder Canyon Project (811,500) | PILT—Arizona and Nevada each receive $300,000 annually | Any payments made for taxes on the project, the electrical energy, or the privilege of operating are deducted before PILT is paid |
| 48 Stat. 66, 16 U.S.C. § 831 Tennessee Valley Authority (Digest LI) | 1933 | Land acquired by TVA (727,100) | PILT—5% of gross revenues—not less than $10,000 to each State, or the two year average of State & local taxes last assessed prior to acquisition by TVA. Payments to counties equal two-year average of taxes assessed before acquisition by TVA & deducted before making payments to States | Payments to counties are deducted before payments to States are made. Proceeds from sale of power to corp. or agency of U.S. not included in gross receipts. |

## Appendix

| Political Subdivision Receiving Payments | Date of Payments According to Statute | Restrictions Placed on the Use of Payments | Administering Agency | Price/Value At Which Share Is Calculated | Method of Assessment of Land for PILT |
|---|---|---|---|---|---|
| States | Biannually, after Dec. 31 and June 30 | Construction and maintenance of public schools. Support of schools as directed by legislature. These restrictions do not apply to 52½% of Alaska's 90% | Dept. of the Interior (BLM) | % of value of products mined | — |
| States | End of fiscal year | None | Federal Power Commission | % of Power sales | — |
| Arizona and Nevada each receive $300,000 annually | On or before July 31 until 1987 | None | Dept. of the Interior (Reclamation Bureau) | Project must generate enough revenue to make payments | — |
| States and counties | Monthly | None | Tennessee Valley Authority | % of revenue from power sales–amount received by each State based ½ on % power sales in state and ½ on % of book value of TVA property in the State | Minimum payments not less than $10,000 to each State or two year average of State and local taxes assessed immediately before acquisition by TVA |

## 6 (cont.)

| Statute | Date Enacted | Type and Acreage of Land or Program Affected by Statute[a] | Type of Statute (RS or PILT (%)) | Deductions Made Before Computation of Payments |
|---|---|---|---|---|
| 48 Stat. 1269, 43 U.S.C. 315 Taylor Grazing Act (Digest LK) | 1934 | Vacant, unappropriated and unreserved Lands of the public domain (except Alaska) excluding National Parks. O&C & CBWR Lands (168,590,300) | RS—Grazing districts—12½% isolated tracks—50% Indian—33⅓% (ceded). Rented—none | None |
| 57 Stat. 19, 16 U.S.C. §835 c-1 (a) Columbia River Basin Project (Digest LL) | 1937 | Land acquired for the Columbia Basin Project (58,900) | PILT—to be negotiated by Secretary of the Interior[6] | None |
| 50 Stat. 522, 7 U.S.C., §1012 Bankhead Jones Farm Tenant Act (Digest LM) | 1937 | Submarginal land acquired under Title III of the Act | RS—25% of net revenue | "Gross receipts less applicable refunds & adjustments" |
| 55 Stat. 650, 33 U.S.C. § 701 c-3 Army Corps of Engineers (Digest LN) | 1941 | Land acquired for flood control purposes (6,734,800) | RS—75% of gross revenues | None |
| 58 Stat. 887, 11 designated Watersheds Under the Dept. of Agriculture (Digest LO) | 1944 | Land acquired for runoff and waterflow retardation by the Sec. of Agriculture | PILT—1% of purchase price or 1% of value when acquired | No payments have ever been made under this legislation |
| 60 Stat. 765, 42 U.S.C. § 2208 Atomic Energy Commission Act (Digest LP) | 1946 | Land acquired by the Atomic Energy Commission (48,500) | PILT | None |

| Political Subdivision Receiving Payments | Date of Payments According to Statute | Restrictions Placed on the Use of Payments | Administering Agency | Price/Value At Which Share Is Calculated | Method of Assessment of Land for PILT |
|---|---|---|---|---|---|
| States, for the benefit of the county in which the land is located | End of fiscal year | Money from the ceded Indian lands must be used for the schools and roads of the county. Others—None | Dept. of the Interior (BLM) | % of grazing fee | — |
| State or political subdivision with whom Sec. of the Interior has negotiated agreements | Annually, no specific date | None | Dept. of the Interior (Reclamation Bureau) | Result of negotiation between Sec. and local officials | 6 |
| Counties in which the land is located | End of calendar year | Shared revenue must be used for school and road purposes | Dept. of Agriculture (Forest Service) and BLM | % of net revenue | — |
| State (to be expended for benefit of counties) | End of fiscal year | State must pay the money to the county having the land for its schools and roads | Dept. of the Army (Corps of Engineers) | % of revenue derived from leasing acquired lands | — |
| County | Annually | None | Dept. of Agriculture (Forest Service) | % of purchase price or 1% of value when acquired | — |
| State and local governments | Discretion of the Commission | None | Atomic Energy Commission | PILT is to be made at the discretion of the AEC | Assessed value of land at time of acquisition |

## 6 (cont.)

| Statute | Date Enacted | Type and Acreage of Land or Program Affected by Statute[a] | Type of Statute (RS or PILT (%)) | Deductions Made Before Computation of Payments |
|---|---|---|---|---|
| 61 Stat. 681, 30 U.S.C. § 601–03 Sale of Materials from Federal Lands (Digest LQ) | 1947 | All public lands under control of Departments of Agriculture and Interior excluding National Parks and Monuments, and Indian lands | RS—Interior— same % as sale of public lands<br><br>Agriculture—% will depend on statute under which land is administered<br><br>O&C statute applies to O&C lands. Coos Bay statute applies to Coos Bay Lands | Depends upon Acts admitting States to Union or particular statute under which other payments from the affected lands are made |
| 61 Stat. 913, 30 U.S.C. § 355 Mineral Leasing on Acquired Lands (Digest LR) | 1947 | All acquired land not covered by existing "mineral leasing laws" but excluding lands acquired for National Parks and Monuments (5,195,421) | RS—% shared varies in the same manner as prescribed for other receipts from lands affected by the lease | Varies depending on applicable statutes |
| 62 Stat. 568, 16 U.S.C. § 577g Superior National Forest ("BWCA") (Digest LS) | 1948 | The Boundary Waters Canoe Area of Superior National Forest (743,700) | PILT—¾ of 1% of the appraised value | None |
| 63 Stat. 377, 40 U.S.C. § 490 General Services Alministration (Digest LT) | 1949 | Real property declared surplus by Government Corporations under Surplus Property Act, 1944 | PILT | No payments ever made under this legislation |

# Appendix

| Political Subdivision Receiving Payments | Date of Payments According to Statute | Restrictions Placed on the Use of Payments | Administering Agency | Price/Value At Which Share Is Calculated | Method of Assessment of Land for PILT |
|---|---|---|---|---|---|
| States or counties depending on the applicable law | Depends upon applicable law | Restrictions vary depending upon applicable statutes | Dept. of the Interior (BLM), Department of Agriculture | Negotiated or bid sale price | |
| States or counties depending on applicable statutes | End of fiscal or calendar year depending on applicable statute | Varies depending on applicable statute | Dept. of the Interior (BLM) | % of products mined | — |
| Minnesota for distribution to Cook, St. Louis and Lake Counties | End of fiscal year | None | Dept. of Agriculture (Forest Service) | % of appraised value of land | Land is reappraised every ten years by the Forest Service |
| Not specified in statute | Not given | None | General Services Administration | Not given in statute | — |

## 6 (cont.)

| Statute | Date Enacted | Type and Acreage of Land or Program Affected by Statute[a] | Type of Statute (RS or PILT (%)) | Deductions Made Before Computation of Payments |
|---|---|---|---|---|
| 64 Stat. 849, 16 U.S.C. § 406d-1 Grand Teton National Park (Digest LU) | 1950 | Land acquired for Grand Teton National Park in Teton County, Wyo. after March 15, 1943 (37,000) | PILT—year of acquisition and next 9 years full taxes paid; next 20 years declining 5% each year. May not exceed 25% of receipts of Park in any one year | Any taxes paid on newly acquired land are deducted from the PILT before payment |
| 64 Stat. 1101, 20 U.S.C. 237 Educational Impact Grants (Public Law 374) (Digest LV) | 1950 | Property acquired after 1938 | PILT | Other financial compensation received |
| 68 Stat. 93, 33 U.S.C. § 981 St. Lawrence Seaway Act (Digest LX) | 1954 | Land acquired by the St. Lawrence Seaway Development Corporation (2,900) | PILT—in discretion of Corp. | None |
| 69 Stat. 719, Trinity River Basin Project (Digest LX) | 1955 | Lands acquired for construction of the Trinity River project (19,800) | PILT | None |
| 69 Stat. 721, 40 U.S.C. §§ 521–24 Payments on RFC Property (Digest LZ) | 1955 | Property formerly held by RFC (800)[b] | PILT | Any other PILT made with respect to the same lands |

186

| Political Subdivision Receiving Payments | Date of Payments According to Statute | Restrictions Placed on the Use of Payments | Administering Agency | Price/Value At Which Share Is Calculated | Method of Assessment of Land for PILT |
|---|---|---|---|---|---|
| Wyoming for further distribution to Teton County | End of fiscal year | None | Dept. of the Interior (Park Service) | Amount of taxes last paid when privately owned is the base used | — |
| School districts | Annually | None | Office of Education | Assessed value all property in school district (10% must be Federally owned) | Local Assessment |
| St. Lawrence County. Massena— Town— Village & School District | None (Local tax due dates) | None | Dept. of Transportation | Based on local tax rates | Local Assessment |
| Trinity County | Annually (Local tax due dates) | None | Dept. of the Interior (Reclamation Bureau) | Payment must equal lost taxes | Local assessment at time of taking is used to establish base figure locally |
| State and local taxing units | Date local taxes due | None | GSA and other "holding" agencies | Local tax rate | Local assessment at time of taking is used to establish base figure locally determined |

187

## 6 (cont.)

| Statute | Date Enacted | Type and Acreage of Land or Program Affected by Statute[a] | Type of Statute (RS or PILT (%)) | Deductions Made Before Computation of Payments |
|---|---|---|---|---|
| 74 Stat. 1024, 43 U.S.C. § 853 Mineral leasing on State selected indemnity lands (Digest LAA) | 1960 | Mineral bearing lands selected by the States as indemnity for school section lands | RS—90% of rents and royalties on the selected lands | None |
| 78 Stat. 701, 16 U.S.C. § 715s Migratory Bird Conservation Act (Digest LAB) | 1964[s] | Migratory Bird Sanctuaries on both public domain and acquired land (7,865,200) | RS-PILT. Public domain 25% of revenue<br><br>Acquired land 25% revenue or ¾ of 1% of appraised value | Necessary expenses are deducted by each sanctuary |
| 78 Stat. 988, 43 U.S.C. § 1421 Public Sale Act as applied to Alaska (Digest LA) | 1964 | Vacant, unreserved lands located in Alaska, required for orderly growth of the community | RS—90% of proceeds from the sale of certain land in Alaska until 12/31/70 | Price paid to publish notice of sale paid by purchaser, and is not considered part of sale price |
| Klamath Wildlife Refuge Act 78 Stat. 859; 16 U.S.C. § 695m (Digest LAC) | 1964 | Lands in Lower Klamath National Wildlife Refuge and the Tule Lake National Wildlife Refuge (172,000) | RS—25% of net revenues received from leasing of lands not to exceed 50% of taxes levied on similar private lands | Cost of collection |

Source: "Revenue Sharing and Payments in Lieu of Taxes on the Public Land," EBS Management Consultants, Inc., Washington, for the Public Land Law Review Commission, July, 1968.

[a] Acreage figures are those supplied by appropriate Federal agencies for 1966 and used in the resource data bank of this study. Acreages are shown in parentheses. It should be remembered that with respect to revenue sharing statutes, the number of acres subject to a particular statute is not determinative of the amount of revenue shared. Rather, it is the amount of revenues produced which determines the shared amounts. In the case of payment in lieu of tax statutes, the amount of the payment is more closely related to the amount of the acreage involved.

[b] Held by GSA only.

1. K-V charges are a separate account and, as such, are not considered in the determination of gross revenues. 16 U.S.C. § 576(b) (1964).

| Political Subdivision Receiving Payments | Date of Payments According to Statute | Restrictions Placed on the Use of Payments | Administer- ing Agency | Price/Value At Which Share Is Calculated | Method of Assessment of Land for PILT |
|---|---|---|---|---|---|
| States | After Dec. 31 and June 30 | None | Dept. of the Interior (BLM) | Based on rents and royalties paid for mineral leases | — |
| Counties | End of fiscal year | Solely for the benefit of schools and roads of the county | Dept. of the Interior (Bureau of Sport Fisheries and Wild- life) | % of revenue or % of ap- praised value | Every five years, using Agriculture Dept. tables of average farm values |
| Alaska | As soon as practicable after June 30 | None | Dept. of the Interior (BLM) | Selling price must at least equal the ap- raised fair market value | Standard real estate appraisal methods |
| Three coun- ties in which Refuges located | Annually (after close of fiscal year) | Must be used for public schools and roads | Dept. of the Interior (Bureau of Reclama- tion) | Leasing proceeds | — |

2. Date of original enactment. Present provisions enacted in 1937, 50 Stat. 874.
3. Date of original enactment. Present provisions enacted in 1939, 53 Stat. 753.
4. 25% is used for administrative costs and any balance is paid into the General Fund of the U.S. Treasury.
5. 87½% of remainder is to pay administration costs.
6. In 1948, agreements were concluded with four counties in Washington which provide for the annual payments to each of the counties of the lesser of (1) the taxes which would have been levied on the land had it remained in private ownership, or (2) 50% of the revenues derived from the leasing of such lands.
7. The remaining 10% is retained by the Federal Government essentially to cover the costs of administering the outstanding leasehold interests to which the selected lands may be subject.
8. Date of amendment, original enactment 1935, 49 Stat. 383.

## 7. Survey of Policies on Payments in Lieu of Taxes in State Capital Cities, 1967

| State | Does State pay Capital City in lieu of tax payment for State government property? How is amount determined? | Does State reimburse Capital City for direct tangible services? How much? | What technical assistance is provided to Capital City by State? | Does Capital City lease State-owned property? Describe | Steps taken in gaining greater State cooperation. Which were most successful? | Steps currently being taken or planned for increased State cooperation | Burden placed on Capital City by existence of non-taxable State offices and other property | Do other cities have problems due to non-taxable State properties? What efforts have been made to solve them? | Analysis of problem of nonprofit organizations |
|---|---|---|---|---|---|---|---|---|---|
| Ala. | No | No | Use of Police Academy | No | At beginning of Geo. Wallace's Adm., (1963) a State-aid program for city streets was initiated. Montgomery got about $900,000 from this program | Ala. League engaged in major effort to secure $12 million per year from State-collected revenues to be used for maintenance and construction of City streets | The providing of fire protection, parking spaces and sanitation | No combined effort | Problem does not exist in Montgomery |
| Alaska | No | No | None; however, proximity to State personnel allows more frequent meetings and sometimes speeding up of projects | No | State is now planning a capital site and assisted in planning a civic center site. In its limited years of statehood, the State hasn't gotten around to viewing local problems | New Adm. very aware of the community's needs for a capital plan. Now facing a period of greater understanding | ⅓ of the City's land area is Federal buildings and schools. The City now provides water, and in the near future, will be levying a sewer charge | Combine forces through Alaska Municipal League. Through this effort, payment in lieu of taxes bill was submitted to the legislature this year | Due to newness of State, headquarters are generally done on basis of rental of office space from privately-owned buildings on which taxes are paid, so presently there is no problem |

# 7 (cont.)

| | | | | | | | | | |
|---|---|---|---|---|---|---|---|---|---|
| Ariz. | No | No | No | None | No | There has been cooperation in areas of highway planning and construction, anti-poverty programs, library construction, improvement of recreation facilities, civil defense emergencies and auto licensing | None | Phoenix provides police and fire protection and sanitary sewerage services for State offices and institutions | There has been no attempt among cities to seek in lieu tax assistance from the State | No such analysis has been made of this problem |
| Calif. | No | No | State and Federal government pay for refuse collection | Staff cooperation between applicable city and state departments. Special projects divided between City, County and State in terms of staff contribution and financing | City leases a unit of State National Guard at $1.00 per year | Cooperation is excellent in local affairs | None | None. City considers State government, its largest industry, as economic asset and therefore has raised no issue of cost to citizens | Unaware of problems in other cities | No analysis of problem. Considers non-profit organizations as economic assets in that they increase employment base |
| Colo. | No | No | 1. $400/mo. for county jail work crew on state highways 2. $4 per day for State prisoner held in county jail | 1. Microfilming program (cost plus 2%) 2. Law Reinforcement Academy available (but not used) | No | Cooperation is tied to relationship with various State agencies. This type of cooperation can only be as effective as | This is something that must be resolved in State legislative chambers. Last year, Urban County concept (which | Real estate valuation of State-owned property: $18,313,740. This is nontaxable | Same problems in other cities | No problem |

**7 (cont.)**

| State | Does State pay Capital City in lieu of tax payment for State government property? How is amount determined? | Does State reimburse Capital City for direct tangible services? How much? | What technical assistance is provided to Capital City by State? | Does Capital City lease State-owned property? Describe | Steps taken in gaining greater State cooperation. Which were most successful? | Steps currently being taken or planned for increased State cooperation | Burden placed on Capital City by existence of nontaxable State offices and other property | Do other cities have problems due to nontaxable State properties? What efforts have been made to solve them? | Analysis of problem of nonprofit organizations |
|---|---|---|---|---|---|---|---|---|---|
| Colo. (cont.) | | | 3. Use of Nat'l. Guard Facility for Police Marksmanship Program 4. Dept. of Local Affairs recently established 5. Cooperation of various State agencies, such as highways, civil defense, etc. | | State laws permit. Problem stems from suburban-core city (Denver) conflict which makes it difficult to bring about statutory reforms | would provide one government for Denver and surrounding suburbs) requiring a Constitutional change did not pass the legislature | | | |
| Conn. | No | No | State provides certain road materials for towns and cities on basis of number of miles of improved roads. State maintains its | No | Cooperative agreement with State concerning planning of capitol complex—$18,750 was given to State-City Plan Committee. There are gov- | City of Hartford currently proposing bill to permit taxing of State-owned property by cities at ½ tax rate for private property. Other | State has $31 million worth of property in Hartford. This is a loss of $1,546,900 in revenue to City per year | | Not significant problem |

Hartford got $14,286 from U. of Conn., Blue Hills Alcoholic Clinic, flood control and airport property. Hartford now proposing

# 7 (cont.)

| | | | | | | | |
|---|---|---|---|---|---|---|---|
| Conn. (cont.) | *that State-owned property of all towns and cities be taxed at 1/3 rate for private property* | roads within boundaries of city | ernment committees to study highway and redevelopment problems. Now being considered is the idea of the U. of Conn. Medical-Dental School to take over city-operated McCook Hospital for 3–4 years pending construction of new hospital after which time municipal hospital will be closed | | | bills include one to provide non-repayable state grants-in-aid to cities for urban renewal and redevelopment and development of stand-by State income tax legislation. Inclusive law for refunding of State gas taxes to municipality on owned or leased equipment | |
| Del. | No | No | Recruit training in State Police school is available without charge, when classes are not filled. The State donates to the volunteer fire dept. Technical assistance of State health depts. is available to City | No | Municipal Street Aid program obtained by Association of Mayors (League of Local Governments) | Continued joint efforts through League of Local Governments | The City charges for sewer and electric service. For all other services there is no charge. These include trash and garbage collection, police protection, street maintenance and repair, mosquito con- | City of Newark has problem due to University — No problem |

| State | Does State pay Capital City in lieu of tax payment for State government property? How is amount determined? | Does State reimburse Capital City for direct tangible services? How much? | What technical assistance is provided to Capital City by State? | Does Capital City lease State-owned property? Describe | Steps taken in gaining greater State cooperation. Which were most successful? | Steps currently being taken or planned for increased State cooperation | Burden placed on Capital City by existence of non-taxable State offices and other property | Do other cities have problems due to non-taxable State properties? What efforts have been made to solve them? | Analysis of problem of nonprofit organizations |
|---|---|---|---|---|---|---|---|---|---|
| Del. (cont.) | | | Municipal Street Aid. Traffic surveys of City are conducted by State Highway Dept. | | | | trol, street cleaning and snow removal | | |
| Fla. | No | City sells electricity, water, gas and sewer services to State. City also provides fire and police protection and parking for State employees | Nothing special. State did construct a 4-lane highway into the capital and provides traffic engineering. State Road Dept. uses City as showplace to demonstrate good ideas to legislators | The reversal is true—City has acted as purchasing agent for the State on land that is desired; and in some cases has paid a portion of the cost out of city funds to assure capital development | City paved way and regulated with property owners for State's construction of legislative building. City and State are jointly planning utility needs | Now negotiating land swap for expansion of FSU—City is getting the State land through urban renewal | There are undetermined tax burdens. There is continuing contact between City and State regarding zoning in neighborhoods of capitol and 2 universities. Utilities, law enforcement and traffic control are also problems | Gainesville has the U. of Fla. There are State headquarters in various cities. Up to now there has been no joint action on the part of the cities affected to secure any State financial relief | Headquarter offices are beneficial, for they bring increased payrolls and business for City and increased utility income. City property is sometimes made available at token price for these organizations |
| Ga. | No | No | None | No for most part. However, State maintains possession of | State has been gradually increasing its aid to municipali- | Support of Georgia Municipal Association. 1968 | This data is not obtainable. Most of property in ques- | Athens has the U. of Georgia (14,000); other cities | No analysis has ever been made. Atlanta's location in SE |

7 (**cont.**)

| | | | | | | | |
|---|---|---|---|---|---|---|---|
| Ga. (cont.) | No | No | new school property until school is paid-in-full | ties. Much of increase is due to participation in Georgia Municipal Association | brings a reapportioned legislature | tion has never been assessed. Over 20% of Central Business District is taken up by government offices. Property is also taken up by Ga. Tech., Interstate Hwy. System, Atlanta Fed. Pen., Ft. MacPherson | have prisons. These situations handled by State Representatives and Georgia Municipal Association | attracts not only State headquarters but also many regional headquarters of nonprofit organizations |
| Hawaii | No | None | Yes. State, by Executive Order, makes available State-owned land for City purposes at no cost | State has cooperated excellently in making lands available for public purposes | Personal contacts and joint meetings involving top officials at both levels of government | County gets 70% of its income from property taxes, so burden of untaxed State properties is significant | Other counties in State have joined in State Association of Counties to work on problem. Hawaii has only one incorporated city and only four counties | No analysis has been made, but it is felt that it isn't a problem. Generally, the City welcomes the opportunity to accommodate such organizations in Capital City and welcomes the activity that they exempt |
| Ida. | No | No | No | None | Have appealed to State legislature to grant City of Boise | Additional burdens include sewer service; increased street | Yes, other cities do have problems | No analysis has been made |

| State | Does State pay Capital City in lieu of tax payment for State government property? How is amount determined? | Does State reimburse Capital City for direct tangible services? How much? | What technical assistance is provided to Capital City by State? | Does Capital City lease State-owned property? Describe | Steps taken in gaining greater State cooperation. Which were most successful? | Steps currently being taken or planned for increased State cooperation | Burden placed on Capital City by existence of non-taxable State offices and other property | Do other cities have problems due to non-taxable State properties? What efforts have been made to solve them? | Analysis of problem of nonprofit organizations |
|---|---|---|---|---|---|---|---|---|---|
| Ida. (cont.) | | | | | | land area, which is presently State-owned, for recreational purposes | travel; increased street lighting; crosswalk signals; sidewalk construction; drainage of surface water | | |
| Ill. | No | Springfield receives following annual payments for fire protection services to State property outside the City limits: State Fair: $1,550,000 (10 days); Ill. Nat'l. Guard $1,500 | None | No | No recent requests made for actual assistance. 1965 Legislature created Capital City planning Commission, as requested by both Governor and Mayor for joint planning affecting both City and State. Financed ⅔ by State and ⅓ by City | None, except for new projects under the Capital City Planning Commission | Burdens are substantial, but don't know how to measure them | Urbana has the U. of Illinois. There has been discussion of the problem but no active combination to get assistance | No analysis has been made |
| Ia. | No | No | None | No | Special provisions for cities | Nothing being proposed spe- | Burden has not been | University and college cities | Question is currently being |

| | | | | | | | | |
|---|---|---|---|---|---|---|---|---|
| Ia. (cont.) | | | | | with State property have not been recently proposed | cifically for cities with State-owned property. Generally, all cities are trying to get a larger share of locally shared taxes | analyzed | have the problem. No effort has been made by individual cities or as a group to secure payments in lieu of taxes | litigated. Iowa Tax Commission recently ruled that property owned by Chambers of Commerce subject to property taxes—the ruling is now being appealed |
| Kan. | No | No | None | No data | No data | League of Kansas Municipalities concentrating on legislature program aimed toward broader tax base for all cities in State. Topeka supporting this legislature and marking time on in-lieu payment plan so as to get the former passed | No data | No data | No data |
| Ky. | No | No cash remuneration. In 1963, State built $500,000 incinerator which was turned over to City to oper- | Technical assistance received is same as for other cities | No | In cooperation with State government, a $50 million governmental complex project is at stage of final con- | No data | Impossible to estimate | Other cities have the problem—nothing has been done to solve it | No problem. City desires to attract these organizations |

| State | Does State pay Capital City in lieu of tax payment for State government property? How is amount determined? | Does State reimburse Capital City for direct tangible services? How much? | What technical assistance is provided to Capital City by State? | Does Capital City lease State-owned property? Describe | Steps taken in gaining greater State cooperation. Which were most successful? | Steps currently being taken or planned for increased State cooperation | Burden placed on Capital City by existence of nontaxable State offices and other property | Do other cities have problems due to nontaxable State properties? What efforts have been made to solve them? | Analysis of problem of nonprofit organizations |
|---|---|---|---|---|---|---|---|---|---|
| **Ky.** (cont.) | | ate. In 1958, State purchased and equipped fire substation and turned over to City | | | struction design | | | | |
| Me. | No | No | None | No | None | No data | Capital City is responsible for maintaining streets, snow removal, cleaning streets, traffic, fire and police protection | No data | No data |
| Md. | No | 1. Sewer service $7,000 per annum 2. Refuse collection $11,500 per annum 3. Fire protection $11,500 per annum These new rates are effective 7/1/67 | None | No | Recent negotiations with Board of Public Works resulted in increased appropriations (see col. 2). Requests for consideration of other municipal serv- | Work being done through Maryland Municipal League and members of State Legislature and State Senate | It is an economic asset to City—every effort is made to encourage their presence and expansion | Information not available | No particular problem |

| | | | | | | | | | |
|---|---|---|---|---|---|---|---|---|---|
| **Md. (cont.)** | | | | | ices (police, street maintenance, sanitation) as well as in-lieu payments received no action | None, as yet | 1/10 of assessed value of Capital City is State property not paying for its services | No—the State Universities pay their share | Does not affect a great deal |
| **Mich.** | No | No | None | One piece is used by the City at no cost for a playground | Only success was grant of money by State Legislature to be used for widening and fitting streets to grades to accommodate new underground ramp facilities (approx. 1/3 of the total cost) | | | | |
| **Mo.** | No | Sanitary sewer service charge, based on water usage | Police officers sent to Highway School. State Highway Department gives assistance. State does small amount of re-printing maps | No | Sewer service charge was instituted 1½ years ago | No steps, except to get appropriation for service charge | No data | It is presumed that the University in Columbia has the same problems | No data |
| **Mont.** | No | No | No | Policemen may attend the schools for the highway patrol but must pay | None | Additional meeting with heads of State and pending legislation | The State pays nothing except its portion in local improvement districts | University cities (Missoula and Bozeman) have the same problem. | There is no problem in Helena. There are some Federal properties |

# 7 (cont.)

| State | Does State pay Capital City in lieu of tax payment for State government property? How is amount determined? | Does State reimburse Capital City for direct tangible services? How much? | What technical assistance is provided to Capital City by State? | Does Capital City lease State-owned property? Describe | Steps taken in gaining greater State cooperation. Which were most successful? | Steps currently being taken or planned for increased State cooperation | Burden placed on Capital City by existence of non-taxable State offices and other property | Do other cities have problems due to non-taxable State properties? What efforts have been made to solve them? | Analysis of problem of nonprofit organizations |
|---|---|---|---|---|---|---|---|---|---|
| Mont. (cont.) | | | their own expenses | | | | (paving and lighting) | has been no joint effort to solve these problems | that are the same problem as the State, but they do not even go along with the local improvements districts |
| Neb. | No | Sewer use free based on water usage | None | No | Very little. State authorized by legislature to contract for fire services; however, Attorney General ruled appropriation illegal | Proposals to State that it assume responsibility for State highways in City limits | Services to State University, State Fair, State Penal Complex, State Capitol, State Hospital | Yes, but to lesser degree | Courts give Federal tax exemptions to such organizations |
| Nev. | No | No | Three fire engines are supplied | No | None | Bill being introduced into Legislature for in-lieu taxes | Police services, fire services, street maintenance, cleaning and snow removal | Nevada Municipal Association tried in-lieu tax bill but failed | None |
| N.H. | No | No | City is billed | No | | Hopefully a case will be | About ¼ of assessable prop- | Hoping to enlist other cities | Currently analyzing |

| | | | | | | | | | |
|---|---|---|---|---|---|---|---|---|---|
| **N.H. (cont.)** | Payments in lieu of taxes by law can be made only if 9% of land area used for State purposes. City does not reach this percentage | No | services rendered, such as fire and police schools and personnel examinations | No | | prepared for 1969 Legislature for in-lieu payments. Survey of value of exempt properties not completed in time for 1967 session | erty is State-owned | support in case for 1969 Legislature | problem |
| **N.J.** | City receives $60,000 for services from State. Each year, City makes request for payment based on services cost; however, amount received does not relate to actual costs incurred | No | Technical assistance received is same as for other cities. However, proximity of State offices facilitates exchange of information and services | No | City has recently improved relationships in planning and development through urban renewal process and planning coordinating committee. Also, close highway planning relationship effected | Working to produce more realistic reimbursement to cities have large number of State facilities | 9.86% of City's assessed valuation is State-owned. Major services are public works and public safety. If City could tax this property, would yield $2.7 million annually | Jersey City and Newark have problems. Mayor of Six Big Cities meet and exchange information concerning this problem | No current analysis available |
| **N.M.** | No | No | None | No | None | None | Unknown | Yes—legislation has been presented but to no avail | None |
| **N.Y.** | On property taken by State for other than highways, State will pay 1% of cost of | Charge based on regular rates | None | No | State legislation in 1965 implemented provision in col. 1 | None | Approximately ½ of all property in City is owned by State | No data | No data |

# 7 (cont.)

| State | Does State pay Capital City in lieu of tax payment for State government property? How is amount determined? | Does State reimburse Capital City for direct tangible services? How much? | What technical assistance is provided to Capital City by State? | Does Capital City lease State-owned property? Describe | Steps taken in gaining greater State cooperation. Which were most successful? | Steps currently being taken or planned for increased State cooperation | Burden placed on Capital City by existence of nontaxable State offices and other property | Do other cities have problems due to nontaxable State properties? What efforts have been made to solve them? | Analysis of problem of nonprofit organizations |
|---|---|---|---|---|---|---|---|---|---|
| N.Y. (cont.) | acquisition and construction of any improvements made by State for 25 years. This 1% is paid in lieu of taxes, and is divided among City, County, and School District | | | | | | | | |
| N.C. | No | No | None | No | 1. Mayor appointed voting member of State Capital Planning Commission 2. Joint Committee established between City and State government. This has been the closest liaison ar- | Continue the effort of educating the general public, business leaders, State officials and State legislators of the unfair burden of tax-free property | Considerable burden | Impact Commission—special legislative study commission to analyze impact of State government property on local areas. Out of study came formula for payment in lieu of taxes | No problem compared to that of State tax-free properties |

7 (cont.)

| | | | | | | | | | |
|---|---|---|---|---|---|---|---|---|---|
| N.C. (cont.) | No | | | | rangement for years | | based on % of value of property of each locality. Report did not meet success in 1965 legislature | | Steps have been taken to limit the tax exempt status of many organizations |
| N.D. | No | State makes monthly payments for water, sewer, and refuse disposal. State does not pay for fire, police, etc. | None specifically for Capital City | No | Practically none | None. In the 1965 Legislature session, the League of North Dakota Municipalities introduced legislation for payments to cities for fire and police protection for State-owned buildings. The legislation was not adopted | 7% of buildings in Bismarck are State-owned | | See col. 6 |
| Ore. | No | State Statute requires Salem to provide police and fire protection to state buildings. No payment is made for these services | None | Small vacant parcel which ultimately will be used for a State office building is leased to City for $1/year. It is used as a temporary park | Most concessions from the State are a result of "horse trading" | Mid-Willamette Council of Governments provides public forum for City-State cooperation. It has not been very successful in discussing financial help | 42% of property in Salem is tax-exempt. Property is subject to sewer, water and street assessments | Cities that are sites of State Universities have problems (Corvallis, population 28,000—10,000 students; Eugene, population 70,000—11,000 students) | This is not a significant problem |

| State | Does State pay Capital City in lieu of tax payment for State government property? How is amount determined? | Does State reimburse Capital City for direct tangible services? How much? | What technical assistance is provided to Capital City by State? | Does Capital City lease State-owned property? Describe | Steps taken in gaining greater State cooperation. Which were most successful? | Steps currently being taken or planned for increased State cooperation | Burden placed on Capital City by existence of nontaxable State offices and other property | Do other cities have problems due to nontaxable State properties? What efforts have been made to solve them? | Analysis of problem of nonprofit organizations |
|---|---|---|---|---|---|---|---|---|---|
| Pa. | No | Commonwealth of Pennsylvania annually contributes $2,500 for fire protection | Commonwealth provides various instructional type meetings in addition to cash contributions for youth-aid assistance for the Police Dept. and recreation cost-sharing programs | No | State representatives have instituted bills in State Legislature to provide for payments in lieu of taxes. These bills have not passed | Efforts to solicit the help of legislators throughout the State are being continued | Burden principally on traffic congestion and parking facilities although Commonwealth has provided extensive underground and street parking for its employees. State property makes up 26% of real estate in City | Philadelphia and Pittsburgh have problems; however, the larger cities are better able to absorb any burdens with their extensive real estate subject to taxation | All tax-exempt property owners were recently required to prove their tax-exempt status |
| R.I. | No | No | Minimal amount of police school training is provided | No | 1. State took over communicable disease hospital 2. State financed 100% of cost of general public assistance 3. State took | 1. Very active Rhode Island Municipal Chief Executives Association 2. Legislation is pending in the general assembly to | ⅓ of real property in City has tax-exempt status. At same time, cost of providing water, sewerage disposal, and garbage collec- | The prison, medical center and State University are in other cities and their problems are as grave as those of Providence | No data |

7 (cont.)

| | | | | | | | | | |
|---|---|---|---|---|---|---|---|---|---|
| R.I. (cont.) | | | | | over health services 4. State aid for redevelopment | authorize inter-governmental cooperation 3. More informal discussions of State and local officials on common problems 4. Continuing cooperation with members of general assembly | tion continues to rise | | No data |
| S.C. | No | No | City uses facilities of State Law Enforcement Division for training. State Highway Department does extensive street surfacings | No | No data | No data | Currently compiling data. There are 640 parcels of property on which no taxes are paid | Yes—other cities have the problem but to a far lesser degree | No data |
| Tenn. | No | No, but water and sewerage services have been placed on a revenue basis partly in order to reach tax-exempt property | Police Academy serving the 95 counties also serves Nashville | Dog pound site temporarily leased while new facility is being built | None | None | The loss due to non-taxable institutions is $3½ million yearly. $1¼ million of this is State property | Yes | Presently analyzing this problem |
| Tex. | No | No. State does use its own trucks for refuse collec- | None | City, has use of city or "public squares" where title is vested | Change from rural dominated Legislature to one | Being a better host city for legislators and helping them | 50% of the city property nontaxable. Of this, 30% be- | No other city in the State has the problem to the | No particular problem |

| State | Does State pay Capital City in lieu of tax payment for State government property? How is amount determined? | Does State reimburse Capital City for direct tangible services? How much? | What technical assistance is provided to Capital City by State? | Does Capital City lease State-owned property? Describe | Steps taken in gaining greater State cooperation. Which were most successful? | Steps currently being taken or planned for increased State cooperation | Burden placed on Capital City by existence of non-taxable State offices and other property | Do other cities have problems due to non-taxable State properties? What efforts have been made to solve them? | Analysis of problem of nonprofit organizations |
|---|---|---|---|---|---|---|---|---|---|
| Tex. (cont.) | | tion, but uses City sanitary fills | | in the State. One is used for Central Fire Station; another for parking lot | of more urban composition has brought success | to understand Austin's unique problems | longs to State government and university | same extent and magnitude as Austin | |
| Vt. | No | Only for fire prevention at rate of $200 per hour for actual time service is rendered | None | No | Hopefully, new attitude of State officials has been created by their desire to have a $15 million State building complex approved. Griffenhagen-Kroeger of San Francisco is making a study on the economic impact of the State Capital to the City | Griffenhagen-Kroeger study will be used as a basis for legislative bill for financial relief from State | 38% of the real estate is tax-exempt | Not much attempt has been made thus far. An attempt to combine forces is planned before the 1968 session of Legislature | Not aware of nonprofit organizations being particular problem in Montpelier |

| State | | | | | | | | | |
|---|---|---|---|---|---|---|---|---|---|
| Va. | No | No | None | No | There has been no success in gaining greater State cooperation regarding payments in lieu of taxes or governmental services | Problems have been called to the attention of the Metropolitan Area Study Commission (appointed by Governor to provide recommendations for alleviating metropolitan area problems | 24% of the real estate in Richmond nontaxable. This represents loss of $1,235,156 in revenue from State-owned property | State colleges are in Fredericksburg, Charlottesville, Radford, Farmville, Petersburg, Harrisburg, Marion, Williamsburg and Blackburg. There has been no effort to combine forces | There is an annual $106,300 loss in revenue from nontaxable properties |
| Wash. | No | No | None | Two-acre park area leased at $10 per year | There has been no particular success except with respect to parking around capitol buildings and use of small piece of state land for park | Attempting closer co-operation with Department of General Administration, which is responsible for all State buildings and grounds | 1. Police protection and traffic control 2. Fire protection 3. Parking 4. Street improvements and signs | Cities with universities, State hospitals and prisons receive compensation to some degree under state tax sharing programs | Presently analyzing this problem |
| W.Va. | No | No | None | No | None | Approach is on an "individual to individual" basis | The Capital City must provide service in case of an emergency | Other cities have the problems but there is no liaison | There are no outstanding problems as such |
| Wis. | No special payments to Capital Cities. State does pay school taxes on | No | Office equipment can be purchased under State contract. State | No | Successful work with Governor's office on problem of parking legis- | Actively support legislation sponsored by Wisconsin League relative | Exact figures not available. Recognize that community benefits eco- | Problem exists in other cities but not to as great an extent | No analysis has been made. Milwaukee proposing legislation |

# 7 (cont.)

| State | Does State pay Capital City in lieu of tax payment for State government property? How is amount determined? | reimburse Capital City for direct tangible services? How much? | What technical assistance is provided to Capital City by State? | Does Capital City lease State-owned property? | Steps taken in gaining greater State cooperation. Which were most successful? | Steps currently being taken or planned for increased State cooperation | Burden placed on Capital City by existence of nontaxable State offices and other property | Do other cities have problems due to nontaxable State properties? What efforts have been made to solve them? | Analysis of problem of organizations which will provide for service charges by tax-exempt organizations |
|---|---|---|---|---|---|---|---|---|---|
| Wis. (cont.) | agricultural land owned by University | | Highway Commission reproduces maps; department heads may attend University courses at nominal charges | | lator's cars. Individual State agency personnel have been extremely helpful and cooperative. Main problem is the expense borne by City taxpayers for services provided to State agencies | to payment for direct services (refuse collection, police and fire protection). Request the Legislature to appropriate money for tuition payments for children of married students who live on State-owned property and whose children attend City of Madison schools | nominally by presence of State offices. Expansion of University resulting in removal of taxable property from City rolls | | |

Source: From data compiled by Richard A. Chandler, City Assessor, Richmond, Va.

## 8. IOWA COUNTY AND CITY ASSESSORS' POLICY ON EXEMPTION OF FRATERNAL ORGANIZATIONS, 1964

| County or City | Do You Exempt Eagles Property? | | | Do You Exempt Elks Lodge? | | | Do You Exempt Moose Lodge? | | |
|---|---|---|---|---|---|---|---|---|---|
| | Yes | No | Partial | Yes | No | Partial | Yes | No | Partial |
| 1 | | | x | — | — | — | — | — | — |
| 2 | x | | | x | | | — | — | — |
| 3 | | x | | | x | | — | — | — |
| 4 | — | — | — | x | | | | | x |
| 5 | | | x | | | x | | | x |
| 6 | | | x | — | — | — | — | — | — |
| 7 | x | | | | | x | x | | |
| 8 | x | | | — | — | — | — | — | — |
| 9 | x | | | x | | | x | | |
| 10 | | | x | | | x | | | x |
| 11 | | x | | | x | | | x | |
| 12 | x | | | x | | | — | — | — |
| 13 | | | x | x | | | — | — | — |
| 14 | | | x | | | x | x | | |
| 15 | | x | | | x | | x | | |
| 16 | | x | | | | x | | x | |
| 17 | | | x | | | x | | | x |
| 18 | | | x | | | x | | | x |
| 19 | x | | | | | x | | | x |
| 20 | | | x | | | x | — | — | — |
| 21 | x | | | — | — | — | — | — | — |
| 22 | x | | | x | | | | | x |
| 23 | | x | | | x | | — | — | — |
| 24 | | x | | | x | | | x | |
| 25 | x | | | | x | | | x | |
| 26 | | | | — | — | — | — | — | — |
| 27 | | | | x | | | — | — | — |
| 28 | x | | | x | | | x | | |
| 29 | x | | | | | x | | | x |
| 30 | | | x | — | — | — | — | — | — |

Source: Data from a Survey made by Andrew S. Regis, Des Moines, Ia., city assessor.

## 9. Percent of Land Owned by the Federal Government in the United States

| | | |
|---|---|---|
| Under 1% | 20 to 29% | |
| 1 to 9% | 30 to 39% | |
| 10 to 19% | 40 to 49% | Over 50% |

Total U.S. 2,271.3 Million Acres (100%)

Federally Owned 755.4 Million Acres (33.3%)

Source: "Inventory Report on Real Property Owned by the United States throughout the World, as of June 30, 1968"; General Services Administration.

## 10. Federally Owned Property in the United States by State, with Total Acreage of States

| State | Total | Number of buildings | Cost (in thousands of dollars) | | | | Acreage of State[a] | Per cent owned by Government[b] |
|---|---|---|---|---|---|---|---|---|
| | | | Land | Buildings | Structures and facilities | Total | | |
| Alabama | 1,097,318.6 | 8,341 | 62,039 | 541,173 | 1,042,817 | 1,646,029 | 32,678,400 | 3.358 |
| Alaska | 348,468,080.0 | 8,443 | 3,294 | 1,018,475 | 1,118,457 | 2,140,226 | 365,481,600 | 95.345 |
| Arizona | 32,432,492.9 | 10,764 | 18,314 | 361,208 | 1,109,028 | 1,488,550 | 72,688,000 | 44.619 |
| Arkansas | 3,151,880.0 | 4,285 | 118,865 | 154,893 | 673,175 | 946,933 | 33,599,360 | 9.381 |
| California | 44,393,847.8 | 60,104 | 371,728 | 3,145,649 | 3,494,674 | 7,012,051 | 100,206,720 | 44.302 |
| Colorado | 24,152,057.6 | 7,218 | 60,873 | 515,451 | 825,269 | 1,401,593 | 66,485,760 | 36.327 |
| Connecticut | 9,303.3 | 2,043 | 35,735 | 152,269 | 66,286 | 254,290 | 3,135,360 | .297 |
| Delaware | 38,256.0 | 871 | 6,900 | 75,016 | 62,677 | 144,593 | 1,265,920 | 3.022 |
| District of Columbia | 11,065.0 | 1,923 | 155,746 | 789,729 | 159,247 | 1,104,722 | 39,040 | 28.343 |
| Florida | 3,391,904.2 | 13,832 | 112,230 | 961,814 | 1,134,282 | 2,208,326 | 34,721,280 | 9.769 |
| Georgia | 2,074,159.1 | 13,820 | 117,472 | 628,494 | 510,263 | 1,256,229 | 37,295,360 | 5.561 |
| Hawaii | 397,278.9 | 11,590 | 25,374 | 514,262 | 511,610 | 1,051,246 | 4,105,600 | 9.677 |
| Idaho | 33,848,889.5 | 4,536 | 38,968 | 206,097 | 507,834 | 752,899 | 52,933,120 | 63.947 |
| Illinois | 523,990.6 | 7,231 | 92,521 | 787,259 | 464,508 | 1,344,288 | 35,795,200 | 1.464 |
| Indiana | 424,958.7 | 6,048 | 81,989 | 309,588 | 405,982 | 797,559 | 23,158,400 | 1.835 |
| Iowa | 211,957.5 | 1,900 | 42,520 | 124,668 | 114,367 | 281,555 | 35,860,480 | .591 |
| Kansas | 666,873.4 | 7,152 | 207,284 | 365,456 | 628,043 | 1,200,783 | 52,510,720 | 1.270 |
| Kentucky | 1,230,725.4 | 7,456 | 261,313 | 495,446 | 956,211 | 1,712,970 | 25,512,320 | 4.824 |
| Louisiana | 1,042,407.6 | 5,230 | 57,374 | 329,589 | 359,157 | 746,120 | 28,867,840 | 3.611 |
| Maine | 130,523.4 | 3,719 | 8,650 | 243,239 | 291,841 | 543,730 | 19,847,680 | .658 |
| Maryland | 189,824.2 | 12,187 | 59,960 | 1,188,583 | 541,271 | 1,789,814 | 6,319,360 | 3.004 |
| Massachusetts | 70,012.5 | 6,292 | 80,799 | 576,973 | 321,109 | 978,881 | 5,034,880 | 1.391 |
| Michigan | 3,316,301.7 | 7,058 | 34,064 | 400,453 | 263,408 | 697,925 | 36,492,160 | 9.088 |
| Minnesota | 3,408,329.0 | 2,449 | 27,889 | 157,066 | 155,758 | 340,713 | 51,205,760 | 6.656 |
| Mississippi | 1,569,327.7 | 4,972 | 68,607 | 269,916 | 420,121 | 758,644 | 30,222,720 | 5.193 |
| Missouri | 1,882,359.3 | 7,754 | 110,013 | 534,015 | 363,254 | 1,007,282 | 44,248,320 | 4.254 |
| Montana | 27,653,766.0 | 6,409 | 42,985 | 197,749 | 892,077 | 1,132,811 | 93,271,040 | 29.649 |
| Nebraska | 718,765.7 | 3,495 | 59,541 | 192,220 | 386,720 | 638,481 | 49,031,680 | 1.466 |

10 (*cont.*)

| State | Total | Number of buildings | Cost (in thousands of dollars) | | | | Acreage of State[a] | Per cent owned by Government[b] |
| | | | Land | Buildings | Structures and facilities | Total | | |
|---|---|---|---|---|---|---|---|---|
| Nevada | 60,725,060.7 | 5,393 | 7,300 | 196,589 | 331,485 | 535,374 | 70,264,320 | 86.424 |
| New Hampshire | 705,689.6 | 1,048 | 25,714 | 73,500 | 86,761 | 185,975 | 5,768,960 | 12.233 |
| New Jersey | 113,019.4 | 8,118 | 47,558 | 585,429 | 407,269 | 1,040,256 | 4,813,440 | 2.348 |
| New Mexico | 26,374,926.0 | 11,459 | 29,519 | 586,071 | 508,592 | 1,124,242 | 77,766,400 | 33.916 |
| New York | 232,684.3 | 10,833 | 153,566 | 1,236,953 | 724,193 | 2,114,712 | 30,680,960 | .758 |
| North Carolina | 1,937,597.0 | 16,232 | 72,126 | 521,717 | 512,548 | 1,106,391 | 31,402,880 | 6.170 |
| North Dakota | 2,119,947.7 | 4,147 | 103,374 | 220,326 | 664,687 | 988,387 | 44,452,480 | 4.769 |
| Ohio | 263,015.7 | 5,101 | 126,898 | 1,014,444 | 704,652 | 1,845,994 | 26,222,080 | 1.003 |
| Oklahoma | 1,423,659.1 | 7,102 | 296,158 | 355,993 | 573,926 | 1,226,077 | 44,087,680 | 3.229 |
| Oregon | 32,182,105.5 | 5,771 | 239,874 | 138,602 | 1,851,716 | 2,230,192 | 61,598,720 | 52.245 |
| Pennsylvania | 597,741.8 | 6,426 | 206,508 | 641,959 | 626,286 | 1,474,753 | 28,804,480 | 2.075 |
| Rhode Island | 7,897.4 | 2,630 | 7,979 | 164,328 | 133,906 | 306,213 | 677,120 | 1.166 |
| South Carolina | 1,128,649.5 | 9,083 | 74,079 | 641,459 | 576,004 | 1,291,542 | 19,374,080 | 5.826 |
| South Dakota | 3,408,270.6 | 3,472 | 137,074 | 168,916 | 874,414 | 1,180,404 | 48,881,920 | 6.972 |
| Tennessee | 1,699,447.8 | 5,960 | 272,899 | 806,774 | 2,058,118 | 3,137,791 | 26,727,680 | 6.358 |
| Texas | 3,003,996.2 | 27,272 | 246,738 | 1,474,727 | 1,275,790 | 2,997,255 | 168,217,600 | 1.786 |
| Utah | 35,060,195.1 | 4,525 | 24,638 | 267,493 | 433,831 | 725,962 | 52,696,960 | 66.532 |
| Vermont | 258,546.4 | 322 | 10,590 | 17,719 | 40,400 | 68,709 | 5,936,640 | 4.355 |
| Virginia | 2,192,117.7 | 19,591 | 132,462 | 1,307,000 | 1,218,750 | 2,658,212 | 25,496,320 | 8.598 |
| Washington | 12,570,420.0 | 17,374 | 167,251 | 837,243 | 2,455,609 | 3,460,103 | 42,693,760 | 29.443 |
| West Virginia | 987,810.4 | 1,247 | 69,595 | 77,979 | 263,969 | 411,543 | 15,410,560 | 6.410 |
| Wisconsin | 1,785,824.7 | 4,111 | 18,018 | 193,435 | 142,145 | 353,598 | 35,011,200 | 5.101 |
| Wyoming | 30,059,582.1 | 3,220 | 48,225 | 71,019 | 355,534 | 474,778 | 62,343,040 | 48.216 |
| Total | 755,344,860.3 | 417,559 | 4,881,250 | 26,836,425 | 34,600,031 | 66,317,706 | 2,271,343,360 | 33.255 |

[a] Source: U.S. Census of Population: 1960 Final Report PC (1)–1A, table 12.  [b] Excludes trust properties.

Source: "Inventory Report on Real Property Owned by the United States Throughout the World, as of June 30, 1968"; General Services Administration.

## 11. REAL PROPERTY LEASED TO THE FEDERAL GOVERNMENT IN THE UNITED STATES, BY STATE

| State | Land—in acres | | | No. of Locations of Buildings | Annual rental |
|---|---|---|---|---|---|
| | Urban | Rural | Total | | |
| Alabama | 621.3 | 10,804.7 | 11,426.0 | 760 | $ 4,538,143 |
| Alaska | 198.1 | 71,622.1 | 71,820.2 | 137 | 1,913,796 |
| Arizona | 53.3 | 137,472.5 | 137,525.8 | 380 | 2,966,206 |
| Arkansas | 433.6 | 3,246.9 | 3,680.5 | 670 | 1,540,902 |
| California | 14,150.0 | 194,356.1 | 208,506.1 | 3,084 | 25,604,303 |
| Colorado | 126.3 | 3,856.7 | 3,983.0 | 1,130 | 4,445,287 |
| Connecticut | 124.4 | 398.8 | 523.2 | 405 | 2,923,620 |
| Delaware | 7.7 | 582.9 | 590.6 | 82 | 434,239 |
| District of Columbia | 11.8 | 0 | 11.8 | 171 | 25,998,481 |
| Florida | 1,484.0 | 10,874.2 | 12,358.2 | 1,102 | 7,073,938 |
| Georgia | 5,232.2 | 6,475.5 | 11,707.7 | 932 | 7,772,212 |
| Hawaii | 27.0 | 29,562.2 | 29,589.2 | 159 | 1,426,834 |
| Idaho | 70.2 | 3,842.0 | 3,912.2 | 403 | 1,529,014 |
| Illinois | 931.9 | 3,867.4 | 4,799.3 | 2,049 | 14,064,584 |
| Indiana | 1,056.6 | 7,920.5 | 8,977.1 | 1,073 | 4,477,714 |
| Iowa | 713.2 | 4,395.8 | 5,109.0 | 1,143 | 3,030,397 |
| Kansas | 371.0 | 1,566.7 | 1,937.7 | 1,056 | 3,155,230 |
| Kentucky | 172.2 | 571.2 | 743.4 | 941 | 2,664,898 |
| Louisiana | 106.0 | 3,041.8 | 3,147.8 | 692 | 3,275,077 |
| Maine | 144.4 | 19,382.2 | 19,526.6 | 484 | 1,114,950 |
| Maryland | 134.8 | 2,748.1 | 2,882.9 | 722 | 14,174,661 |
| Massachusetts | 214.1 | 21,023.0 | 21,237.1 | 587 | 6,275,360 |
| Michigan | 1,164.2 | 10,081.2 | 11,245.4 | 1,347 | 9,128,413 |
| Minnesota | 1,692.6 | 7,961.6 | 9,654.2 | 1,404 | 4,073,843 |
| Mississippi | 871.4 | 19,981.8 | 20,853.2 | 886 | 2,714,105 |
| Missouri | 743.9 | 2,641.5 | 3,385.4 | 1,302 | 5,533,922 |
| Montana | 531.1 | 6,650.7 | 7,181.8 | 549 | 1,523,504 |
| Nebraska | 448.1 | 2,827.8 | 3,275.9 | 757 | 2,289,236 |
| Nevada | 203.6 | 9,793.3 | 9,996.9 | 174 | 1,278,383 |
| New Hampshire | 74.5 | 104.6 | 179.1 | 262 | 584,987 |
| New Jersey | 411.1 | 20,239.6 | 20,650.7 | 1,221 | 6,814,779 |
| New Mexico | 81.4 | 636,655.8 | 636,737.2 | 338 | 2,731,931 |
| New York | 458.6 | 4,160.9 | 4,619.5 | 2,703 | 28,074,637 |
| North Carolina | 544.9 | 50,452.9 | 50,997.8 | 995 | 4,778,749 |
| North Dakota | 1,215.7 | 10,078.0 | 11,293.7 | 531 | 1,044,442 |
| Ohio | 1,337.9 | 2,419.1 | 3,757.0 | 1,649 | 9,405,023 |
| Oklahoma | 515.5 | 6,534.5 | 7,050.0 | 785 | 5,765,817 |
| Oregon | 142.1 | 3,064.8 | 3,206.9 | 733 | 5,178,450 |

## 11 (cont.)

| State | Urban | Rural | Total | No. of Locations of Build-ings | Annual rental |
|---|---|---|---|---|---|
| Pennsylvania | 279.9 | 55,127.6 | 55,407.5 | 2,381 | 12,997,167 |
| Rhode Island | 74.7 | 30.1 | 104.8 | 148 | 2,499,473 |
| South Carolina | 525.7 | 10,411.7 | 10,937.4 | 507 | 2,394,703 |
| South Dakota | 149.1 | 5,033.0 | 5,182.1 | 492 | 1,063,601 |
| Tennessee | 359.5 | 13,707.9 | 14,067.4 | 810 | 3,629,095 |
| Texas | 1,774.9 | 125,555.0 | 127,329.9 | 2,152 | 12,051,149 |
| Utah | 44.2 | 38,600.1 | 38,644.3 | 340 | 1,238,516 |
| Vermont | 31.4 | 395.1 | 426.5 | 295 | 559,783 |
| Virginia | 555.3 | 2,937.4 | 3,492.7 | 1,236 | 18,799,612 |
| Washington | 138.5 | 38,470.6 | 38,609.1 | 942 | 5,858,721 |
| West Virginia | 125.8 | 987.2 | 1,113.0 | 703 | 1,945,838 |
| Wisconsin | 778.8 | 6,931.6 | 7,710.4 | 1,149 | 3,946,935 |
| Wyoming | 16.8 | 3,933.1 | 3,949.9 | 259 | 629,267 |
| Total | 41,675.3 | 1,633,379.8 | 1,675,055.1 | 45,212 | 298,933,927 |

Source: "Inventory Report on Real Property Leased to the United States Throughout the World, as of June 30, 1968"; General Services Administration.

*Appendix*

## 12. Predominant Usage of Federal Land in the U.S. as of June 30, 1968

| Category | Million Acres | Per Cent |
|---|---|---|
| Forest and wildlife | 497.8 | 65.9 |
| Grazing | 164.3 | 21.8 |
| Parks and historic sites | 23.3 | 3.1 |
| Alaska oil and gas reserves | 23.0 | 3.0 |
| Military (except airfields) | 15.9 | 2.1 |
| Reclamation and irrigation | 7.5 | 1.0 |
| Flood control and navigation | 7.4 | 0.9 |
| Industrial | 2.8 | 0.4 |
| Alaska native reserves | 2.8 | 0.4 |
| Military functions in Alaska and Hawaii | 2.7 | 0.3 |
| Airfields | 2.9 | 0.4 |
| Power development and distribution | 2.1 | 0.3 |
| Research and development | 1.6 | 0.2 |
| Other usages | 1.3 | 0.2 |
| Total | 755.4 | 100.0 |

Source: "Inventory Report on Real Property Owned by the United States Throughout the World, as of June 30, 1968"; General Services Administration.

## 13. Per Cent of all Tax Revenue of State and Local Governments Provided by Property Taxes, by States, 1966

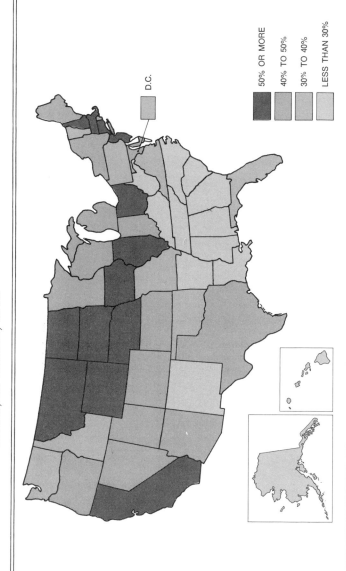

D.C.

50% OR MORE

40% TO 50%

30% TO 40%

LESS THAN 30%

*Source:* "Taxable Property Values," 1967 U.S. Census of Governments, U.S. Department of Commerce, Bureau of the Census.

## 14. Estimated Yearly Tax Bill Attributable to Exemptions, California, for Four Hypothetical Taxpayers

| Property and Market Value | Assessed Value | Total Tax Payment due to Exemptions | Payment due to: | | | |
|---|---|---|---|---|---|---|
| | | | Veterans | Churches | Colleges | Welfare |
| $ 10,000 | $ 2,330 | $ 8.33 | $ 5.48 | $ 1.10 | $ 0.51 | $ 1.24 |
| 16,000 | 3,728 | 13.31 | 8.76 | 1.75 | .82 | 1.98 |
| 40,000 | 9,320 | 33.27 | 21.90 | 4.38 | 2.05 | 4.94 |
| 100,000 | 23,330 | 83.30 | 54.83 | 10.97 | 5.13 | 12.37 |

Source: Report of the Senate Fact Finding Committee on Revenue and Taxation, Part 9; California Legislature; March, 1965. Based on yearly average assessment ratio of 23.3 per cent, the approximate statewide average for 1954–1963.

## 15. Exempt Property, Connecticut, 1909–1965

| Year | Amount[a] | Per Cent Increase | Per Cent Exempt to Taxable Property | Public Property Valuation | Public Property Per Cent Increase | Private Property Valuation | Private Property Per Cent Increase | Per Cent Private to Total Exempt |
|------|-----------|-------------------|-------------------------------------|---------------------------|-----------------------------------|----------------------------|------------------------------------|----------------------------------|
| 1909 | $ 144,200,941 |       | 17.23% | $ 66,455,399 |       | $ 77,745,542 |       | 53.9% |
| 1913 | 168,268,897 | 16.7% | 15.80 | 82,562,096 | 24.2% | 85,706,801 | 10.2% | 50.9 |
| 1917 | 200,281,957 | 19.0 | 14.56 | 102,218,933 | 23.8 | 98,063,024 | 14.4 | 49.0 |
| 1921 | 280,887,014 | 40.2 | 14.31 | 147,892,212 | 44.7 | 132,994,802 | 35.6 | 47.3 |
| 1925 | 403,033,410 | 43.5 | 16.67 | 213,875,189 | 44.6 | 189,158,221 | 42.2 | 46.9 |
| 1929 | 479,146,428 | 18.9 | 15.92 | 241,881,540 | 13.1 | 237,264,888 | 25.4 | 49.5 |
| 1933 | 546,419,346 | 14.0 | 18.46 | 264,009,947 | 9.1 | 282,409,399 | 19.0 | 51.7 |
| 1937 | 579,074,468 | 6.0 | 19.02 | 280,817,567 | 6.4 | 298,256,901 | 5.6 | 51.5 |
| 1941 | 655,840,135 | 13.3 | 19.88 | 348,129,266 | 24.0 | 307,710,869 | 3.2 | 46.9 |
| 1945 | 749,292,673 | 14.2 | 21.52 | 408,811,192 | 17.4 | 340,481,481 | 10.6 | 45.4 |
| 1949 | 922,683,907 | 23.1 | 20.74 | 473,904,803 | 15.9 | 448,779,104 | 31.8 | 48.6 |
| 1953 | 1,261,379,429 | 36.7 | 21.47 | 685,974,446 | 44.7 | 575,404,983 | 28.2 | 45.6 |
| 1957 | 1,666,298,937 | 32.1 | 21.57 | 921,030,487 | 34.3 | 745,269,450 | 29.6 | 44.7 |
| 1961 | 2,301,801,952 | 38.1 | 22.18 | 1,293,858,889 | 40.5 | 1,007,943,063 | 35.2 | 43.8 |
| 1965 | 2,864,990,493 | 24.5 | 21.95 | 1,633,252,232 | 26.2 | 1,231,738,261 | 22.2 | 43.0 |

[a] 1929 and succeeding years figures are not strictly comparable with preceding years, because practically all personal property has been excluded in the 1929 and succeeding years figures.

Source: Quadrennial Statement by the Tax Commissioner of Real Estate Exempted from Taxation; State of Connecticut; 1966.

*Appendix*

## 16. RATIO OF EXEMPT TO TAXABLE REAL PROPERTY, MARYLAND COUNTIES, 1969–1970

| County | Per Cent Exempt | County | Per Cent Exempt |
|---|---|---|---|
| Allegheny | 21.5% | Howard | 16.1% |
| Anne Arundel | 22.7 | Kent | 23.2 |
| Baltimore | 12.6 | Montgomery | 17.7 |
| Calvert | 25.7 | Prince George's | 28.1 |
| Caroline | 15.3 | Queen Anne's | 14.3 |
| Carroll | 21.2 | St. Mary's | 61.2 |
| Cecil | 36.4 | Somerset | 24.3 |
| Charles | 36.4 | Talbot | 12.1 |
| Dorchester | 25.2 | Washington | 23.0 |
| Frederick | 28.6 | Wicomico | 18.3 |
| Garrett | 46.0 | Worcester | 9.5 |
| Harford | 40.5 | Baltimore City | 24.8 |
| | Statewide avg. 22.8% | | |

Source: Maryland Department of Assessments and Taxation.

## 17. Exempt Property, Massachusetts, 1966[a]

| Property of | Valuation |
|---|---:|
| United States | $ 322,761,991 |
| Housing authorities | 299,101,963 |
| Commonwealth of Massachusetts | 625,104,907 |
| Literary organizations | 777,730,596 |
| Benevolent organizations | 176,621,162 |
| Charitable organizations | 242,076,404 |
| Scientific organizations | 49,855,036 |
| Temperance organizations | 79,430 |
| Agricultural societies | 4,423,360 |
| War veterans' organizations | 7,784,318 |
| Militia organizations | — |
| Fraternal societies | — |
| Retirement associations | — |
| Religious organizations | — |
| Houses of religious worship | 336,081,652 |
| Parsonages | 23,949,655 |
| Cemeteries | 18,190,331 |
| Property held for perpetual cemetery care | — |
| Water companies | 1,500 |
| Credit unions | — |
| City or town | 1,879,671,129 |
| County | 35,349,220 |
| District | 63,841,681 |
| Total exempt valuations | $4,862,624,335 |

[a] Reporting is at five-year intervals.
Source: Commonwealth of Massachusetts.

Appendix

## 18. Exempt Property, New York State, 1894–1965

| | Assessed Value of Property (in millions) | | | Exempt Property as Percentage of Total |
|---|---|---|---|---|
| | Exempt | Taxable | Total | |
| **New York City** | | | | |
| 1894 | $ 308[a] | $ 1,613 | $ 1,921 | 16.2% |
| 1910 | 1,359 | 7,044 | 8,303 | 16.4 |
| 1920 | 2,321 | 9,973 | 12,294 | 18.9 |
| 1930 | 5,118 | 19,717 | 24,835 | 20.6 |
| 1940 | 4,860 | 16,539 | 21,399 | 22.7 |
| 1950 | 5,868 | 18,112 | 23,980 | 24.5 |
| 1957 | 8,803 | 21,943 | 30,746 | 28.6 |
| 1965 | 15,250 | 30,902 | 46,152 | 33.0 |
| **Outside New York City** | | | | |
| 1894 | 273 | 2,228 | 2,501 | 10.9 |
| 1910 | 439 | 2,595 | 2,924 | 15.1 |
| 1920 | 676 | 4,623 | 5,299 | 12.8 |
| 1930 | 1,579 | 9,406 | 10,985 | 14.3 |
| 1940 | 1,996 | 8,985 | 11,031 | 18.1 |
| 1950 | 2,412 | 10,284 | 12,696 | 19.0 |
| 1957 | 3,801 | 14,743 | 18,544 | 20.6 |
| 1965 | 5,821 | 18,667 | 24,488 | 23.8 |
| **Statewide** | | | | |
| 1894 | 581[a] | 3,841 | 4,422 | 13.2 |
| 1910 | 1,788 | 9,639 | 11,427 | 15.7 |
| 1920 | 2,997 | 14,596 | 17,593 | 17.0 |
| 1930 | 6,697 | 29,123 | 35,826 | 18.7 |
| 1940 | 6,856 | 25,574 | 32,430 | 21.2 |
| 1950 | 8,280 | 28,396 | 36,676 | 22.6 |
| 1957 | 12,604 | 36,686 | 49,290 | 25.6 |
| 1965 | 21,071 | 49,568 | 70,640[b] | 29.8 |

[a] Real and personal property.    [b] Does not add because of rounding.
Sources of data: 1894 Constitutional Convention, Revised Record, Vol. V, pp. 720–24; N.Y. State Board of Tax Commissioners, Annual Report (1900), pp. 185–7; N.Y. State Legislative Committee on Taxation and Retrenchment, Legis. Doc. 1927, No. 86, p. 37; N.Y. State Tax Commission, Annual Reports, 1910, pp. 76–77, 303; 1920, pp. 125–27, 260–61; 1930, pp. 104, 246; 1936, p. 127; 1940, pp. 131, 150, 282; N.Y. State Comptroller, Legis. Doc. 1950, No. 13A, p. 3; data furnished by the N.Y. State Office for Local Government, Board of Equalization and Assessment for 1957 and 1965. Source of table: "Local Finance"; Temporary State Commission on the Constitutional Convention; State of New York; 1967.

# 19. Growth of Tax-Exempt Property in New York State by Category, 1957–1965

| | New York City | | | Outside New York City | | | Statewide | | |
|---|---|---|---|---|---|---|---|---|---|
| | 1957[a] | 1965 | Percentage Increase | 1957[b] | 1965 | Percentage Increase | 1957[a] | 1965 | Percentage Increase |
| | | | | (in millions) | | | | | |
| **Public** | | | | | | | | | |
| *A. Not taxable by local governments:* | | | | | | | | | |
| Foreign | $ 71.6 | $ 89.2 | | $ 2.5 | $ 4.0 | | $ 74.1 | $ 93.2 | |
| Federal | 392.5 | 519.2 | | 503.0 | 626.9 | | 895.5 | 1,146.1 | |
| Subtotal | 464.1 | 608.4 | 31 | 505.5 | 630.9 | 25 | 969.6 | 1,239.3 | 28 |
| *B. Would not add to aggregate revenue even if taxed:* | | | | | | | | | |
| Municipal | 4,057.2 | 7,219.4 | 78 | 1,306.2 | 2,144.1 | 64 | 5,363.5 | 9,363.5 | 74 |
| *C. Would add to aggregate local revenue, if taxed:* | | | | | | | | | |
| New York State | 102.2 | 217.8 | | 507.9 | 872.0 | | 610.0 | 1,089.8 | |
| Authority | 2,645.4 | 4,536.4 | | 32.6 | 79.9 | | 2,678.0 | 4,616.3 | |
| Subtotal | 2,747.6 | 4,754.2 | 73 | 540.5 | 951.9 | 76 | 3,288.1 | 5,706.1 | 73 |
| **Private** | | | | | | | | | |
| *D. Protected by Constitution:* | | | | | | | | | |
| Religious | 482.2 | 625.7 | | 314.1 | 493.3 | | 796.3 | 1,214.7 | |
| Educational | 198.8 | 673.3 | | 395.5 | 541.4 | | 485.3 | 1,119.0 | |
| Charitable | 207.7 | 232.5 | | 61.5 | 87.0 | | 269.1 | 319.5 | |
| Subtotal | 879.7 | 1,531.5 | 74 | 671.1 | 1,121.7 | 67 | 1,550.7 | 2,653.2 | 71 |

19 (Cont.)

| | New York City | | | Outside New York City | | | Statewide | | |
|---|---|---|---|---|---|---|---|---|---|
| | 1957[a] | 1965 | Percentage Increase | 1957[b] | 1965 | Percentage Increase | 1957[a] | 1965 | Percentage Increase |
| | | | | (in millions) | | | | | |
| E. *Not protected by Constitution:* | | | | | | | | | |
| Veterans | 111.2 | 187.6 | | 338.6 | 572.7 | | 449.8 | 760.3 | |
| Hospital | 260.4 | 478.0 | | 123.7 | 208.1 | | 383.5 | 686.1 | |
| Other private | 283.1 | 471.0 | | 98.4 | 191.8 | | 381.5 | 662.8 | |
| Subtotal | 654.7 | 1,136.6 | 73 | 560.7 | 972.6 | 73 | 1,214.8 | 2,109.2 | 73 |
| Grand Total: | | | | | | | | | |
| Exempt property | $8,802.1 | $15,250.0 | 73% | $3,800.8 | $5,821.2 | 53% | $12,603.5 | $21,071.3 | 67% |

[a] Will not add because of unavailable breakdown from Nassau County of some $217 million. The percentages were readjusted.
[b] Will not add because of rounding.
Source of data: N.Y. State Office for Local Government, Board of Equilization and Assessment.
Source of Table: "Local Finance"; Temporary State Commission on the Constitutional Convention; State of New York; 1967.

## 20. Ownership of Exempt Property, New York State, 1965

(in millions)

| | New York City | | Outside New York City | | Statewide | |
|---|---|---|---|---|---|---|
| | Assessed Value | Percentage of Total | Assessed Value | Percentage of Total | Assessed Value | Percentage of Total |
| **Public** | | | | | | |
| A. Exempt property beyond the taxing jurisdiction of state and local governments: | $ 608.4 | 4.0% | $ 630.9 | 10.8% | $ 1,239.3 | 5.9% |
| B. Exempt property owned by municipal corporations: | 7,219.4 | 47.3 | 2,144.1 | 36.8 | 9,363.5 | 44.4 |
| C. Exempt property which would add to aggregate local revenues, if taxed: | | | | | | |
| Authorities | 4,536.4 | | 79.9 | | 4,616.3 | |
| New York State | | | | | | |
| Administration | 72.8 | | 132.2 | | 205.0 | |
| Airport | 0.0 | | 0.3 | | 0.3 | |
| Conservation | 0.0 | | 2.9 | | 2.9 | |
| Correction | 0.0 | | 29.4 | | 29.4 | |
| Education | 0.0 | | 186.1 | | 186.1 | |
| Flood control | 0.0 | | 1.1 | | 1.1 | |
| Hospital | 112.6 | | 158.3 | | 270.9 | |
| Housing | 0.0 | | 17.2 | | 17.2 | |
| Protection | 12.7 | | 52.0 | | 64.7 | |
| Recreation | 0.0 | | 37.2 | | 37.2 | |
| Utility | 19.8 | | 247.7 | | 267.5 | |
| Welfare | 0.0 | | 1.6 | | 1.6 | |
| Miscellaneous | 0.0 | | 5.8 | | 5.8 | |
| Total state-owned | 217.9 | | 872.0 | | 1,089.8 | |
| Subtotal (C) | 4,754.2 | 31.2 | | | 5,706.1 | |
| Subtotal: Publicly owned ex- | 12,582.0 | 82.5 | 3,726.9 | 64.0 | 16,308.9 | 77.4 |

|  | New York City | | Outside New York City | | Statewide | |
|---|---|---|---|---|---|---|
|  | Assessed Value | Percentage of Total | Assessed Value | Percentage of Total | Assessed Value | Percentage of Total |
|  | (in millions) | | | | | |
| Private | | | | | | |
| D. Exempt property protected by present Constitution: | | | | | | |
|   Educational | 625.7 | | 493.3 | | 1,119.0 | |
|   Religious | 673.3 | | 541.4 | | 1,214.7 | |
|   Charitable | 232.5 | | 87.0 | | 319.5 | |
|   Subtotal (D) | 1,531.5 | 10.0 | 1,121.7 | 19.3 | 2,653.2 | 12.6 |
| E. Exempt property not protected by present Constitution: | | | | | | |
|   Cemetery | 157.0 | | 51.2 | | 208.2 | |
|   Conservation | 0.0 | | 0.1 | | 0.1 | |
|   Fraternal | 0.0 | | 49.1 | | 49.1 | |
|   Hospital | 478.0 | | 208.1 | | 686.1 | |
|   Recreation | 0.0 | | 0.9 | | 0.9 | |
|   Utility | 292.5 | | 68.7 | | 361.2 | |
|   Veterans | 187.6 | | 572.7 | | 760.3 | |
|   Miscellaneous | 21.5 | | 21.8 | | 43.3 | |
|   Subtotal (E) | 1,136.6 | 7.5 | 972.6 | 16.7 | 2,109.2 | 10.0 |
| Subtotal: Privately owned exempt property (D, E) | 2,668.1 | 17.5 | 2,094.3 | 36.0 | 4,762.4 | 22.6 |
| Grand Total: All exempt property | $15,250.1 | 100.0% | $5,821.2 | 100.0% | $21,071.3 | 100.0% |

Source of data: N.Y. State Office for Local Government, Board of Equalization and Assessment.
Source of Table: "Local Finance"; Temporary State Commission on the Constitutional Convention; State of New York; 1967.

## 21. Projection of Added Revenues if Certain Exempt Property Had Been Taxed, New York State, 1964

(in millions)

| Owner | New York City[a] | | Outside New York City[b] | | Statewide | |
|---|---|---|---|---|---|---|
| | Assessed Value | Projected Revenue | Assessed Value | Projected Revenue | Value Assessed | Projected Revenue |
| New York State | $ 193.4 | $ 8.5 | $ 847.2 | $ 72.6 | $1,040.6 | $ 81.1 |
| Authorities | 4,300.8 | 189.7 | 114.4 | 9.8 | 4,415.2 | 199.5 |
| Religious, educational, charitable | 1,496.7 | 63.8 | 1,080.6 | 92.6 | 2,527.3 | 156.4 |
| Other private | 1,093.3 | 48.2 | 900.4 | 77.1 | 1,993.7 | 126.3 |
| Total | $7,034.2 | $310.2 | $2,942.6 | $252.1 | $9,976.8 | $562.3 |

[a] 1964 tax rate at $44.10 per $1,000 of assessed valuation.
[b] 1964 tax rate at $85.65 per $1,000 of assessed valuation as an average of all tax rates outside New York City.
Source of data: N.Y. State Office for Local Government, Board of Equalization and Assessment.
Source of Table: "Local Finance"; Temporary State Commission on the Constitutional Convention; State of New York; 1967

Appendix

## 22. CITIES IN NEW YORK WITH 25% OR MORE OF REAL PROPERTY VALUATION EXEMPT, 1969

| Name of City | Rates of Exempt to Total Valuation | Name of City | Rates of Exempt to Total Valuation |
|---|---|---|---|
| Watervliet | 78.0% | New York City | 33.2% |
| Ithaca | 60.2 | Buffalo | 32.7 |
| Hudson | 57.8 | Elmira | 32.5 |
| Albany | 46.5 | Kingston | 32.2 |
| Niagara Falls | 44.7 | Beacon | 31.7 |
| Troy | 44.6 | Little Falls | 31.1 |
| Cortland | 43.7 | Salamanca | 30.4 |
| Ogdensburg | 42.7 | Binghamton | 30.1 |
| Plattsburgh | 42.6 | Syracuse | 29.9 |
| Johnstown | 40.1 | Watertown | 29.7 |
| Rome | 37.6 | Batavia | 29.5 |
| Oswego | 37.4 | Cohoes | 29.4 |
| Saratoga Springs | 37.3 | Gloversville | 29.1 |
| Middletown | 36.4 | Mechanicville | 28.8 |
| Canandaigua | 35.9 | Schenectady | 28.3 |
| Fulton | 34.3 | Auburn | 27.9 |
| Utica | 34.3 | Glens Falls | 26.4 |
| Norwich | 34.2 | Olean | 25.7 |
| Geneva | 33.3 | Newburgh | 25.4 |
| | | Peekskill | 25.3 |

Source: New York State Board of Equalization and Assessment.

227

## 23. Exempt Real Property Valuations, Ohio, 1959–1966

*(Percentage Distribution by Ownership Classes)*

| Year | Public Ownership Classes | | | | | | | | Private Ownership Classes | | | | |
|------|--------------------------|----------------|-----------|-------|----------|----------------|-----------|--------|----------|-----------|----------------------|------------|--------|
| | Boards of Education | United States | Municipal | State | Counties | Park Districts | Townships | Total | Churches | Charities | Colleges & Academies | Cemeteries | Total |
| 1959 | 25.78% | 13.69% | 12.85% | 7.75% | 4.84% | 1.75% | 1.72% | 68.38% | 16.20% | 9.52% | 4.33% | 1.57% | 31.62% |
| 1960 | 26.58 | 14.37 | 12.04 | 8.03 | 4.50 | 1.64 | 1.46 | 68.62 | 16.16 | 9.07 | 4.62 | 1.53 | 31.38 |
| 1961 | 26.70 | 14.94 | 11.71 | 7.15 | 4.48 | 1.42 | 1.51 | 67.91 | 16.38 | 8.90 | 5.33 | 1.48 | 32.09 |
| 1962 | 27.22 | 15.71 | 11.55 | 6.90 | 4.11 | 1.37 | 0.92 | 67.78 | 16.65 | 8.67 | 5.43 | 1.47 | 32.22 |
| 1963 | 27.68 | 13.24 | 11.32 | 8.18 | 4.07 | 1.22 | 0.83 | 66.54 | 17.15 | 9.21 | 5.60 | 1.50 | 33.46 |
| 1964 | 27.50 | 12.63 | 11.72 | 6.06 | 3.95 | 1.61 | 1.27 | 64.74 | 17.27 | 9.00 | 7.85 | 1.14 | 35.26 |
| 1965 | 27.41 | 12.45 | 11.52 | 6.27 | 4.12 | 1.58 | 1.25 | 64.60 | 17.37 | 9.04 | 7.87 | 1.12 | 35.40 |
| 1966 | 27.16 | 12.13 | 12.74 | 6.37 | 4.23 | 1.53 | 0.31 | 64.47 | 17.68 | 8.71 | 8.00 | 1.14 | 35.53 |

## 24. Distribution of Valuations by Ownership Classifications, Ohio

(Amounts in millions; items may not add because of rounding)

Property Under Public Ownership

| Year | Boards of Education | United States | Municipal | State | Counties | Park Districts | Townships | Total |
|---|---|---|---|---|---|---|---|---|
| 1959 | $661.4 | $351.1 | $329.7 | $198.9 | $124.2 | $45.0 | $44.0 | $1,754.3 |
| 1960 | 718.7 | 388.6 | 325.4 | 217.1 | 121.8 | 44.2 | 39.6 | 1,855.4 |
| 1961 | 748.3 | 418.7 | 328.2 | 200.4 | 125.6 | 39.9 | 42.3 | 1,903.4 |
| 1962 | 782.1 | 451.4 | 331.7 | 198.4 | 118.0 | 39.5 | 26.4 | 1,947.5 |
| 1963 | 849.6 | 406.5 | 347.4 | 251.1 | 125.0 | 37.3 | 25.3 | 2,042.2 |
| 1964 | 920.2 | 422.6 | 392.0 | 202.8 | 132.2 | 53.8 | 42.5 | 2,166.1 |
| 1965 | 945.9 | 429.7 | 397.5 | 216.4 | 142.2 | 54.5 | 43.3 | 2,229.5 |
| 1966 | 970.0 | 433.3 | 455.0 | 227.5 | 151.0 | 54.5 | 11.0 | 2,302.3 |
| 7-Year Change | $308.6 (+46.66%) | $82.2 (+23.41%) | $125.3 (+38.00%) | $28.6 (+14.38%) | $26.8 (+21.58%) | $9.5 (+21.11%) | $33.0 (−75.00%) | $548.0 (+31.24%) |

## 24 (Cont.)

| Year | Property Under Private Ownership | | | | | Grand Total |
|---|---|---|---|---|---|---|
| | Churches | Charities | Schools & Colleges | Cemeteries | Total | |
| 1959 | $415.7 | $244.2 | $111.2 | $40.3 | $ 811.5 | $2,565.7 |
| 1960 | 437.0 | 245.2 | 125.0 | 41.3 | 848.5 | 2,703.9 |
| 1961 | 459.0 | 249.3 | 149.4 | 41.4 | 899.1 | 2,802.4 |
| 1962 | 478.4 | 249.0 | 156.0 | 42.3 | 925.7 | 2,873.1 |
| 1963 | 526.6 | 282.6 | 172.0 | 46.0 | 1,027.2 | 3,069.4 |
| 1964 | 577.8 | 301.2 | 262.8 | 38.1 | 1,179.9 | 3,346.0 |
| 1965 | 599.5 | 311.8 | 271.5 | 38.7 | 1,221.5 | 3,450.9 |
| 1966 | 631.2 | 311.2 | 285.7 | 40.8 | 1,268.9 | 3,571.3 |
| 7-Year Change | $215.5 (+51.84%) | $ 67.0 (+27.44%) | $174.5 (+156.92%) | $ 0.5 (+.012%) | $ 457.4 (+56.36%) | $1,005.6 (+39.19%) |

*Source:* Annual Report of the Ohio Department of Taxation for Fiscal Year Ended June 30, 1967.

Appendix

## 25. Twelve Ohio Cities Having the Largest Amount of Real Property Exempted from Taxation in the 1967 Tax Year

| City | Real Property Exempted from Taxation (in millions) | | | | |
|---|---|---|---|---|---|
| | Governmental[a] | Churches | Other[b] | Total | Percentage |
| Cleveland | $313.7 | $75.6 | $132.3 | $521.6 | 24.0 |
| Columbus | 219.6 | 35.9 | 26.5 | 282.0 | 21.2 |
| Toledo | 76.1 | 33.4 | 35.6 | 145.1 | 15.7 |
| Cincinnati | 83.5 | 23.2 | 18.3 | 125.0 | 10.3 |
| Dayton | 56.8 | 25.0 | 38.0 | 119.8 | 19.1 |
| Akron | 44.8 | 22.9 | 22.1 | 89.8 | 12.5 |
| Youngstown | 29.5 | 13.2 | 10.8 | 53.5 | 15.4 |
| Canton | 19.2 | 8.5 | 8.7 | 36.4 | 14.3 |
| Cleveland Hts. | 13.2 | 12.5 | 7.6 | 33.3 | 15.8 |
| Springfield | 15.3 | 7.8 | 9.9 | 33.0 | 19.6 |
| Hamilton | 16.9 | 5.3 | 6.4 | 28.6 | 18.0 |
| Athens | 27.1 | 1.2 | .2 | 28.5 | 50.7([c]) |

[a] Includes Federal, State, County, Township, Park District, School District, and Municipal exempt property.
[b] Includes private colleges and academies, charitable institutions and graveyards, monuments, and cemeteries.
[c] Highest in state.
Source: Service Letter, Ohio Public Expenditure Council, Columbus, O.; December, 1968.

## 26. EXEMPT VALUATIONS, ALBANY, N.Y., 1963, 1969

| Classification | (in millions; items rounded) | |
| --- | --- | --- |
| | 1963 | 1969 |
| U.S. Government | $ 21.5 | $ 21.3 |
| State of New York | 112.1 | 101.2 |
| Albany County | 1.9 | 10.5 |
| City | 46.9 | 54.8 |
| Albany Port District | 10.6 | 11.5 |
| Churches | 18.7+ | 20.4 |
| Parsonages | .790+ | .861 |
| Veterans organizations | .267 | .427 |
| Private schools and colleges | 15.5 | 18.2 |
| Moral associations | 3.2 | 3.4 |
| Hospitals and orphanages | 15.5 | 22.1 |
| Veterans exemptions | 3.25 | 3.3 |
| Over 65 exemptions | — | .676 |
| Total Exempt | $253,764,059 | $288,155,191 |
| Taxable | | $286,379,892 |
| Ratio of Exempt to Total | | 50.2% |

Source: Board of Assessors, City of Albany.

## 27. SAMPLE EXEMPT PROPERTY LISTINGS PUBLISHED IN ALBANY, N.Y., 1968

| Description of Property, Ownership and Use | Full Value of Real Property | Value of Land Excl. Building |
|---|---|---|
| *United States—Wholly Exempt* | | |
| Steel Bldg., 172 Euclid Ave. | 7,500 | |
| Federal Bldg., 441 Broadway | 930,000 | 500,000 |
| Federal Bldg., Internal Revenue, 445 Broadway | 2,225,000 | 658,000 |
| Veterans Hospital, Holland Ave. | 17,770,000 | 421,835 |
| River Gauge, Recreation Pier | 1,000 | |
| U.S. Army Reserve, 90 No. Main Ave. | 200,000 | 12,000 |
| U.S. Navy Reserve, 780 Washington Ave. | 178,500 | 25,000 |
| U.S. Air Reserve, 80 No. Main Ave. | 50,000 | 12,000 |
| *State of New York—Wholly Exempt* | | |
| Education Bldg., 89 Washington Ave. | 8,600,000 | 575,000 |
| Property, 8 Thurlow Terr. | 55,000 | 44,250 |
| Property, 7 Thurlow Terr. | 46,600 | 35,000 |
| Adm. Mall, 263–267 Hudson Ave. | 22,200 | 11,400 |
| Parking, 55–7 Elk St. | 57,800 | 57,800 |
| Campus, 1220 Washington Ave. | 10,763,300 | 620,900 |
| State Hall, 21 Eagle St. | 3,000,000 | 190,000 |
| State Land, 186–262 Southern Blvd. | 28,080 | 29,080 |
| Parking, 167 Elk St. | 293,000 | 290,000 |
| Boiler House, 91 Sheridan Ave. | 705,000 | 20,940 |
| Property, 10 Thurlow Terr. | 26,500 | 18,000 |
| Exec. Mansion, 134 Eagle St. | 250,000 | 49,960 |
| Research Found., 411–13 State St. | 69,500 | 22,000 |
| Vacant, 654 Washington Ave. | 7,500 | 1,980 |
| Adm. Mall, 130–132 Jay St. | 37,000 | 13,500 |
| Adm. Mall, Market St. | 2,000 | 2,000 |
| Adm. Mall, 154–160 Hamilton St. | 17,000 | 17,000 |
| Vacant, 50 Westbrook St. | 200 | 200 |
| Vacant, 47 Westbrook St. | 800 | 800 |
| Vacant, North St. | 1,105 | 1,105 |
| Vacant, 108 Broadway, Rear | 15,000 | 15,000 |
| State Office Bldg., 86 Swan St. | 10,000,000 | 261,000 |
| Highway Dept., 353 Broadway | 500,000 | 16,000 |
| Vacant, Quay St. | 13,600 | 13,800 |
| Vacant, Church St. | 1,000 | 1,000 |
| Vacant, Church St. | 6,000 | 6,000 |
| Vacant, Church St. | 5,000 | 5,000 |
| Vacant, 100 Church St. | 53,700 | 53,700 |

## 27 (*Cont.*)

| Description of Property, Ownership and Use | Full Value of Real Property | Value of Land Excl. Building |
|---|---|---|
| Vacant, 118 Broadway | 21,900 | 21,900 |
| Vacant, 108 Broadway | 19,000 | 19,000 |
| Vacant, 90 Broadway | 19,300 | 19,300 |
| State Laboratory, 138 New Scotland Ave. | 560,000 | 40,000 |
| Brick Bldg., 48 Marion Ave. | 50,315 | 6,800 |
| Vacant, 143–51 Kenosha St. | 3,450 | 3,450 |
| State Capitol Bldg., Eagle St. | 47,000,000 | 1,000,000 |
| Vacant, Quay St., Rear | 13,800 | 13,000 |
| Property, 9 Thurlow Terr. | 30,000 | 14,000 |
| Proposed Site, 1225 Washington Ave. | 135,000 | 135,000 |
| Vacant, 151 Broadway | 1,000 | 1,000 |
| College, 161 Partridge St. | 225,000 | 23,400 |
| N. Y. S. Teach., Col., 143 Washington Ave. | 350,000 | 39,000 |
| Normal College, 115 Western Ave. | 2,582,000 | 252,700 |
| N. Y. S. Teach. Col., 84 Holland Ave. | 3,000,000 | 175,000 |
| College, Teach., 279–307 Western Ave. | 1,125,000 | 106,500 |
| College Dormitory, 1220 Washington Ave., Rear | 3,000,000 | 500,000 |
| N. Y. S. Teach. Col., 213–25 Ontario St. | 229,300 | 26,800 |
| College, 1560 Madison Ave. | 10,000 | 10,000 |
| College, 1265 Western Ave. | 30,000 | 30,000 |
| College, 750 State St. | 450,000 | 25,800 |
| N. Y. S. Teach. Col., 10 No. Hawk St. | 1,750,000 | 25,000 |
| College, 41 Fuller Road | 15,000 | 15,000 |
| N. Y. S. Teachers Assoc., 203 Ontario St. | 2,500 | 2,500 |
| Schuyler Mansion, 37 Clinton St. | 100,000 | 7,670 |
| Recreation Pier | 22,100 | 22,100 |
| State Hall Pk., 8 Pine St. | 40,000 | 40,000 |
| Urban Dev., 205–207 Livingston Ave. | 6,000 | 1,400 |
| Urban Dev., 159–229 Livingston Ave. | 5,500 | 5,000 |
| Urban Dev., 211 and 229 Livingston Ave. | 2,200 | 2,200 |
| Urban Dev., 186–190 Colonie St. | 9,200 | 1,900 |
| Urban Dev., 171 Colonie St. | 3,500 | 3,500 |
| 167–171 No. Pearl St. | 169,000 | 26,450 |
| Vacant, 909 Central Ave., rear | 1,000 | 1,000 |
| Vacant, 935 Central Ave., rear | 1,500 | 1,500 |
| Port Dist., Westerlo Island | 11,500,000 | 4,000,000 |
| Housing, 37 Morton Ave. | 500,000 | 15,000 |
| Housing, 134 Franklin St. | 65,000 | 10,000 |
| Housing, 63 Morton Ave. | 500,000 | 22,000 |
| Housing, 2 Warren St. | 400,000 | 15,000 |

## 27 (*Cont.*)

| Description of Property, Ownership and Use | Full Value of Real Property | Value of Land Excl. Building |
|---|---|---|
| Housing, 230 Green St. | 500,000 | 14,700 |
| Housing, 31 Lawrence St. | 1,500 | 1,500 |
| Housing, Manning Blvd. | 200 | 200 |
| Housing, 252 No. Pearl St. | 38,000 | 38,000 |
| Housing, 20 Warren St. | 400,000 | 18,000 |
| St. Joseph Orphanage, 261 North Pearl St. | 17,000 | 7,200 |
| St. Vincent's, 391 Western Ave. | 500,000 | 90,000 |
| Albany Home for Children, 490 Hudson Ave. | 15,000 | 1,650 |
| Albany Orphanage, 60 Academy Rd. | 275,000 | 65,000 |
| Albany Home for Children, 715 Myrtle Ave. | 8,500 | 3,000 |
| *Morale Associations* | | |
| Albany Catholic Association, 342 First St. | 30,000 | 3,200 |
| YMCA Rail., 605 Broadway | 111,000 | 18,920 |
| YWCA, 2 Lodge St. | 425,000 | 73,000 |
| Family Society, 12 South Lake Ave. | 19,000 | 7,750 |
| First Scientist, 109 State St. | 65,250 | |
| Masonic Hall, 67 Maiden Lane | 77,300 | |
| Albany Catholic Association, 741 Madison Ave. | 305,000 | 19,200 |
| Soc. Prop. Faith, 9 Elk St. | 18,000 | |
| Trinity Institute, 13 Trinity Pl. | 59,000 | 6,510 |
| Albany Inter-Racial Council, 126 Second St. | 3,500 | 3,500 |
| YMCA, 296 Partridge St. | 42,300 | 20,000 |
| Boys' Club, 31 Delaware Ave. | 190,000 | 19,600 |
| YMCA, 415 State St. | 704,500 | 44,000 |
| Roman Catholic Diocese, 465 State St. | 95,000 | 36,000 |
| Salvation Army, 59 Orange St. | 4,500 | 4,500 |
| St. Peter's Guild, 107 State St. | 216,620 | 129,640 |
| Boys' Club, 516 Livingston Ave. | 110,000 | 9,000 |
| Albany Comm. Chest, 877 Madison Ave. | 62,000 | 7,300 |
| American Red Cross, 2 Clara Barton Dr. | 20,000 | 1,200 |
| Roman Catholic Diocese, 150 Hamilton St. | 80,000 | 6,250 |
| *Benevolent Associations* | | |
| Salvation Army, 88 Madison Ave. | 4,000 | 1,500 |
| St. Vincent, 200–202 Partridge St. | 18,000 | 4,000 |
| League Lutheran Women, 688 Madison Ave. | 125,000 | 21,000 |
| League Lutheran Women, 690 Madison Ave. | 50,000 | 9,000 |
| Association of the Blind, 301 Washington Ave. | 150,000 | 7,000 |
| St. Vincent's Child Care, 115 Grand St. | 21,000 | 1,000 |
| St. Andrew's Society, 150 Washington Ave. | 30,000 | 14,000 |

## 27 (*Cont.*)

| Description of Property, Ownership and Use | Full Value of Real Property | Value of Land Excl. Building |
|---|---|---|
| Salvation Army, 468 Clinton Ave. | 14,500 | 2,000 |
| Albany International Center, 22 Willett St. | 20,000 | 6,600 |
| Mohawk Hudson Humane Society, 7 Elk St. | 28,000 | 14,500 |
| Albany Guild of Public Nursing, 245 Lark St. | 28,500 | 6,600 |
| Family Rosary Society, 773 Madison Ave. | 93,000 | 12,600 |
| Sisters of the Poor, 379 Central Ave. | 295,000 | 82,000 |
| Salvation Army, 22 Clinton Ave. | 215,000 | 6,100 |
| Salvation Army, 460 Clinton Ave. | 251,500 | 28,200 |
| Home for the Friendless, 553 Clinton Ave. | 82,000 | 10,500 |
| Albany Jewish Soc., 291 State St. | 20,000 | 13,500 |
| *Private Schools* | | |
| St. James, 16 St. James Place | 400,000 | 6,000 |
| Blessed Sacrament, 609 Central Ave. | 300,000 | |
| Boys Academy, 89 Academy Road | 1,300,000 | 75,500 |
| Catholic Diocese, 180 So. Hawk St. | 1,300,000 | 75,500 |
| Catholic Diocese, 44 So. Dove St. | 2,500 | 2,500 |
| Catholic Diocese, 98–100 Slingerland St. | 70,000 | 5,000 |
| Roman Catholic Diocese, 30 Anne St. | 1,000 | 1,000 |
| Catholic Diocese, 166 Delaware St. | 100 | 100 |
| Sacred Heart Convent, 799 So. Pearl St. | 800,000 | 64,000 |
| Christian Brothers Academy, 1 De Salle Road | 775,000 | 60,000 |

Source: *City Record*, December 4, 1968, p. 2083. Assessors Report of Real Property Exempt from Taxation, 1967 Real Property Tax Law, Sec. 496–1, County of Albany, City of Albany, N.Y.

## 28. GROWTH OF EXEMPT PROPERTY, BALTIMORE, 1958–1968/69

| Classification | 1958 Valuation | 1968/69 Valuation |
|---|---|---|
| Federal | $  23,027,230 | $  36,059,690 |
| State | 11,064,200 | 28,042,360 |
| City | 198,869,930 | 293,234,260 |
| Churches, synagogues, parsonages, and schools | 68,338,485 | 95,563,770 |
| Colleges, universities, and academies | 21,790,740 | 44,397,550 |
| Cemeteries | 4,361,230 | 5,438,740 |
| Lodges, benevolent and cultural societies | 7,354,370 | 8,677,060 |
| Hospitals, infirmaries, and dispensaries | 23,559,380 | 44,455,260 |
| Fire Insurance salvage corps | 53,650 | — |
| New Marsh Wholesale Produce Market Authority | — | 776,600 |
| Railroads | 12,171,360 | 13,946,330 |
| Housing Authority of Baltimore City | 54,479,740 | 41,042,900 |
| Homes and asylums | 9,326,130 | 17,168,920 |
| Miscellaneous | 5,280,170 | 8,933,040 |
| Lexington Market Authority | 4,187,960 | 4,272,200 |
| Blind persons | 667,520 | 1,526,230 |
| Maryland Port Authority | — | 27,188,560 |
| Nonprofit housing for elderly persons | — | 4,160,120 |
| Totals | $  444,532,095 | $  674,883,590 |
| Taxable Real Property | $2,075,409,008 | $2,381,020,188 |
| Ratio of Exempt to Total | 17.6% | 22.3% |

*Source:* Annual Report of Department of Assessments, City of Baltimore, January 1, 1958; January 1, 1968.

## 29. EXEMPT REAL PROPERTY VALUATIONS, BOSTON, 1968

| Classification | Valuation | Classification | Valuation |
|---|---|---|---|
| U.S.A. | $ 112,213,500 | Railroads | $ 41,300 |
| Commonwealth of Mass. | 233,193,100 | Mass. Hospital Service/ Blue Cross, Blue Shield | 2,500,000 |
| Metropolitan Transit Authority | 18,637,600 | Knights of Columbus | 315,800 |
| Mystic Bridge Authority | 384,600 | Schools | 59,140,600 |
| Mass. Turnpike Authority | 15,104,600 | Fire | 4,567,000 |
| Mass. Port Authority | 289,700 | All others | 15,084,200 |
| Mass. Parking Authority | 146,200 | City Hall and Annex | 26,549,000 |
| Metropolitan District Commission | 13,801,900 | Commonwealth lease to City for parking areas | 5,059,300 |
| Literary | 154,722,500 | Parks and playgrounds | 90,322,500 |
| Benevolent | 107,014,800 | Libraries | 6,425,900 |
| Charitable | 43,784,800 | Foreclosures | 3,524,400 |
| Scientific | 3,632,700 | Boston Housing Authority | 102,952,800 |
| Incorporated Temperance Societies | 8,000 | Health | 1,251,600 |
| U.S. Veterans incorporated organizations | 766,600 | Hospitals | 12,115,600 |
| Fraternal societies | 39,500 | Institutions | 10,463,000 |
| Religious organizations | 83,900 | Boston Redevelopment Authority | 40,426,300 |
| Houses of religious worship, parsonages | 46,573,500 | Boston Redevelopment Authority 121A | 97,759,400 |
| Cemeteries | 5,395,700 | Police | 3,596,100 |
| American Red Cross | 235,000 | Printing | 360,000 |
| General Laws 59 Section 6 Brookline | 59,000 | Public buildings and off-street parking | 15,856,600 |
| Crabtreet Estates | 380,000 | Public Works Department | 9,569,000 |
| Farm and trade schools | 1,069,900 | Welfare | 1,002,600 |
| Old South Church | 514,000 | Code V | 593,200 |
| | | | $1,267,527,300 |

Source: Annual Report of the Assessing Department, City of Boston.

## 30. EXEMPT REAL PROERTY VALUATIONS, BUFFALO, N.Y., 1969

| Classification | Valuation |
|---|---|
| U.S.A. | $   29,110,910 |
| N.Y. State | 70,826,060 |
| Erie County | 21,706,320 |
| City of Buffalo | 89,991,250 |
| City of Buffalo (schools) | 57,283,930 |
| Religious | 43,981,150 |
| Charitable | 9,255,010 |
| Hospitals except public-owned | 31,855,590 |
| Veterans | 18,881,430 |
| Port Authority | 8,397,300 |
| Public housing | 52,176,260 |
| Cemeteries | 6,455,310 |
| Private schools | 33,386,880 |
| Limited & nonprofit housing | 2,434,340 |
| Parsonages | 2,332,360 |
| State retirement system | 2,275,790 |
| Railroads | 38,466,345 |
| Miscellaneous | 986,890 |
| Total | $   519,803,105 |
| Taxable | $1,024,156,571 |
| Ratio of Exempt to Total Valuations | 33.6% |

Source: City of Buffalo, Department of Assessment.

## 31. Exempt Real Property Valuations, Denver, 1968

| Classification | Valuation (in millions) |
|---|---|
| U.S. Government | $ 37.9 |
| State of Colorado | 19.1 |
| Denver Housing Authority | 9.7 |
| Denver Stapleton Airport | 11.0 |
| Colorado Seminary (Denver University) | 13.8 |
| Private schools | 4.5 |
| Parochial schools | 9.0 |
| Churches, other places of worship | 18.2 |
| Hospitals | 16.2 |
| Fraternal organizations | 2.2 |
| Other charitable organizations | 10.2 |
| Parsonages | 1.3 |
| Senior Citizens' Homes | 2.3 |
| Total Exempt | $231.8 |
| Taxable | $936.9 |
| Ratio of Exempt to Total Valuations | 19.7% |

Source: Denver City assessor data.

## 32. Exempt Property Valuations, Milwaukee, 1968–1969

| Classification | Valuation | Classification | Valuation |
|---|---|---|---|
| *Religious* | | *Milwaukee County* | |
| Churches | $ 136,392,440 | General | $ 37,135,000 |
| Parsonages | 4,270,420 | Airports | 37,500,000 |
| Separate schools | 25,507,000 | Parks | 87,641,900 |
| Miscellaneous | 11,981,690 | Tax deed & | |
| Total | 178,151,550 | welfare | 753,200 |
| | | Total | $ 163,030,100 |
| *Educational* | | | |
| Colleges | $ 143,433,000 | *City of Milwaukee* | |
| Other | 2,800,000 | General | $ 63,000,000 |
| Total | $ 146,233,000 | Redevelopment | |
| | | (Subject to | |
| *Cemeteries* | $ 15,039,600 | resale) | 15,000,000 |
| | | Parking | 20,000,000 |
| *Fraternal* | | Playgrounds | 8,000,000 |
| Lodges, etc. | $ 6,200,000 | Tax deed | 1,000,000 |
| Memorial halls | 775,000 | Land bank | 2,539,000 |
| Total | $ 6,975,000 | Milwaukee Technical | |
| *Benevolent* | | College | 12,100,000 |
| Hospitals | $ 128,131,000 | Total | $ 121,688,000 |
| Children's homes | 8,000,000 | | |
| Homes for aged | 10,776,000 | *Sewer system* | $ 16,000,000 |
| Miscellaneous | 17,275,000 | (Underground work | |
| Total | $ 164,182,000 | not included) | |
| | | *Street lighting* | |
| *Miscellaneous* | | (All property) | $ 13,500,000 |
| Women's clubs | $ 300,000 | *Fire department* | $ 5,500,000 |
| Labor temples | 3,900,000 | | |
| Total | $ 4,200,000 | *Public schools* | $ 181,000,000 |
| *U.S. Government* | $ 61,500,000 | Grand Total | |
| | | Exempt | $1,085,872,150 |
| *State of Wisconsin* | | | |
| General | $ 8,697,000 | Total Taxable | |
| Dept. Veterans | | Valuation | $3,606,796,000 |
| Affairs | 176,000 | Ratio of Exempt | |
| Total | $ 8,873,000 | to Total | 21.3% |

*Source:* Office of the Tax Commissioner, City of Milwaukee.

## 33. EXEMPT REAL PROPERTY VALUATIONS, MINNEAPOLIS, 1968

| Classification | Valuation (in millions; items rounded) |
|---|---|
| Public schools | $ 37.1 |
| Private and church schools | 10.7 |
| Academy, college, and university | 50.3 |
| Public property | 101.4 |
| Churches and church property | 41.4 |
| Public hospitals | 44.6 |
| Charitable institutions | 14.0 |
| Cemeteries | 10.6 |
| Railroads | 28.1 |
| Telephone company | 7.5 |
| Total Exempt | $346.1 |
| Taxable | $954.7 |
| Ratio of Exempt to Total | 26.3% |
| Ratio of Exempt to Total, 1962 | 23.9% |
| Ratio of Exempt to Total, 1956 | 21.8% |

Source: City of Minneapolis, Department of Assessor.

Appendix

## 34. EXEMPT PROPERTIES IN NEW YORK CITY, 1968–1969

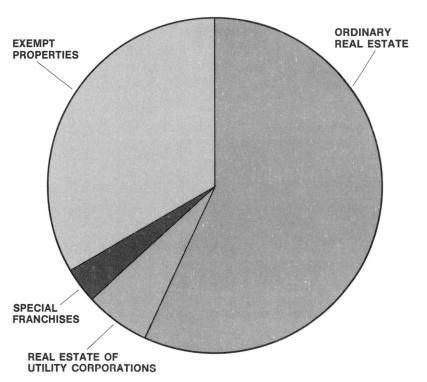

| Classification | Assessed Valuation | 1968–1969 Percentage | 1958–1959 Percentage |
|---|---|---|---|
| Ordinary real estate | $28,523,172,555 | 56.9 | 59.5 |
| Real estate of utility corporations | 3,279,514,998 | 6.5 | 6.6 |
| Special franchises (fixed by State Board of Equalization and Assessment) | 1,502,190,905 | 3.0 | 3.3 |
| Total Taxable Property | $33,304,878,458 | 66.4 | 69.4 |
| Total Exempt Property | 16,854,832,911 | 33.6 | 30.6 |
| Total Value of All Property | $50,159,711,369 | 100.0 | 100.0 |

Source: City of New York Annual Report of the Tax Commission, 1968–1969.

243

## 35. EXEMPT PROPERTIES BY OWNERSHIP, NEW YORK CITY, 1968–1969

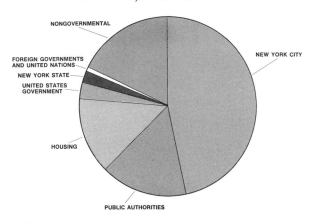

| Classification | Assessed Valuation | Percentage |
|---|---|---|
| *Governmental* | | |
| New York City | $ 7,790,007,858 | 46.2 |
| Public authorities | 2,662,792,690 | 15.8 |
| Housing | 2,334,250,971 | 13.9 |
| U.S. Government | 569,439,200 | 3.4 |
| New York State | 336,365,585 | 2.0 |
| Foreign governments and United Nations | 89,707,000 | 0.5 |
| Total | $13,782,563,304 | 81.8 |
| *Nongovernmental* | | |
| Religious | $ 726,010,645 | 4.3 |
| Hospitals and asylums | 631,905,320 | 3.7 |
| Schools and libraries | 808,368,030 | 4.8 |
| Benevolent organizations | 188,311,950 | 1.1 |
| Cemeteries | 163,032,010 | 1.0 |
| Veterans, clergy, parsonages, etc. | 286,493,905 | 1.7 |
| Exemption railroads | 268,135,647 | 1.6 |
| Fallout shelters | 12,100 | 0.0 |
| Total | $ 3,072,269,607 | 18.2 |
| Grand Total of Exempt Property | $16,854,832,911 | 100.0 |

Source: City of New York Annual Report of the Tax Commission, 1968–1969.

Appendix

## 36. DETAILS OF OWNERSHIP CATEGORIES, EXEMPT PROPERTY IN NEW YORK CITY, 1968–1969

| Classification | No. Parcels | Valuation |
|---|---|---|
| *City of New York* | | |
| Borough Presidents | 194 | $ 10,163,093 |
| Department of Real Estate | 74 | 4,833,765 |
| Board of Education and | | |
|   Higher Education | 1,140 | 1,566,076,300 |
| Fire Department | 253 | 45,983,250 |
| Department of Sanitation | 118 | 92,895,470 |
| Department of Water Supply, | | |
|   Gas and Electricity | 114 | 708,917,705 |
| Department of Marine and Aviation | 354 | 432,903,950 |
| Airfields (leased to Port of | | |
|   N.Y. Authority) | 49 | 565,165,700 |
| Department of Public Works | 322 | 1,372,713,045 |
| Department of Correction | 7 | 65,180,000 |
| Department of Welfare | 15 | 22,397,000 |
| Department of Parks | 1,443 | 1,565,178,140 |
| Armories | 13 | 18,206,000 |
| Department of Health | 42 | 28,077,600 |
| Libraries and museums | 116 | 104,952,000 |
| Police Department | 104 | 29,130,375 |
| Department of Traffic | 54 | 56,757,900 |
| Department of Markets | 25 | 57,327,000 |
| Department of Hospitals | 38 | 369,831,600 |
| Department of Highways | 108 | 673,239,215 |
| Board of Water Supply | 2 | 78,750 |
| Total | 4,585 | $ 7,790,007,858 |
| *Public Authorities* | | |
| Transit Authority | 242 | $ 1,438,791,315 |
| Triborough Bridge and | | |
|   Tunnel Authority | 115 | 694,839,270 |
| Port of New York Authority | 83 | 428,903,550 |
| Metropolitan Commuter | | |
|   Transport Authority | 78 | 76,629,205 |
| Municipal railroads | 3 | 2,872,950 |
| PATH | 7 | 20,756,400 |
| Total | 528 | $ 2,662,792,690 |

## 36 (Cont.)

| Classification | No. Parcels | Valuation |
|---|---|---|
| *Housing* | | |
| PUBLIC HOUSING | | |
| Federal-aided | 187 | $ 759,204,231 |
| State-aided | 88 | 665,230,000 |
| City-aided | 82 | 322,921,600 |
| Old Federal emergency | 2 | 400,000 |
| Total Public Housing | 359 | $ 1,747,755,831 |
| NONPUBLIC HOUSING | | |
| Limited dividends | 27 | $ 80,341,600 |
| Redevelopment | 37 | 215,954,640 |
| Limited profit | 131 | 290,198,900 |
| Total Nonpublic Housing | 195 | $ 586,495,140 |
| Total Housing | 554 | $ 2,334,250,971 |
| *Nongovernmental* | | |
| Veterans | 104,701 | $ 200,435,980 |
| Churches, synagogues, monasteries, convents, etc. | 4,883 | 726,010,645 |
| Asylums and homes | 144 | 85,908,300 |
| Hospitals, infirmaries, and dispensaries | 403 | 545,997,020 |
| Religious, mental, moral, fire and benevolent assns. | 752 | 188,311,950 |
| Colleges and schools | 1,137 | 801,790,530 |
| Cemeteries | 239 | 163,032,010 |
| Libraries (other than city) | 11 | 6,577,500 |
| Parsonages | 1,383 | 25,844,325 |
| Clergy | 931 | 1,399,400 |
| Exemption railroads | 129 | 268,135,647 |
| Alterations | 3,390 | 58,814,200 |
| Fallout shelters | 9 | 12,100 |
| Total | 118,112 | $ 3,072,269,607 |
| *United States Government* | | |
| Army | 29 | $ 160,515,800 |
| Navy | 14 | 133,226,000 |
| Post Offices | 43 | 84,661,800 |
| Lighthouses | 5 | 104,500 |
| Cemeteries | 2 | 577,500 |
| Hospitals | 7 | 56,463,300 |
| Government land and buildings | 46 | 133,890,300 |
| Total | 146 | $ 569,439,200 |

## 36 (Cont.)

| Classification | No. Parcels | Valuation |
|---|---|---|
| *State of New York* | | |
| Militia | 10 | $ 9,654,500 |
| Hospitals | 21 | 194,675,000 |
| State land and buildings | 358 | 70,283,950 |
| Public Works | 113 | 19,863,135 |
| Labor Department | 1 | 615,000 |
| Dormitory Authority | 23 | 41,274,000 |
| Total | 526 | $ 336,365,585 |
| *Foreign Governments and United Nations* | | |
| Foreign governments | 8 | $ 1,207,000 |
| United Nations | 1 | 88,500,000 |
| Total | 9 | $ 89,707,000 |
| *Valuation of Exempt Real Estate by Boroughs* | | |
| Manhattan | 5,955 | $ 6,665,332,460 |
| The Bronx | 11,169 | 2,272,815,104 |
| Brooklyn | 33,877 | 3,873,678,322 |
| Queens | 55,926 | 3,205,903,265 |
| Richmond | 17,533 | 837,103,760 |
| Total | 124,460 | $16,854,832,911 |

Source: City of New York Annual Report of the Tax Commission, 1968–1969.

## 37. MONETARY COST OF REAL ESTATE TAX EXEMPTION IN NEW YORK CITY, 1957–1958 TO 1966–1967

| | | | | | (000,000 omitted) |
|---|---|---|---|---|---|

| Fiscal Year | (1) Tax Exempt | (2) Basic Tax Rate | (3) Real Estate Taxes Actually Collected | (4) Real Estate Taxes Foregone | (5) Sum of Real Estate Taxes Collected and Foregone |
|---|---|---|---|---|---|
| 1966–67 | $15,665 | $4.957 | $1,573 | $777 | $2,350 |
| 1965–66 | 15,250 | 4.56 | 1,408 | 695 | 2,103 |
| 1964–65 | 14,442 | 4.41 | 1,312 | 637 | 1,949 |
| 1963–64 | 13,713 | 4.27 | 1,219 | 586 | 1,805 |
| 1962–63 | 12,578 | 4.16 | 1,133 | 523 | 1,656 |
| 1961–62 | 11,872 | 4.10 | 1,069 | 487 | 1,556 |
| 1960–61 | 11,193 | 4.12 | 1,027 | 461 | 1,488 |
| 1959–60 | 10,756 | 4.16 | 978 | 447 | 1,425 |
| 1958–59 | 9,880 | 4.16 | 932 | 411 | 1,343 |
| 1957–58 | 8,803 | 3.99 | 875 | 351 | 1,226 |

Source: "Real Estate Tax Exemption in New York City: A Design for Reform," Citizens Budget Commission, Inc., New York City, April, 1967.

*Appendix*

## 38. EXEMPT REAL PROPERTY, PHILADELPHIA, 1969

| Title | Total Value |
|---|---|
| Federal Government | $   222,015,600 |
| State of Pennsylvania | 95,792,260 |
| City of Philadelphia | 389,859,600 |
| School District of Philadelphia | 198,037,800 |
| Philadelphia Housing Authority | 94,995,900 |
| Redevelopment Authority | 50,126,900 |
| Naval Housing | 3,183,000 |
| Museums, libraries, etc. | 30,844,400 |
| Special total disabled veterans | 174,700 |
| Veteran posts | 1,723,300 |
| Public utilities | 52,428,800 |
| Philadelphia Housing Development Corporation | 2,736,700 |
| Miscellaneous authorities | 16,406,300 |
| Miscellaneous exempt property | 50,496,300 |
| Institutions of learning | 151,448,900 |
| Churches | 147,809,900 |
| Cemeteries | 8,851,900 |
| Hospitals | 105,006,400 |
| Total Exempt | $1,621,938,660 |
| Taxable | $4,546,895,360 |
| Ratio of Exempt to Total | 24.7% |

Source: City of Philadelphia Board of Revision of Taxes.

## 39. GROWTH OF EXEMPT REAL PROPERTY VALUATIONS, PHILADELPHIA, 1915–1966

| Year | Valuation (*in millions*) | | | Exempt Valuation as Percentage of Valuation of All Real Estate |
| | Taxable Real Estate | Exempt Real Estate | All Real Estate | |
|---|---|---|---|---|
| 1915 | $1,670 | $ 253 | $1,922 | 13.1% |
| 1920 | 1,941 | 306 | 2,248 | 13.6 |
| 1925 | 2,769 | 480 | 3,249 | 14.8 |
| 1930 | 3,452 | 648 | 4,099 | 15.8 |
| 1935 | 3,072 | 705 | 3,768 | 19.5 |
| 1940 | 2,522 | 698 | 3,220 | 21.7 |
| 1945 | 2,426 | 698 | 3,124 | 22.3 |
| 1950 | 2,909 | 766 | 3,675 | 20.8 |
| 1955 | 3,662 | 920 | 4,583 | 20.1 |
| 1956 | 3,732 | 946 | 4,678 | 20.2 |
| 1957 | 3,817 | 984 | 4,801 | 20.5 |
| 1958 | 3,864 | 991 | 4,856 | 20.4 |
| 1959 | 3,892 | 1,113 | 5,005 | 22.2 |
| 1960 | 3,951 | 1,155 | 5,067 | 22.8 |
| 1961 | 4,029 | 1,188 | 5,216 | 22.8 |
| 1962 | 4,098 | 1,217 | 5,315 | 22.9 |
| 1963 | 4,180 | 1,244 | 5,424 | 22.9 |
| 1964 | 4,257 | 1,280 | 5,537 | 23.1 |
| 1965 | 4,309 | 1,345 | 5,655 | 23.8 |
| 1966 | 4,383 | 1,407 | 5,790 | 24.3 |

Source: "The Problem of Tax-Exempt Property in Philadelphia," Report #1, Pennsylvania Economy League, Eastern Division, Philadelphia, 1966.

*Appendix*

## 40. EXEMPT REAL PROPERTY, ST. LOUIS, 1968

| Ownership category | Valuation (*in millions*) | % of Total Exempt |
|---|---|---|
| City | $ 115.0 | 21.2% |
| U.S. | 114.0 | 20.9 |
| Redevelopment Authority | 93.0 | 17.0 |
| Schools | 74.0 | 13.8 |
| Churches | 42.5 | 7.8 |
| Hospitals | 35.0 | 6.4 |
| State | 17.0 | 3.1 |
| Metropolitan School District | 9.0 | 1.6 |
| Institutions, other | 44.6 | 8.2 |
| Total[a] | $ 544.2 | |
| Taxable Valuation | $1,278.5 | |
| Ratio of Exempt to Total Valuation | | 30.0% |

[a] May not add due to rounding.
*Source:* Office of the Assessor, St. Louis.

## 41. GROWTH OF EXEMPT REAL PROPERTY, ST. LOUIS, 1958–1968

| Year | Taxable | Exempt | % Exempt to Total |
|---|---|---|---|
| 1958 | $1,253,793,880 | $394,463,220 | 23.8 |
| 1959 | 1,272,974,770 | 402,358,490 | 23.9 |
| 1963 | 1,273,129,390 | 443,743,510 | 25.8 |
| 1964 | 1,276,582,240 | 450,862,020 | 26.1 |
| 1968 | 1,268,521,020 | 544,283,550 | 30.0 |

*Source:* Office of the Assessor, St. Louis.

251

## 42. EXEMPT VALUATIONS, WASHINGTION, D.C., 1969

| Category | Assessed Valuations | Tax Foregone | % of Land Area | % of Total Valuation |
|---|---|---|---|---|
| *Taxable Property* | | | | |
| Total Taxable | $3,672,533,933 | $113,848,552 | 45.1 | 47.7 |
| *Exempt Property* | | | | |
| United States | 3,070,817,806 | 95,195,352 | 43.3 | 39.9 |
| District of Columbia | 329,873,366 | 10,226,075 | 4.4 | 4.3 |
| Other Exempt: | | | | |
| Religious | 183,191,116 | 5,678,925 | | |
| Educational | 150,245,718 | 4,657,617 | | |
| Charitable | 30,238,050 | 937,380 | | |
| Hospitals | 84,774,036 | 2,627,995 | | |
| Libraries | 3,134,181 | 97,160 | | |
| Foreign | 50,563,401 | 1,567,465 | | |
| Cemeteries | 15,075,660 | 467,345 | | |
| Miscellaneous | 108,327,723 | 3,358,159 | | |
| Total Other Exempt | $ 625,549,885 | $ 19,392,046 | 7.2 | 8.1 |
| Total Exempt | $4,026,241,057 | $124,813,473 | 54.9 | 52.3[a] |
| Total Taxable and Exempt | $7,698,774,990 | $238,662,025 | 100.0 | 100.0 |

[a] 1959 ratio of exempt to total valuation was 40%.
*Source:* District of Columbia Department of Finance and Revenue.

Appendix

## 43. U.S. Supreme Court Opinion

### Walz v. Tax Commission of the City of New York

May 4, 1970

Abridged

Appellant, owner of real estate in Richmond County, New York, sought an injunction in the New York courts to prevent the New York City Tax Commission from granting property tax exemptions to religious organizations for religious properties used solely for religious worship.

Mr. Chief Justice Burger delivered the opinion of the Court.

\*    \*    \*

The course of constitutional neutrality in this area cannot be an absolutely straight line; rigidity could well defeat the basic purpose of these provisions, which is to insure that no religion be sponsored or favored, none commanded, and none inhibited. The general principle deducible from the First Amendment and all that has been said by the Court is this: that we will not tolerate either governmentally established religion or governmental interference with religion. Short of those expressly proscribed governmental acts there is room for play in the joints productive of a benevolent neutrality which will permit religious exercise to exist without sponsorship and without interference.

Each value judgment under the Religion Clauses must therefore turn on whether particular acts in question are intended to establish or interfere with religious beliefs and practices or have the effect of doing so. Adherence to the policy of neutrality that derives from an accommodation of the Establishment and Free Exercise Clauses has prevented the kind of involvement that would tip the balance toward government control of churches or governmental restraint on religious practice. . . .

In *Everson* the Court declined to construe the Religion Clauses with a literalness that would undermine the ultimate constitutional objective as illuminated by history. Surely, bus transportation and police protection to pupils who receive religious instruction "aid" that particular religion to maintain schools that plainly tend to assure future adherents to a particular faith by having control of their total education at an early age. No religious body that maintains schools would deny this as an affirmative if not dominant policy of church schools. But if as in *Everson* buses can be provided to carry and policemen to protect church school pupils, we fail to see how a broader range of police and fire protection given equally to all churches, along with nonprofit hospitals, art galleries, and libraries receiving the same tax exemption, is different for purposes of the religion clauses.

253

Similarly, making textbooks available to pupils in parochial schools in common with public schools was surely an "aid" to the sponsoring churches because it relieved those churches of an enormous aggregate cost for those books. Supplying of costly teaching materials was not seen either as manifesting a legislative purpose to aid or as having a primary effect of aid contravening the First Amendment. [*Board of Education* v. *Allen*.] In so doing the Court was heeding both its own prior holdings and our religious tradition. Mr. Justice Douglas, in Zorach v. Clauson, after recalling that we "are a religious people whose institutions presuppose a Supreme Being," went on to say:

> We make room for as wide a variety of beliefs and creeds as the spiritual needs of man deem necessary. . . . *When the state encourages religious instruction . . . it follows the best of our traditions.* For it then respects the religious nature of our people and accommodates the public service to their spiritual needs. (Emphasis added.)

With all the risks inherent in programs that bring about administrative relationships between public education bodies and church-sponsored schools, we have been able to chart a course that preserved the autonomy and freedom of religious bodies while avoiding any semblance of established religion. This is a "tight rope" and one we have successfully traversed.

The legislative purpose of the property tax exemption is neither the advancement nor the inhibition of religion; it is neither sponsorship nor hostility. New York, in common with the other states, has determined that certain entities that exist in a harmonious relationship to the community at large, and that foster its "moral or mental improvement," should not be inhibited in their activities by property taxation or the hazard of loss of those properties for nonpayment of taxes. It has not singled out one particular church or religious group or even churches as such; rather, it has granted exemption to all houses of religious worship within a broad class of property owned by nonprofit quasi-public corporations which include hospitals, libraries, playgrounds, scientific, professional, historical and patriotic groups. The State has an affirmative policy that considers these groups as beneficial and stabilizing influences in community life and finds this classification useful, desirable, and in the public interest. Qualification for tax exemption is not perpetual or immutable; some tax-exempt groups lose that status when their activities take them outside the classification and new entities can come into being and qualify for exemption.

Governments have not always been tolerant of religious activity, and hostility toward religion has taken many shapes and forms—economic, political, and sometimes harshly oppressive. Grants of exemption historically reflect the concern of authors of constitutions and statutes as to the

254

latent dangers inherent in the imposition of property taxes: exemption constitutes a reasonable and balanced attempt to guard against those dangers. . . . We cannot read New York's statute as attempting to establish religion; it is simply sparing the exercise of religion from the burden of property taxation levied on private profit institutions.

We find it unnecessary to justify the tax exemption on the social welfare services or "good works" that some churches perform for parishioners and others—family counseling, aid to the elderly and the infirm, and to children. Churches vary substantially in the scope of such services; programs expand or contract according to resources and need. As public-sponsored programs enlarge, private aid from the church sector may diminish. The extent of social services may vary, depending on whether the church serves an urban or rural, a rich or poor constituency. To give emphasis to so variable an aspect of the work of religious bodies would introduce an element of governmental evaluation and standards as to the worth of particular social welfare programs, thus producing a kind of continuing day-to-day relationship which the policy of neutrality seeks to minimize. Hence, the use of a social welfare yardstick as a significant element to qualify for tax exemption could conceivably give rise to confrontations that could escalate to constitutional dimensions.

Determining that the legislative purpose of tax exemption is not aimed at establishing, sponsoring, or supporting religion does not end the inquiry, however. We must also be sure that the end result—the effect—is not an excessive government entanglement with religion. The test is inescapably one of degree. Either course, taxation of churches or exemption, occasions some degree of involvement with religion. Elimination of exemption would tend to expand the involvement of government by giving rise to tax valuation of church property, tax liens, tax foreclosures, and the direct confrontations and conflicts that follow in the train of those legal processes.

Granting tax exemptions to churches necessarily operates to afford an indirect economic benefit and also gives rise to some, but yet a lesser, involvement than taxing them. In analyzing either alternative the questions are whether the involvement is excessive, and whether it is a continuing one calling for official and continuing surveillance leading to an impermissible degree of entanglement. Obviously a direct money subsidy would be a relationship pregnant with involvement and, as with most governmental grant programs, could encompass sustained and detailed administrative relationships for enforcement of statutory or administrative standards, but that is not this case. The hazards of churches supporting government are hardly less in their potential than the hazards of governments supporting churches; each relationship carries some involvement rather than the desired insulation and separation. We cannot ignore the instances in history when church support of government led to the kind of involvement we seek to avoid.

The grant of a tax exemption is not sponsorship since the government does not transfer part of its revenue to churches but simply abstains from demanding that the church support the state. No one has ever suggested that tax exemption has converted libraries, art galleries, or hospitals into arms of the state or employees "on the public payroll." There is no genuine nexus between tax exemption and establishment of religion. As Mr. Justice Holmes commented in a related context "a page of history is worth a volume of logic." [*New York Trust Co. v. Eisner.*] The exemption creates only a minimal and remote involvement between church and state and far less than taxation of churches. It restricts the fiscal relationship between church and state, and tends to complement and reinforce the desired separation insulating each from the other.

Separation in this context cannot mean absence of all contact; the complexities of modern life inevitably produce some contact and the fire and police protection received by houses of religious worship are no more than incidental benefits accorded all persons or institutions within a State's boundaries, along with many other exempt organizations. The appellant has not established even an arguable quantitative correlation between the payment of an ad valorem property tax and the receipt of these municipal benefits.

All of the fifty states provide for tax exemption of places of worship, most of them doing so by constitutional guarantees. For so long as federal income taxes have had any potential impact on churches—over seventy-five years—religious organizations have been expressly exempt from the tax. Such treatment is an "aid" to churches no more and no less in principle than the real estate tax exemption granted by states. Few concepts are more deeply embedded in the fabric of our national life, beginning with pre-Revolutionary colonial times, than for the government to exercise at the very least this kind of benevolent neutrality toward churches and religious exercise generally so long as none was favored over others and none suffered interference.

It is significant that Congress, from its earliest days, has viewed the religion clauses of the Constitution as authorizing statutory real estate tax exemption to religious bodies. . . . It is obviously correct that no one acquires a vested or protected right in violation of the Constitution by long use, even when that span of time covers our entire national existence and indeed predates it. Yet an unbroken practice of according the exemption to churches, openly and by affirmative state action, not covertly or by state inaction, is not something to be lightly cast aside. . . . Nothing in this national attitude toward religious tolerance and two centuries of uninterrupted freedom from taxation has given the remotest sign of leading to an established church or religion and on the contrary it has operated affirmatively to help guarantee the free exercise of all forms of religious beliefs. Thus, it is hardly useful to suggest that tax exemption is but the "foot in the door" or the "nose of the camel in the tent" leading to an established church. If tax exemption can be seen as this first step toward "establishment" of religion, as Mr. Justice Douglas fears, the second step has been long in coming. Any move which realistically "establishes" a church or tends to do so can be dealt with "while this Court sits." . . .

It is interesting to note that while the precise question we now decide has not been directly before the Court previously, the broad question was discussed by the Court in relation to real estate taxes assessed nearly a century ago on land owned by and adjacent to a church in Washington, D.C. At that time Congress granted real estate tax exemptions to buildings devoted to art, to institutions of public charity, libraries, cemeteries, and "church buildings, and grounds actually occupied by such buildings." In denying tax exemption as to land owned by but not used for the church, but rather to produce income, the Court concluded:

> In the exercise of this [taxing] power, Congress, like any State legislature unrestricted by constitutional provisions, may at its discretion wholly exempt certain classes of property from taxation or may tax them at a lower rate than other property." *Gibbons* v. *District of Columbia* (1886).

It appears that at least up to 1885 this Court, reflecting more than a century of our history and uninterrupted practice, accepted without discussion the proposition that federal or state grants of tax exemption to churches were not a violation of the Religious Clauses of the First Amendment. As to the New York statute, we now confirm that view.

(Concurring opinions were written by Justices Brennan and Harlan; Justice Douglas dissented.)

# Index

260

Churches (cont.)
payment-in-lieu of taxes and, 123
restrictions on exemptions and, 25–
26, 27, 30
retirement homes and, 82–85
service charges to, 43
state-supported, 21, 22–23
subsidies to, 28
taxes levied on, 21–22
variability of exemptions by states,
30–37
wealth of, 20–21, 39–42
See also individual church groups
Churches: Their Riches, Revenues, and
Immunities, The, 11
Church of England, 23
Church of Jesus Christ of Latter Day
Saints. See Mormon Church
Church-state separation, 24, 82
Cities. See Metropolitan core cities
City of Detroit v. the Murray Corpora-
tion, 54
Civil defense, 135
Civil War, 24–25, 26, 90
Clark, Douglas H., 162
Clawson, Marion, 51, 153
Cleveland, 15, 42, 123
Cleveland Municipal Stadium, 68
Cline, Denzel C., 55
Clubs. See Social clubs
Cody (Wo.), 115
College Park (Md.), 121
Colleges and universities, 4, 14n., 17,
62–72, 73n., 75, 113, 133, 136,
137, 141, 144, 167
adjacent lands and, 63–68
business ventures and, 63–66, 69–70
charters to, 63–65
exemptions for, 22
housing requirements of, 66–68
increase in, 62–64
land development and, 69–70
payment-in-lieu of taxes and, 119–
122
payments to local governments, 170–
172

Colleges and Universities (cont.)
properties of, 23
sports stadiums, 68
tax and tax related payments (1969),
173–174
Colorado, vi, 12, 30, 47n., 52, 77, 79,
82, 83, 87, 141
acreage of federally-leased land, 213
acreage of federally-owned land, 211
survey of exemption practices, 165–
169
survey of policy on payment-in-lieu
of taxes, 191–192
Colorado Medical School, University
of, 82
Colorado Springs, 137
Columbia University, 66, 68, 138
Commager, Henry Steele, 150
Commission for the Revision of the
Statutes of the State (N.Y.), 27
Commission on Financing Higher
Education, 66
Commission to Study Tax Exemption
Laws, (R.I.), 56, 142
Committee on Tax Exempt Property
(Colo.), 82–83
Commodity Credit Corporation, 53
Commuter areas, 103
Competition with private industry, 107
Computers, 17
Confederate Soldiers Home (Miss.), 74
Confiscation Acts (1799 and 1802), 24
Congress of Cities, 129
Connecticut, 16, 30, 36, 38, 90n., 104,
121, 124, 171
acreage of federally-leased land, 213
acreage of federally-owned land, 211
exempt property valuations, 218
survey of exempt practices, 165–169
survey of policy on payment-in-lieu
of taxes, 192–193
Conser, Eugene P., 7, 147
Conservation lands, 123–125
Constantine, 21
Continental Motors Corp. v. Town-
ship of Muskegon (Mich.), 54

271